Why You're Going to Love This Book

Decisions, decisions. Which comes first: choosing a college major or choosing a career? The truth is that this is a chicken-and-egg problem and people disagree about it.

Some people say that first you should decide what career you want to pursue and then choose a major that helps you prepare for it. They tell you success stories about students who graduated with degrees in accounting, computer science, or some other career-oriented major and then got high-paying, fast-track career offers from businesses.

Other people take the opposite approach. They say that you should first decide on a major you really love and then choose a career that can take advantage of what you've learned. They tell you horror stories about students who declared a major in a career-oriented field such as engineering or business, only to discover that the coursework was so boring that they dropped out of college or changed majors and delayed graduation by one or more years.

Both approaches have upsides and downsides. *The reason this book is so special* is that it lets you choose a four-year college major and a career *simultaneously*, instead of considering just one or the other. It links 127 majors to 263 careers. It informs you about what the career is like and also about what you would study in the major. It tells you which careers are commonly associated with each major and, in some cases, how graduates might go into careers in unexpected fields.

So the choice is yours: You can sign up for an expensive battery of personality tests and counseling sessions; you can dig through piles of college catalogs, examining and comparing the requirements for the majors; you can search through massive databases of career information, taking pains to determine the skill requirements and the income you can expect—or you can use this book to obtain self-understanding and get concise and authoritative facts about majors and careers that might suit you.

If the choice is not obvious already, turn to part I and start the exercises. You'll be surprised by how quickly you'll start seeing the connections between who you are and where you want to go.

Dedication

Dedicated to the memory of Sidney Shatkin, who completed his college major (history) at age 58.

 # Contents

Introduction: How to Use This Book

This section shows you how to use this book for your specific needs. First it explains who will benefit most from reading the book, as well as how it can help you. Then it details the different elements of parts I and II. Finally, it describes how you can get the most out of this book depending on your needs.

Who Really Needs This Book?

Lots of people need to make decisions about college majors and careers. Read over the following list to see where you fit in:

- **You are a young person choosing a major or career who doesn't have a clear idea which major or career might be best for you.** This book can help you look at yourself and see what majors or careers might be good choices for you. For example, you might be a high school student trying to decide which college to go to. Your choice might depend partly on your intended career and major. This book can help you narrow your choices by getting you interested in some specific careers and majors. It can also *broaden* your choices by informing you about certain majors and careers that are new to you.

- **Or perhaps you're not even sure you want to go to college at all,** but you are exploring your options. This book might get you excited about certain college-related career paths and help make the decision easier.

- **You have a major in mind but are not yet certain about it.** With this book, you can get facts that will help you make up your mind and start planning. For example, you might be a college student who will soon have to declare a major. Maybe you're at a two-year college and you're thinking about going on for a four-year degree, but in what major? This book might suggest majors and careers that you haven't considered before, and it gives you concrete facts to help you evaluate majors that you already have in mind.

- **You are a midlife career changer.** You can find ways to use your accumulated skills and experience in a new career. For example, perhaps you're considering taking college classes and want to find a major that can help advance your career. This book gives you dollar figures about careers and useful information about coursework in college majors.

- **Or perhaps you already have a degree** and want to (or need to) change careers while still taking advantage of your educational credentials. You don't have to let yourself be boxed in by traditional connections between majors and careers. With the information about skills and work groups in this book, you might explore nontraditional career pathways that you have not previously considered.

- **You are making the transition from college to a career.** You can see which careers might make good use of what you've learned. For example, perhaps you're a college student who will graduate soon, and you're wondering how you might "use" the degree you're about to get. Be sure to look at the career suggestions in this book and think about using the information about skills when you start preparing your resume.

- **You are planning the transition from military to civilian life.** This book can help you identify college majors for which your military training has already given you a head start. You can also find careers that make use of the skills you've acquired in the military.

- **You are applying for jobs.** You can get ideas for your resume, cover letter, or job interviews. For example, you can review the Career Snapshots in the book so that you will use appropriate job-related terms when you write your letters and resumes.

- **You are a professional helping others make decisions about majors and careers.** For example, maybe you're a guidance counselor, academic advisor, or librarian and need to help other people make these decisions. You can help them clarify their priorities, explore options, and plan their next steps.

You can see from the preceding bulleted items that this book can help a broad variety of people.

What's in This Book?

This book is set up so that you can find information quickly in a variety of ways. Looking at the table of contents, you'll see that the book is divided into two main parts. Part I asks "Which Majors and Careers Might Suit You?" Each section in it offers an exercise to help you assemble a Hot List of majors to explore in part II. Part II offers "Facts About College Majors and Careers," and it lists the 127 college majors alphabetically.

Here's what you'll find for each college major in part II:

- **Definition:** A brief summary of what the major covers.

- **Career Snapshot:** A one-paragraph description of the subject and an explanation of what sorts of careers (and additional education) graduates typically go into.

- **Related Specialties and Careers:** A list of areas of concentration that people in this field pursue, both in college and later in jobs. Depending on your interests, you could go in many different directions.

- **Related Job Titles, Earnings, Projected Growth, and Openings:** Here's where you'll get very specific facts about the jobs that the major most frequently leads to. You'll see the average income for everyone in the job, the projected growth rate for the job, and how many annual job openings are projected. You'll also see the O*NET-SOC code number for each job. This number is the government's standard classification code for the job and makes it easy for you to look up additional details in other career information sources, such as JIST's _O*NET Dictionary of Occupational Titles_.

- **Typical Sequence of College Courses:** This is a list of the college courses that are often required for this major. Naturally, each college has its own set of requirements, but this is a general look at what to expect. If you have some college credits on your record, this list might indicate programs for which you have already completed some of the requirements.

- **Typical Sequence of High School Courses:** If you're still in high school, this list can recommend coursework that would be good preparation.

If you're beyond high school, you'll see whether you have an appropriate background.

- **Personality Type:** This is the one type that best describes the environment common to the related careers and the personality of people working in them. For definitions of the six personality types and a listing of majors linked to each type, see the appendix. Remember that most careers and people are associated with one or more secondary personality types in addition to a primary type; the appendix lists majors by both the primary and the highest-rated secondary type.

- **Other Characteristics:** These characteristics can help you decide whether the careers related to the major are consistent with your abilities and preferences. Included are the interest areas (also known as career clusters), work groups, skills, values, and work environment that best describe the careers. Keep in mind that being in the major is usually a different experience from being in the related careers, because being in college requires you to attend classes, do research, write papers, and so on. The GOE (short for Guide for Occupational Exploration) is a way of organizing careers that appeal to similar interests into large interest areas (also called career clusters) and more-specific work groups. The 16 GOE interest areas are based on the 16 career clusters that the U.S. Department of Education developed around 1999 as a way to explore occupations and plan for related education and training.

- **Related Titles in the Classification of Instructional Programs (CIP):** Here each major is linked to one or more programs in the Classification of Instructional Programs (CIP), a naming scheme used by the U.S. Department of Education and by some colleges. You can get additional information about any CIP program on the Web at http://nces.ed.gov/pubsearch/pubsinfo.asp?pubid=2002165.

Note that you can also use the index to look up occupations, high school courses, interest areas/career clusters, or work groups and find the related majors in part II.

How You Can Benefit from This Book

This isn't the only book about careers or college majors, but it is specially designed to knit the two tightly together so that you can decide about both at the same time.

You can benefit from using the book in the following ways:

- Do the quick exercises in part I to help you zero in on what is most important to you in a major and a career. Tables that accompany the exercises will help you assemble a "Hot List" of majors that may offer what you want.

- Browse the book for quick and effective information. This is easy because the description of each major begins with a quick definition of the major and the "Career Snapshot" explains how the major relates to various career tracks.

- Use the suggestions in the next section on how to follow the link from a career to a major and then to a different career.

- See specific and up-to-date facts about careers, derived from the databases of the U.S. Department of Labor.

- Easily compare majors and careers with a consistent naming scheme used for work-related skills, values, and environments (derived from the Department of Labor's databases).

- Use the handy appendix to locate majors and careers that are a good match for your personality type.

How to Make This Book Work for You

Different people will use this book differently. The following section explains how you can use this book to serve several different functions, depending on your particular needs.

Use it as a complete guide. Starting with part I, work your way through the exercises and assemble your Hot List of majors. Then move into part II to explore the majors and annotate your Hot List with notes about the related careers. This method is particularly useful for people who are undecided and like to do things in an orderly way. Or you can merely do one or two exercises to quickly generate majors to investigate.

Use it as an evaluation tool. Go directly to part II to review a major and its related careers. Take note of the required courses and skills, the value rewards, and the work environment. Then you may want to do some or all of the exercises in part I to see whether your choice is a good fit for your personality. Or create a Hot List for a more thorough evaluation; then compare your tentative choice to other majors on that list. This method is particularly useful to those who are decided on but not 100 percent committed to a major.

Use it as a skill identifier. Use the index to locate a major you have already taken or that corresponds to your career. If it is not there, use the "Your Interests" exercise in part I to find the appropriate work group for your career and then go to the majors listed in part II to find the closest equivalent(s) to your experience. Jot down the skill requirements for the major(s). Then use the "Your Skills" exercise to find majors and careers that use those skills. This method is particularly useful for people who wish to make a career change.

Use it as a major-to-career linker. Jump directly to part II to see which careers are associated with specific majors. The "Related Job Titles, Earnings, Projected Growth, and Openings" table lists the careers most commonly linked to the major. The "Career Snapshot" may suggest additional career paths to consider.

If you really want to open up your thinking, make a note of the GOE work groups listed under the "Other Characteristics" heading and then go to the "Your Interests" exercise in part I to see what other majors are associated with each work group. Look up these majors to see the related careers. This method is particularly useful for people who want to see which careers "use" a major that they have already completed (or will soon).

Use it as a resume stimulus. Go to part II and look at the major you have completed (or will soon). Make note of the skills listed for the related careers. If you have these skills, use those terms on your resume—or in cover letters and job interviews. Also, look at "Related Specialties in Majors and Careers" and "Typical Sequence of College Courses." This method is most useful for people who are looking for a job.

Where Does This Information Come From?

The information in this book comes from the best and most current sources available.

The links between majors and careers are based on a crosswalk created by the National Crosswalk Service Center and used by the U.S. Department of Labor (DOL) to search in its Occupational Information Network (O*NET) database. It is important for you to understand that the occupations listed for a major are not the *only* ones open to degree holders; they are simply the ones most commonly associated with that major. Also keep in mind that when several careers are listed for a major, they probably do not attract an equal number of degree holders. The postsecondary teaching jobs—which are listed for almost every major in this book—attract only the small number of people who pursue their study of the subject as far as a master's or doctoral degree.

The DOL is the nation's number-one source of information about careers. For valuable facts about the skills, values, satisfactions, and working environments of careers, the *Quick Guide to College Majors and Careers* draws on the most recent release of the DOL's O*NET database. The information about job growth and job openings comes from the DOL's Office of Occupational Statistics and Employment Projections. The information regarding the average earnings in each career comes from another office of the DOL, Occupational Employment Statistics. Finally, much of the information about career paths and opportunities comes from the DOL's best-selling *Occupational Outlook Handbook*. Taken together, these facts give you a good introduction to the wide range of careers linked to the majors in this book.

The information for "Typical Sequence of College Courses" is derived from research of actual college catalogs. The author examined and compared several catalogs and identified commonly required courses. You may notice some variation in the number of courses listed. Some majors have fairly standard requirements that can be listed in detail; in some cases, a professional association mandates that certain courses be included. For other majors, notably the interdisciplinary subjects, requirements are either so minimal or so varied that it is difficult to list more than a handful of typical courses.

The "Typical Sequence of High School Courses" sections are based on a general understanding of which high school courses are considered prerequisites for the college-level courses required by the major. They are suggestions: often helpful for entering the major but not always required.

When you read the information in this book about a major or career, keep in mind that the description covers what is *average* or *typical*—but in the real world plenty of exceptions exist. For example, one college may offer a major with an unusual emphasis not mentioned here. And if you start looking at "help wanted" advertisements, you may learn about jobs that require a somewhat different mix of skills than the ones listed here. Use this book as an introduction to the majors and careers. When you've found some choices that interest you, explore them in greater detail. You may be able to find a way to carve out a niche within a major or career to suit your particular abilities and interests.

PART I

What Majors and Careers Might Suit You?

Before you can figure out where you're going, it helps to understand who you are. This section will help you do that. Through some quick and easy exercises, you'll take a look at yourself and what matters most to you. You'll examine your priorities from several different angles:

- Your interests

- Your skills

- Your favorite high school courses

- Your work-related values

Each time you draw conclusions about your priorities, you'll get immediate feedback in terms of *college majors* and *work groups* (families of careers) that you should consider.

Then in "Your Hot List of College Majors and Careers," you'll put together the suggestions from the exercises for all four factors to create a Hot List of college majors that you should explore in part II.

As you do the exercises in the following sections, keep in mind that for exercises about career planning there are no "right" or "wrong" answers. The most important thing these exercises require is honesty.

Your Interests

Surely you have been in a situation where someone you knew, perhaps even a close friend, was bored by something that you found fascinating. Different people have different interests. Becoming aware of your interests is an important first step in career planning.

It is important not to exaggerate the importance of interests. In the past, people have attempted to base career guidance entirely on interests. Yet most of us are happy enough with jobs that fail to satisfy all of our interests because we can compensate by pursuing those extra interests in our spare time as *hobbies*. Therefore, the *Quick Guide to College Majors and Careers* does not suggest that your interests alone should determine your choices. You will have the chance to evaluate majors and careers using three other sets of criteria: your skills, your high school courses, and your work-related values.

In examining your interests, you will not review just any kind of interests but *work-related* interests. You will consider the interests described in the *New Guide for Occupational Exploration (GOE)*, Fourth Edition (JIST Works, 2006), which expands and updates the work originally done by a Department of Labor task force and makes it consistent with a widely used career clustering scheme developed by the Department of Education. Under this interest classification, the world of work is divided into 16 broad areas of interest (career clusters). Each interest area/cluster is further divided into work groups, for a total of 117.

Therefore, you'll follow a two-step process: First you'll identify the interest areas/clusters that appeal most to you. Then you'll zero in on interesting GOE work groups within the most appealing interest areas/clusters and you'll see the college majors linked to each work group.

Interest Areas/Clusters That Most Appeal to You

The following table names and defines the 16 interest areas/clusters. Read over the table and find one, two, or even three different interest areas/clusters that deal with the kinds of work that most interest you. Then write the names of these appealing interest areas/clusters in the blank spaces that follow the table.

Interest Areas/Clusters

Interest Area/ Cluster	Definition
01 Agriculture and Natural Resources	An interest in working with plants, animals, forests, or mineral resources for agriculture, horticulture, conservation, extraction, and other purposes.
02 Architecture and Construction	An interest in designing, assembling, and maintaining components of buildings and other structures.
03 Arts and Communication	An interest in creatively expressing feelings or ideas, in communicating news or information, or in performing.
04 Business and Administration	An interest in making a business organization or function run smoothly.
05 Education and Training	An interest in helping people learn.
06 Finance and Insurance	An interest in helping businesses and people to be assured of a financially secure future.
07 Government and Public Administration	An interest in helping a government agency serve the needs of the public.
08 Health Science	An interest in helping people and animals to be healthy.
09 Hospitality, Tourism, and Recreation	An interest in catering to the personal wishes and needs of others, so that they might enjoy a clean environment, good food and drink, comfortable lodging away from home, and recreation.
10 Human Service	An interest in improving people's social, mental, emotional, or spiritual well-being.
11 Information Technology	An interest in designing, developing, managing, and supporting information systems.
12 Law and Public Safety	An interest in upholding people's rights or in protecting people and property by using authority, inspecting, or investigating.
13 Manufacturing	An interest in processing materials into intermediate or final products or maintaining and repairing products by using machines or hand tools.

(continued)

(continued)

Interest Areas/Clusters	
Interest Area/ Cluster	**Definition**
14 Retail and Wholesale Sales and Service	An interest in bringing others to a particular point of view by personal persuasion and by sales and promotional techniques.
15 Scientific Research, Engineering, and Mathematics	An interest in discovering, collecting, and analyzing information about the natural world; in applying scientific research findings and technology; and in imagining and manipulating quantitative data.
16 Transportation, Distribution, and Logistics	An interest in operations that move people or materials.

List, in order of appeal, as many as three interest areas/clusters where you would find the most satisfaction.

1. _____

2. _____

3. _____

GOE Work Groups and Majors That You Find Most Interesting

In the following table, look for the interest areas/clusters that you wrote in the preceding blank spaces. For each interest area/cluster, note the specific GOE work groups included; the table defines them in terms of what the workers do. If a GOE work group appeals to you, scan the names of the related college majors. Circle the college majors that seem intriguing. Then, in the blank spaces that follow the table, write down the four-digit codes of the most interesting GOE work groups and the names of related college majors that you might want to explore. **Hint:** Try to include not just the "definitely" majors but also the "maybe" majors. In the exercises that follow, you'll be able to narrow down your choices further.

Interest Areas/Clusters with GOE Work Groups and Related College Majors

01 Agriculture and Natural Resources

GOE Work Group	Workers in This Field...	Related College Majors
Managerial Work in Agriculture and Natural Resources, 01.01	Manage and coordinate businesses or workers who tend plants and animals or who drill or dig for oil or minerals.	Agricultural business and economics, agronomy and crop science, forestry, horticulture, wildlife management
Resource Science/Engineering for Plants, Animals, and the Environment, 01.02	Do research to find out more about plants, animals, and natural resources.	Agricultural engineering, agronomy and crop science, animal science, forestry, petroleum engineering, soil science, wildlife management, zoology
Resource Technologies for Plants, Animals, and the Environment, 01.03	Handle technical duties as part of a team doing research or engineering in the field of plants, animals, or natural resources.	Environmental science, food science
General Farming, 01.04	Raise plants or animals in a farm or ranch setting.	Horticulture
Nursery, Groundskeeping, and Pest Control, 01.05	Care for trees, shrubs, and lawns or apply chemicals to control pests.	Horticulture
Forestry and Logging, 01.06	Maintain forests and extract wood from them.	Forestry

02 Architecture and Construction

GOE Work Group	Workers in This Field...	Related College Majors
Managerial Work in Architecture and Construction, 02.01	Directly supervise and coordinate activities of the workers who construct buildings, roads, or other structures.	Business management, operations management
Architectural Design, 02.02	Plan and design buildings and landscapes and help supervise construction.	Architecture, landscape architecture

(continued)

(continued)

Interest Areas/Clusters with GOE Work Groups and Related College Majors

03 Arts and Communication

GOE Work Group	Workers in This Field...	Related College Majors
Managerial Work in Arts and Communication, 03.01	Manage people who work in the arts and communication.	Drama/theater arts, film/cinema studies, graphic design/commercial art/illustration, public relations
Writing and Editing, 03.02	Write or edit prose or poetry.	Journalism and mass communications
News, Broadcasting, and Public Relations, 03.03	Write, edit, translate, and report factual or persuasive information.	Chinese, classics, French, German, Japanese, journalism and mass communications, modern foreign language, public relations, Russian, Spanish
Studio Art, 03.04	Draw, paint, or sculpt works of art.	Art
Design, 03.05	Design consumer goods and interior spaces in which visual appeal is important.	Family and consumer sciences, graphic design/commercial art/illustration, horticulture, industrial design, interior design
Drama, 03.06	Direct dramatic works, perform in them for the public, provide essential services for actors, or use actors' voices to make announcements.	Drama/theater arts, film/cinema studies
Music, 03.07	Direct, compose, or perform instrumental or vocal music for the public.	Drama/theater arts, film/cinema studies, music
Dance, 03.08	Plan or perform works of dance.	Dance
Media Technology, 03.09	Perform technical tasks associated with broadcasting and technological forms of art.	Film/cinema studies, graphic design/commercial art/illustration, photography

Interest Areas/Clusters with GOE Work Groups and Related College Majors

04 Business and Administration

GOE Work Group	Workers in This Field...	Related College Majors
Managerial Work in General Business, 04.01	Are top-level and middle-level administrators who direct all or part of the activities in business establishments.	Business management, human resources management, industrial and labor relations, international business, international relations, public administration
Managerial Work in Business Detail, 04.02	Supervise and coordinate certain high-level business activities: contracts for buying or selling goods and services, office support services, facilities planning and maintenance, customer service, administrative support.	Business management, public administration
Human Resources Support, 04.03	Help a business or government agency by identifying skills that the business needs, selecting the best job candidates, training and rewarding them appropriately, and evaluating their performance.	Human resources management, industrial and labor relations
Accounting, Auditing, and Analytical Support, 04.05	Use mathematics, logic, computerized tools, and knowledge of industry practices and government regulations to help businesses and government agencies make decisions.	Accounting, business management, finance, operations management, operations research, transportation and logistics management

05 Education and Training

GOE Work Group	Workers in This Field...	Related College Majors
Preschool, Elementary, and Secondary Teaching and Instructing, 05.02	Do general and specialized teaching in classrooms, working with young children or teenagers.	Business education, early childhood education, elementary education, family and consumer sciences, industrial/ technology education, physical education, secondary education, special education

(continued)

(continued)

Interest Areas/Clusters with GOE Work Groups and Related College Majors

05 Education and Training

GOE Work Group	Workers in This Field...	Related College Majors
Postsecondary and Adult Teaching and Instructing, 05.03	Teach specialized subjects to adults.	Related to most majors, because any subject can be taught at the college level.
Library Services, 05.04	Provide library services that connect people with information.	Library science
Archival and Museum Services, 05.05	Acquire and preserve items of lasting value for the benefit of researchers or the general public.	Art history, history
Counseling, Health, and Fitness Education, 05.06	Help people lead healthy and well-directed lives.	Physical education, sports management

06 Finance and Insurance

GOE Work Group	Workers in This Field...	Related College Majors
Managerial Work in Finance and Insurance, 06.01	Manage an organization's financial forecasting and reporting, investments, and cash.	Finance
Finance/Insurance Investigation and Analysis, 06.02	Analyze and evaluate financial information to help managers make decisions and plans regarding financial transactions such as investments and insurance claims.	Accounting, business management, economics, finance, insurance, mechanical engineering
Finance/Insurance Sales and Support, 06.05	Sell services such as investment counseling, insurance, and advertising.	Finance, insurance

07 Government and Public Administration

GOE Work Group	Workers in This Field...	Related College Majors
Managerial Work in Government and Public Administration, 07.01	Are top-level and middle-level administrators who direct all or part of the activities in government agencies or community outreach organizations.	Business management, public administration

Interest Areas/Clusters with GOE Work Groups and Related College Majors

07 Government and Public Administration

GOE Work Group	Workers in This Field...	Related College Majors
Public Planning, 07.02	Plan the development or redevelopment of cities, towns, and rural areas or help the professionals who lead the planning projects.	Urban studies
Regulations Enforcement, 07.03	Protect the public by assuring that people are not exposed to unsafe products, facilities, or practices.	Accounting, criminal justice/law enforcement, occupational health and industrial hygiene, wildlife management
Public Administration Clerical Support, 07.04	Perform clerical tasks that contribute to the functioning of courts, city governments, and licensing bureaus.	Journalism and mass communications

08 Health Science

GOE Work Group	Workers in This Field...	Related College Majors
Managerial Work in Medical and Health Services, 08.01	Manage health-care activities.	Health information systems administration, hospital/health facilities administration
Medicine and Surgery, 08.02	Diagnose and treat human diseases, disorders, and injuries.	Medicine, nursing (RN training), pharmacy, physician assisting
Dentistry, 08.03	Provide health care for patients' teeth and mouth tissues.	Dentistry
Health Specialties, 08.04	Are health professionals who specialize in certain parts of the human body.	Chiropractic, optometry, podiatry
Animal Care, 08.05	Care for and train animals of many kinds.	Veterinary medicine
Medical Technology, 08.06	Use technology to detect signs of disease and to assist in treatment of patients.	Clinical laboratory technology, health information systems administration, orthotics/prosthetics

(continued)

(continued)

Interest Areas/Clusters with GOE Work Groups and Related College Majors

08 Health Science

GOE Work Group	Workers in This Field...	Related College Majors
Medical Therapy, 08.07	Care for, treat, or train people to improve their physical and emotional well-being.	Occupational therapy, physical therapy, speech pathology and audiology
Health Protection and Promotion, 08.09	Help people maintain good health.	Dietetics

09 Hospitality, Tourism, and Recreation

GOE Work Group	Workers in This Field...	Related College Majors
Managerial Work in Hospitality and Tourism, 09.01	Manage all or part of the activities in restaurants, hotels, resorts, and other places where people expect good personal service.	Hotel/motel and restaurant management
Recreational Services, 09.02	Provide services to help people enjoy their leisure activities.	Recreation and parks management, sports management
Sports, 09.06	Compete or officiate in athletic events or improve the athletic skills of teams and individual competitors.	Physical education, sports management

10 Human Service

GOE Work Group	Workers in This Field...	Related College Majors
Counseling and Social Work, 10.01	Help people deal with their problems and major life events.	Hotel/motel and restaurant management, psychology, social work
Religious Work, 10.02	Conduct worship services, help people deal with spiritual problems, and provide religious education.	Philosophy, religion/religious studies

11 Information Technology

GOE Work Group	Workers in This Field...	Related College Majors
Managerial Work in Information Technology, 11.01	Manage complex computer resources and the people who work with those resources.	Computer science, management information systems, operations management

Interest Areas/Clusters with GOE Work Groups and Related College Majors

11 Information Technology

GOE Work Group	Workers in This Field...	Related College Majors
Information Technology Specialties, 11.02	Use computer hardware and software to process information, solve problems, and conduct research.	Computer engineering, computer science, management information systems

12 Law and Public Safety

GOE Work Group	Workers in This Field...	Related College Majors
Managerial Work in Law and Public Safety, 12.01	Manage fire and police departments.	Public administration
Legal Practice and Justice Administration, 12.02	Provide legal advice and representation to clients, hear and make decisions on court cases, and help individuals and groups reach agreements.	Law
Legal Support, 12.03	Conduct investigations into legal matters and prepare drafts of legal documents.	Law
Law Enforcement and Public Safety, 12.04	Enforce laws and investigate suspicious persons and acts.	Criminal justice/law enforcement
Safety and Security, 12.05	Protect people, animals, and property.	Criminal justice/law enforcement

13 Manufacturing

GOE Work Group	Workers in This Field...	Related College Majors
Managerial Work in Manufacturing, 13.01	Manage manufacturing and repair processes.	Business management, operations management
Production Precision Work, 13.06	Manufacture products with precise requirements for size, shape, color, freedom from contamination, or some other characteristic.	Orthotics/prosthetics
Graphic Arts Production, 13.08	Produce printed materials and photographic reproductions.	Graphic design/commercial art/illustration

(continued)

(continued)

Interest Areas/Clusters with GOE Work Groups and Related College Majors

13 Manufacturing

GOE Work Group	Workers in This Field...	Related College Majors
Hands-On Work, Assorted Materials, 13.09	Perform manufacturing tasks, mostly by hand, but with some use of tools and equipment.	Graphic design/commercial art/illustration

14 Retail and Wholesale Sales and Service

GOE Work Group	Workers in This Field...	Related College Majors
Managerial Work in Retail/Wholesale Sales and Service, 14.01	Direct or manage various kinds of selling and/or advertising operations—either a department within a business or a specialized business firm that contracts to provide selling and/or advertising services.	Advertising, business management, family and consumer sciences, horticulture, marketing, public relations
General Sales, 14.03	Sell and solicit orders for products and services of many kinds.	Advertising, horticulture, insurance
Personal Soliciting, 14.04	Appeal to people directly and sell them merchandise or services.	Insurance
Purchasing, 14.05	Buy goods and services, either for a business to use or for resale.	Family and consumer sciences, insurance

15 Scientific Research, Engineering, and Mathematics

GOE Work Group	Workers in This Field...	Related College Majors
Managerial Work in Scientific Research, Engineering, and Mathematics, 15.01	Manage scientists who do research, engineers who apply scientific principles to solve real-world problems, and workers who study and apply the principles of mathematics.	Aeronautical/aerospace engineering, agricultural engineering, architecture, astronomy, biochemistry, bioengineering, biology, botany, chemical engineering, chemistry, civil engineering, computer engineering, earth sciences, electrical engineering, geology, industrial engineering, landscape architecture,

Interest Areas/Clusters with GOE Work Groups and Related College Majors

15 Scientific Research, Engineering, and Mathematics

GOE Work Group	Workers in This Field...	Related College Majors
		materials science, mathematics, mechanical engineering, metallurgical engineering, meteorology, microbiology/bacteriology, oceanography, operations research, petroleum engineering, physics, statistics, urban studies, zoology
Physical Sciences, 15.02	Are concerned mostly with nonliving things such as chemicals, rocks, metals, and movements of the earth and stars.	Astronomy, chemistry, earth sciences, geography, geology, materials science, meteorology, oceanography, physics
Life Sciences, 15.03	Do research and conduct experiments to find out more about plants, animals, and other living things.	Biochemistry, environmental science, microbiology/bacteriology
Social Sciences, 15.04	Gather, study, and analyze information about individuals, groups, or entire societies.	Agricultural business and economics, anthropology, archeology, classics, economics, history, international relations, political science, psychology, sociology, urban studies
Physical Science Laboratory Technology, 15.05	Use special laboratory techniques and equipment to perform tests in such fields as chemistry and physics and then record information resulting from experiments and tests.	Food science
Mathematics and Data Analysis, 15.06	Use advanced math, statistics, and computer programs to solve problems and conduct research.	Actuarial science, mathematics, statistics

(continued)

(continued)

Interest Areas/Clusters with GOE Work Groups and Related College Majors

15 Scientific Research, Engineering, and Mathematics

GOE Work Group	Workers in This Field...	Related College Majors
Research and Design Engineering, 15.07	Plan, design, and direct the development and construction of buildings, bridges, roads, airports, dams, sewage systems, air conditioning systems, mining machinery, and other structures and equipment.	Aeronautical/aerospace engineering, bioengineering, chemical engineering, civil engineering, computer engineering, electrical engineering, mechanical engineering, metallurgical engineering
Industrial and Safety Engineering, 15.08	Utilize scientific principles to improve the functioning of a business or to make its processes and products safer.	Industrial engineering

16 Transportation, Distribution, and Logistics

GOE Work Group	Workers in This Field...	Related College Majors
Managerial Work in Transportation, 16.01	Manage transportation services.	Business management, public administration, transportation and logistics management

Write down the three GOE work groups in which you have the greatest interest, using the left column of the list that follows. In the right column, put the most interesting college majors that are related to the work groups that interest you.

Work Groups and College Majors That Relate to My Interests

1. _____   _____

          _____

          _____

          _____

          _____

2. _____   _____

                                _____

                                _____

                                _____

                                _____

3. _____   _____

                                _____

                                _____

                                _____

                                _____

Your Skills

Different kinds of work demand different skills. Most people want to find work that is generally consistent with their skills so they will be competent to meet the skill requirements. Of course, you don't yet *have* all the skills you will need for your career—that's why you are planning to get further education. Nevertheless, based on your experience in school, you probably have a good idea of which skills you learn easily and which come harder. You may also have work experience that indicates some of your skills.

The following chart lists and defines 34 skills that the U.S. Department of Labor (DOL) describes in the O*NET database. For each skill in the chart, ask yourself, "What things have I done in which I've used this skill at a high level and *enjoyed* using it?" If you can think of several good examples, mark the name of the skill with a plus sign or an underline; otherwise, move on to another skill.

Which Skills Are Most Important to You?

Skill	Description
Active Learning	Working with new material or information to grasp its implications
Active Listening	Listening to what other people are saying and asking questions as appropriate
Complex Problem-Solving	Identifying complex problems, reviewing the options, and implementing solutions
Coordination	Adjusting actions in relation to others' actions
Critical Thinking	Using logic and analysis to identify the strengths and weaknesses of different approaches
Equipment Maintenance	Performing routine maintenance and determining when and what kind of maintenance is needed
Equipment Selection	Determining the kind of tools and equipment needed to do a job
Installation	Installing equipment, machines, wiring, or programs to meet specifications
Instructing	Teaching others how to do something
Judgment and Decision Making	Weighing the relative costs and benefits of a potential action
Learning Strategies	Using multiple approaches when learning or teaching new things
Management of Financial Resources	Determining how money will be spent to get the work done and accounting for these expenditures
Management of Material Resources	Obtaining and seeing to the appropriate use of equipment, facilities, and materials needed to do certain work
Management of Personnel Resources	Motivating, developing, and directing people as they work, identifying the best people for the job
Mathematics	Using mathematics to solve problems
Monitoring	Assessing how well one is doing when learning or doing something
Negotiation	Bringing others together and trying to reconcile differences
Operation Monitoring	Watching gauges, dials, or other indicators to make sure a machine is working properly
Operations Analysis	Analyzing needs and product requirements to create a design

Which Skills Are Most Important to You?	
Persuasion	Persuading others to approach things differently
Programming	Writing computer programs for various purposes
Quality Control Analysis	Evaluating the quality or performance of products, services, or processes
Reading Comprehension	Understanding written sentences and paragraphs in work-related documents
Repairing	Repairing machines or systems, using the needed tools
Science	Using scientific methods to solve problems
Service Orientation	Actively looking for ways to help people
Social Perceptiveness	Being aware of others' reactions and understanding why they react the way they do
Speaking	Talking to others to effectively convey information
Systems Analysis	Determining how a system should work and how changes will affect outcomes
Systems Evaluation	Looking at many indicators of system performance, taking into account their accuracy
Technology Design	Generating or adapting equipment and technology to serve user needs
Time Management	Managing one's own time and the time of others
Troubleshooting	Determining what is causing an operating error and deciding what to do about it
Writing	Communicating effectively with others in writing as indicated by the needs of the audience

Now that you've looked at all the skills, determine the three skills that you would most like to use in your career and list them below.

The Most Desirable Skills for My Career
1. _____
2. _____
3. _____

The following table relates each of the 34 skills to college majors and to the 5 *New Guide for Occupational Exploration (GOE)* work groups for which the skill is most important. (It might also be used by other work groups, but at a lower level.) For a skill to be linked to a work group, it must be important for *all* the careers in the work group, not just the careers linked to the majors in this book. Using the three skills that you just listed, find the corresponding college majors and work groups. At the end of this section, enter the college majors and work groups that match your skills.

A skill applies to a college major because it is required by the occupations to which the major is linked. You do not necessarily need this skill *in* the college major, but it is likely that learning this skill will be part of what you do in the major.

Relationship of Skills to College Majors and Work Groups		
Skill	**College Majors**	**Work Groups (GOE)**
Active Learning	African American studies, American studies, anthropology, archeology, area studies, Asian studies, astronomy, biochemistry, biology, botany, dentistry, earth sciences, geology, Hispanic American studies, medicine, microbiology/bacteriology, oceanography, physics, podiatry, political science, sociology, veterinary medicine, women's studies	Legal Practice and Justice Administration, 12.02 Life Sciences, 15.03 Mathematics and Data Analysis, 15.06 Physical Sciences, 15.02 Postsecondary and Adult Teaching and Instructing, 05.03
Active Listening	Anthropology, English, law, medicine, optometry, podiatry, psychology	Health Specialties, 08.04 Legal Practice and Justice Administration, 12.02 Life Sciences, 15.03 Medicine and Surgery, 08.02 Social Sciences, 15.04
Complex Problem Solving	Animal science, anthropology, archeology, architecture, astronomy, biochemistry, chemical engineering, chiropractic, civil engineering, computer engineering, computer science, dentistry, electrical engineering, international relations, materials science, medicine, microbiology/bacteriology, occupational health and industrial hygiene, operations research, orthotics/	Architectural Design, 02.02 Managerial Work in Scientific Research, Engineering, and Mathematics, 15.01 Physical Sciences, 15.02 Life Sciences, 15.03 Research and Design Engineering, 15.07

Relationship of Skills to College Majors and Work Groups

Skill	College Majors	Work Groups (GOE)
	prosthetics, petroleum engineering, physician assisting, physics, podiatry, veterinary medicine	
Coordination	International relations, religion/religious studies	Architectural Design, 02.02 Music, 03.07 Religious Work, 10.02 Research and Design Engineering, 15.07 Resource Science/Engineering for Plants, Animals, and the Environment, 01.02
Critical Thinking	African American studies, American studies, anthropology, archeology, area studies, art history, Asian studies, biochemistry, chiropractic, dentistry, English, Hispanic American studies, hospital/health facilities administration, law, medicine, microbiology/bacteriology, orthotics/prosthetics, physician assisting, podiatry, political science, sociology, veterinary medicine, women's studies	Health Specialties, 08.04 Legal Practice and Justice Administration, 12.02 Life Sciences, 15.03 Managerial Work in Medical and Health Services, 08.01 Postsecondary and Adult Teaching and Instructing, 05.03
Equipment Maintenance	Agronomy and crop science, podiatry	Dentistry, 08.03 Forestry and Logging, 01.06 Graphic Arts Production, 13.08 Managerial Work in Agriculture and Natural Resources, 01.01 Physical Science Laboratory Technology, 15.05
Equipment Selection	Podiatry	Dentistry, 08.03 Industrial and Safety Engineering, 15.08

(continued)

(continued)

Relationship of Skills to College Majors and Work Groups		
Skill	**College Majors**	**Work Groups (GOE)**
		Managerial Work in Agriculture and Natural Resources, 01.01
		Physical Sciences, 15.02
		Research and Design Engineering, 15.07
Installation	Agricultural business and economics, agricultural engineering, bioengineering, chemical engineering, civil engineering, computer engineering, computer science, electrical engineering, industrial engineering, landscape architecture, management information systems, materials science, mechanical engineering, metallurgical engineering, petroleum engineering, urban studies	Information Technology Specialties, 11.02
		Managerial Work in Architecture and Construction, 02.01
		Managerial Work in Information Technology, 11.01
		Managerial Work in Scientific Research, Engineering, and Mathematics, 15.01
		Research and Design Engineering, 15.07
Instructing	Actuarial science, African American studies, American studies, anthropology, archeology, area studies, art history, Asian studies, biochemistry, business education, chiropractic, dance, dentistry, elementary education, English, geography, Hispanic American studies, humanities, industrial/technology education, medicine, occupational health and industrial hygiene, occupational therapy, orthotics/prosthetics, physical education, physical therapy, physician assisting, political science, secondary education, sociology, speech pathology and audiology, veterinary medicine, women's studies	Counseling, Health, and Fitness Education, 05.06
		Dance, 03.08
		Medicine and Surgery, 08.02
		Postsecondary and Adult Teaching and Instructing, 05.03
		Preschool, Elementary, and Secondary Teaching and Instructing, 05.02
Judgment and Decision Making	Aeronautical/aerospace engineering, civil engineering, dentistry, international relations, law, medicine, microbiology/bacteriology, optometry, petroleum engineering,	Health Specialties, 08.04
		Legal Practice and Justice Administration, 12.02

Relationship of Skills to College Majors and Work Groups

Skill	College Majors	Work Groups (GOE)
	philosophy, podiatry, religion/religious studies, veterinary medicine	Life Sciences, 15.03 Religious Work, 10.02 Research and Design Engineering, 15.07
Learning Strategies	African American studies, American studies, area studies, art, Asian studies, business education, chiropractic, elementary education, English, Hispanic American studies, hospital/health facilities administration, humanities, industrial/technology education, orthotics/prosthetics, physical education, physical therapy, political science, psychology, secondary education, sociology, special education, speech pathology and audiology, veterinary medicine, women's studies	Medicine and Surgery, 08.02 Postsecondary and Adult Teaching and Instructing, 05.03 Preschool, Elementary, and Secondary Teaching and Instructing, 05.02 Religious Work, 10.02 Social Sciences, 15.04
Management of Financial Resources	Accounting, aeronautical/aerospace engineering, agricultural business and economics, agricultural engineering, agronomy and crop science, animal science, anthropology, archeology, architecture, biochemistry, bioengineering, business management, chemical engineering, civil engineering, dentistry, earth sciences, electrical engineering, finance, forestry, geology, hospital/health facilities administration, hotel/motel and restaurant management, industrial engineering, international business, international relations, landscape architecture, library science, marketing, materials science, medicine, metallurgical engineering, microbiology/bacteriology, oceanography, petroleum engineering, philosophy, podiatry, public administration, recreation and parks management, soil science, urban studies	Accounting, Auditing, and Analytical Support, 04.05 Architectural Design, 02.02 Managerial Work in Finance and Insurance, 06.01 Managerial Work in General Business, 04.01 Religious Work, 10.02

(continued)

(continued)

Relationship of Skills to College Majors and Work Groups		
Skill	**College Majors**	**Work Groups (GOE)**
Management of Material Resources	Agricultural business and economics, agronomy and crop science, business management, dentistry, hospital/health facilities administration, international business, international relations, library science, optometry, public administration, recreation and parks management, soil science	Managerial Work in General Business, 04.01 Managerial Work in Medical and Health Services, 08.01 Managerial Work in Agriculture and Natural Resources, 01.01 Physical Sciences, 15.02 Religious Work, 10.02
Management of Personnel Resources	Animal science, astronomy, business management, dentistry, earth sciences, geology, hospital/health facilities administration, hotel/motel and restaurant management, international business, international relations, marketing, medicine, meteorology, microbiology/bacteriology, oceanography, operations management, optometry, philosophy, public administration, recreation and parks management, religion/religious studies, soil science	Religious Work, 10.02 Managerial Work in General Business, 04.01 Managerial Work in Manufacturing, 13.01 Managerial Work in Law and Public Safety, 12.01 Managerial Work in Government and Public Administration, 07.01
Mathematics	Accounting, actuarial science, aeronautical/aerospace engineering, agricultural engineering, animal science, astronomy, bioengineering, chemical engineering, chemistry, civil engineering, computer engineering, earth sciences, electrical engineering, geology, industrial engineering, landscape architecture, materials science, mathematics, mechanical engineering, metallurgical engineering, meteorology, oceanography, operations research, petroleum engineering, physics, soil science, statistics, urban studies	Mathematics and Data Analysis, 15.06 Research and Design Engineering, 15.07 Managerial Work in Scientific Research, Engineering, and Mathematics, 15.01 Physical Sciences, 15.02 Resource Science/Engineering for Plants, Animals, and the Environment, 01.02
Monitoring	Business education, dentistry, hospital/health facilities administration, industrial/technology education, international business, international relations, medicine, physical education, secondary education	Managerial Work in General Business, 04.01 Health Specialties, 08.04 Managerial Work in Government and Public Administration, 07.01

Relationship of Skills to College Majors and Work Groups		
Skill	**College Majors**	**Work Groups (GOE)**
		Religious Work, 10.02
		Postsecondary and Adult Teaching and Instructing, 05.03
Negotiation	Advertising, anthropology, architecture, civil engineering, criminal justice/law enforcement, international business, international relations, law, marketing, philosophy, psychology, religion/religious studies	Legal Practice and Justice Administration, 12.02
		Religious Work, 10.02
		Social Sciences, 15.04
		Law Enforcement and Public Safety, 12.04
		Managerial Work in General Business, 04.01
Operation Monitoring	Agricultural business and economics, food science	Physical Science Laboratory Technology, 15.05
		Graphic Arts Production, 13.08
		Resource Technologies for Plants, Animals, and the Environment, 01.03
		Physical Sciences, 15.02
		Managerial Work in Manufacturing, 13.01
Operations Analysis	Aeronautical/aerospace engineering, agricultural engineering, animal science, architecture, bioengineering, chemical engineering, civil engineering, computer engineering, computer science, electrical engineering, international relations, landscape architecture, management information systems, materials science, mechanical engineering, metallurgical engineering, operations research, petroleum engineering, urban studies	Architectural Design, 02.02
		Research and Design Engineering, 15.07
		Managerial Work in Scientific Research, Engineering, and Mathematics, 15.01
		Managerial Work in Information Technology, 11.01
		Information Technology Specialties, 11.02

(continued)

(continued)

Relationship of Skills to College Majors and Work Groups

Skill	College Majors	Work Groups (GOE)
Persuasion	Aeronautical/aerospace engineering, African American studies, American studies, area studies, Asian studies, business education, civil engineering, criminal justice/law enforcement, English, Hispanic American studies, hospital/health facilities administration, industrial/technology education, interior design, international relations, law, medicine, optometry, philosophy, photography, physical education, political science, public relations, religion/religious studies, secondary education, women's studies	Legal Practice and Justice Administration, 12.02 Religious Work, 10.02 Law Enforcement and Public Safety, 12.04 Health Specialties, 08.04 Finance/Insurance Sales and Support, 06.05
Programming	Animal science, computer engineering, computer science, electrical engineering, management information systems, operations research	Information Technology Specialties, 11.02 Mathematics and Data Analysis, 15.06 Managerial Work in Information Technology, 11.01 Physical Sciences, 15.02 Research and Design Engineering, 15.07
Quality Control Analysis	Aeronautical/aerospace engineering, agricultural engineering, architecture, bioengineering, chemical engineering, chemistry, civil engineering, clinical laboratory technology, computer engineering, computer science, electrical engineering, food science, hospital/health facilities administration, landscape architecture, materials science, metallurgical engineering, petroleum engineering	Physical Sciences, 15.02 Physical Science Laboratory Technology, 15.05 Managerial Work in Scientific Research, Engineering, and Mathematics, 15.01 Resource Technologies for Plants, Animals, and the Environment, 01.03 Research and Design Engineering, 15.07
Reading Comprehension	African American studies, American studies, animal science, anthropology, archeology, area studies, Asian studies, astronomy, biochemistry, biology, botany, chiropractic,	Legal Practice and Justice Administration, 12.02 Health Specialties, 08.04 Life Sciences, 15.03

Relationship of Skills to College Majors and Work Groups

Skill	College Majors	Work Groups (GOE)
	dentistry, English, geography, Hispanic American studies, law, medicine, microbiology/bacteriology, occupational health and industrial hygiene, occupational therapy, operations research, optometry, orthotics/prosthetics, pharmacy, physical therapy, physician assisting, physics, podiatry, political science, sociology, soil science, speech pathology and audiology, veterinary medicine, women's studies, zoology	Postsecondary and Adult Teaching and Instructing, 05.03 Medicine and Surgery, 08.02
Repairing	Agricultural business and economics, agronomy and crop science, horticulture	Managerial Work in Agriculture and Natural Resources, 01.01 Managerial Work in Architecture and Construction, 02.01 General Farming, 01.04 Forestry and Logging, 01.06 Managerial Work in Information Technology, 11.01
Science	Aeronautical/aerospace engineering, agricultural engineering, animal science, anthropology, archeology, architecture, astronomy, biochemistry, bioengineering, biology, botany, chemical engineering, chemistry, chiropractic, civil engineering, clinical laboratory technology, computer engineering, computer science, dentistry, earth sciences, electrical engineering, environmental science, food science, forestry, geography, geology, industrial engineering, landscape architecture, materials science, mathematics, mechanical engineering, medicine, metallurgical engineering, meteorology, microbiology/bacteriology, nursing (RN training), occupational health and industrial hygiene, occupational therapy, oceanography, operations research, optometry, orthotics/prosthetics, petroleum engineering, pharmacy, physical therapy,	Physical Sciences, 15.02 Life Sciences, 15.03 Research and Design Engineering, 15.07 Managerial Work in Scientific Research, Engineering, and Mathematics, 15.01 Health Specialties, 08.04

(continued)

(continued)

Relationship of Skills to College Majors and Work Groups		
Skill	**College Majors**	**Work Groups (GOE)**
	physician assisting, physics, podiatry, sociology, soil science, speech pathology and audiology, statistics, urban studies, veterinary medicine, wildlife management, zoology	
Service Orientation	Hospital/health facilities administration, medicine, nursing (RN Training), philosophy, public relations, recreation and parks management, religion/religious studies	Religious Work, 10.02 Managerial Work in Government and Public Administration, 07.01 Health Specialties, 08.04 Medicine and Surgery, 08.02 Managerial Work in Law and Public Safety, 12.01
Social Perceptiveness	African American studies, American studies, anthropology, area studies, Asian studies, business education, criminal justice/law enforcement, English, Hispanic American studies, humanities, industrial/technology education, medicine, nursing (RN training), philosophy, physical education, psychology, religion/religious studies, secondary education, social work, sociology, special education, women's studies	Social Sciences, 15.04 Counseling and Social Work, 10.01 Religious Work, 10.02 Managerial Work in Government and Public Administration, 07.01 Medicine and Surgery, 08.02
Speaking	African American studies, American studies, anthropology, area studies, Asian studies, chiropractic, dentistry, English, Hispanic American studies, humanities, law, orthotics/prosthetics, political science, religion/religious studies, sociology, speech pathology and audiology, veterinary medicine, women's studies	Legal Practice and Justice Administration, 12.02 Postsecondary and Adult Teaching and Instructing, 05.03 Religious Work, 10.02 Drama, 03.06 Managerial Work in Medical and Health Services, 08.01
Systems Analysis	Aeronautical/aerospace engineering, animal science, computer engineering, computer science, electrical engineering, international relations, management information systems, operations research	Research and Design Engineering, 15.07 Managerial Work in Information Technology, 11.01

Relationship of Skills to College Majors and Work Groups		
Skill	**College Majors**	**Work Groups (GOE)**
		Information Technology Specialties, 11.02 Accounting, Auditing, and Analytical Support, 04.05 Physical Sciences, 15.02
Systems Evaluation	Aeronautical/aerospace engineering, animal science, computer engineering, computer science, electrical engineering, health information systems administration, hospital/health facilities administration, international relations, management information systems, operations research	Managerial Work in Information Technology, 11.01 Research and Design Engineering, 15.07 Information Technology Specialties, 11.02 Managerial Work in Government and Public Administration, 07.01 Physical Sciences, 15.02
Technology Design	Aeronautical/aerospace engineering, agricultural engineering, animal science, architecture, bioengineering, chemical engineering, chemistry, civil engineering, computer engineering, computer science, electrical engineering, industrial engineering, landscape architecture, management information systems, materials science, metallurgical engineering, petroleum engineering, urban studies	Managerial Work in Scientific Research, Engineering, and Mathematics, 15.01 Research and Design Engineering, 15.07 Information Technology Specialties, 11.02 Managerial Work in Information Technology, 11.01 Physical Sciences, 15.02
Time Management	Biochemistry, dentistry, international relations, microbiology/bacteriology, secondary education	Legal Practice and Justice Administration, 12.02 Physical Sciences, 15.02 Life Sciences, 15.03 Managerial Work in Finance and Insurance, 06.01 Managerial Work in Scientific Research, Engineering, and Mathematics, 15.01

(continued)

(continued)

Relationship of Skills to College Majors and Work Groups		
Skill	**College Majors**	**Work Groups (GOE)**
Troubleshooting	Computer engineering, computer science, electrical engineering	Information Technology Specialties, 11.02 Managerial Work in Information Technology, 11.01 Research and Design Engineering, 15.07 Managerial Work in Architecture and Construction, 02.01 Physical Sciences, 15.02
Writing	African American studies, American studies, animal science, anthropology, archeology, area studies, Asian studies, astronomy, biochemistry, biology, botany, chiropractic, English, geography, Hispanic American studies, history, humanities, law, microbiology/bacteriology, occupational health and industrial hygiene, occupational therapy, orthotics/prosthetics, physical therapy, physician assisting, physics, political science, sociology, soil science, speech pathology and audiology, veterinary medicine, women's studies, zoology	Legal Practice and Justice Administration, 12.02 Postsecondary and Adult Teaching and Instructing, 05.03 Social Sciences, 15.04 Writing and Editing, 03.02 News, Broadcasting, and Public Relations, 03.03

Write down the college majors and work groups that correspond with the three skills you listed earlier in this section. If there are many, try to find college majors and work groups that are linked to *more than one* of your important skills. Write these names in the following box.

College Majors and Work Groups That Relate to My Skills
_____   _____ _____   _____ _____   _____

_____   _____

_____   _____

_____   _____

_____   _____

_____   _____

_____   _____

_____   _____

_____   _____

Your Favorite High School Courses

A good way to predict how well people will like college courses is to ask them how much they liked similar high school courses. Also, most people earn their highest grades in college courses similar to the high school courses in which they did well. Therefore, it can be useful to take note and write down the names of three high school courses that you liked and in which you earned high grades.

My Best High School Courses
1. _____
2. _____
3. _____

Next, with those courses in mind, look over the information in the following table and find related college majors and work groups from the GOE Work Groups column. As you review this information, mark the items that most closely match your best high school courses. At the end of this section, you can make a list of the best matches.

In the following table, high school courses are matched with college majors and work groups that require similar skills and appeal to similar interests. In some cases a high school course may be listed in part II of this book as common preparation for a major even though the major is not linked to the course in the following table.

The Relationship of High School Courses to College Majors and Work Groups

High School Course	College Majors	GOE Work Groups
Algebra	See Pre-Calculus	
Art	Advertising, architecture, art, art history, geography, graphic design/commercial art/illustration, industrial design, interior design, journalism and mass communications, landscape architecture, photography, public relations	Architectural Design, 02.02 Archival and Museum Services, 05.05 Design, 03.05 General Sales, 14.03 Graphic Arts Production, 13.08 Hands-On Work, Assorted Materials, 13.09 Managerial Work, 03.01, 14.01 Media Technology, 03.09 News, Broadcasting, and Public Relations, 03.03 Postsecondary and Adult Teaching and Instructing, 05.03 Public Administration Clerical Support, 07.04 Studio Art, 03.04
Biology	Agricultural business and economics, agricultural engineering, agronomy and crop science, animal science, anthropology, archeology, biochemistry, bioengineering, biology, botany, chiropractic, clinical laboratory technology, dance, dentistry, dietetics, environmental science, food science, forestry, health information systems administration, horticulture, hospital/health facilities administration, landscape architecture, medicine,	Animal Care, 08.05 Counseling and Social Work, 10.01 Dance, 03.08 Dentistry, 08.03 Forestry and Logging, 01.06 General Farming, 01.04 Health Protection and Promotion, 08.09 Health Specialties, 08.04 Life Sciences, 15.03

The Relationship of High School Courses to College Majors and Work Groups

High School Course	College Majors	GOE Work Groups
	microbiology/bacteriology, nursing (RN training), occupational therapy, oceanography, optometry, orthotics/prosthetics, pharmacy, physical therapy, physician assisting, podiatry, psychology, recreation and parks management, social work, soil science, speech pathology and audiology, veterinary medicine, wildlife management, zoology	Managerial Work, 01.01, 08.01, 15.01 Medical Technology, 08.06 Medical Therapy, 08.07 Medicine and Surgery, 08.02 Nursery, Groundskeeping, and Pest Control, 01.05 Physical Science Laboratory Technology, 15.05 Physical Sciences, 15.02 Postsecondary and Adult Teaching and Instructing, 05.03 Recreational Services, 09.02 Regulations Enforcement, 07.03 Resource Science/Engineering for Plants, Animals, and the Environment, 01.02 Resource Technologies for Plants, Animals, and the Environment, 01.03
Calculus	Actuarial science, aeronautical/aerospace engineering, agricultural engineering, architecture, astronomy, biochemistry, bioengineering, biology, botany, chemical engineering, chemistry, civil engineering, computer engineering, computer science, earth sciences, economics, electrical engineering, geology, industrial engineering, landscape architecture, materials science, mathematics, mechanical engineering, metallurgical engineering, meteorology, microbiology/bacteriology, oceanography, operations management, operations research, optometry, petroleum engineering, physics, statistics	Accounting, Auditing, and Analytical Support, 04.05 Architectural Design, 02.02 Industrial and Safety Engineering, 15.08 Information Technology Specialties, 11.02 Life Sciences, 15.03 Managerial Work, 11.01, 15.01 Mathematics and Data Analysis, 15.06 Physical Sciences, 15.02 Postsecondary and Adult Teaching and Instructing, 05.03 Research and Design Engineering, 15.07

(continued)

(continued)

The Relationship of High School Courses to College Majors and Work Groups

High School Course	College Majors	GOE Work Groups
		Resource Science/Engineering for Plants, Animals, and the Environment, 01.02
Chemistry	Aeronautical/aerospace engineering, agricultural business and economics, agricultural engineering, agronomy and crop science, animal science, anthropology, astronomy, biochemistry, bioengineering, biology, botany, chemical engineering, chemistry, chiropractic, civil engineering, clinical laboratory technology, computer engineering, computer science, dentistry, dietetics, earth sciences, electrical engineering, environmental science, food science, forestry, geology, health information systems administration, horticulture, hospital/health facilities administration, industrial engineering, materials science, mechanical engineering, medicine, metallurgical engineering, meteorology, microbiology/bacteriology, nursing (RN Training), occupational health and industrial hygiene, occupational therapy, oceanography, operations research, optometry, orthotics/prosthetics, petroleum engineering, pharmacy, physical therapy, physician assisting, physics, podiatry, recreation and parks management, soil science, speech pathology and audiology, veterinary medicine, wildlife management, zoology	Animal Care, 08.05 Dentistry, 08.03 Forestry and Logging, 01.06 General Farming, 01.04 General Sales, 14.03 Health Protection and Promotion, 08.09 Health Specialties, 08.04 Industrial and Safety Engineering, 15.08 Life Sciences, 15.03 Managerial Work, 01.01, 08.01, 15.01 Medical Technology, 08.06 Medical Therapy, 08.07 Medicine and Surgery, 08.02 Nursery, Groundskeeping, and Pest Control, 01.05 Physical Science Laboratory Technology, 15.05 Physical Sciences, 15.02 Postsecondary and Adult Teaching and Instructing, 05.03 Regulations Enforcement, 07.03 Research and Design Engineering, 15.07 Resource Science/Engineering for Plants, Animals, and the Environment, 01.02 Resource Technologies for Plants, Animals, and the Environment, 01.03

The Relationship of High School Courses to College Majors and Work Groups

High School Course	College Majors	GOE Work Groups
Computer Science	Accounting, actuarial science, aeronautical/aerospace engineering, agricultural business and economics, agricultural engineering, astronomy, biochemistry, bioengineering, business management, chemical engineering, chemistry, civil engineering, clinical laboratory technology, computer engineering, computer science, earth sciences, electrical engineering, environmental science, finance, geography, geology, graphic design/commercial art/illustration, health information systems administration, hospital/health facilities administration, hotel/motel and restaurant management, human resources management, industrial design, industrial engineering, insurance, interior design, international business, landscape architecture, library science, management information systems, marketing, materials science, mathematics, mechanical engineering, metallurgical engineering, meteorology, occupational health and industrial hygiene, oceanography, operations management, operations research, petroleum engineering, physics, public administration, soil science, statistics, transportation and logistics management, wildlife management, zoology	Accounting, Auditing, and Analytical Support, 04.05 Architectural Design, 02.02 Design, 03.05 Finance/Insurance Investigation and Analysis, 06.02 Finance/Insurance Sales and Support, 06.05 Forestry and Logging, 01.06 General Sales, 14.03 Graphic Arts Production, 13.08 Hands-On Work, Assorted Materials, 13.09 Human Resources Support, 04.03 Industrial and Safety Engineering, 15.08 Information Technology Specialties, 11.02 Library Services, 05.04 Life Sciences, 15.03 Managerial Work, 01.01, 02.01, 04.01, 06.01, 07.01, 08.01, 09.01, 11.01, 13.01, 14.01, 15.01, 16.01 Mathematics and Data Analysis, 15.06 Media Technology, 03.09 Medical Technology, 08.06 Physical Science Laboratory Technology, 15.05 Physical Sciences, 15.02

(continued)

(continued)

The Relationship of High School Courses to College Majors and Work Groups		
High School Course	**College Majors**	**GOE Work Groups**
		Postsecondary and Adult Teaching and Instructing, 05.03
		Purchasing, 14.05
		Research and Design Engineering, 15.07
		Resource Science/Engineering for Plants, Animals, and the Environment, 01.02
		Resource Technologies for Plants, Animals, and the Environment, 01.03
		Safety and Security, 12.05
		Social Sciences, 15.04
Dance	Dance, physical education	Dance, 03.08
		Preschool, Elementary, and Secondary Teaching and Instructing, 05.02
		Postsecondary and Adult Teaching and Instructing, 05.03
		Counseling, Health, and Fitness Education, 05.06
		Sports, 09.06
English	See Literature	
Family and Consumer Sciences	Family and consumer sciences	Design, 03.05
		Managerial Work in Retail/Wholesale Sales and Service, 14.01
		Postsecondary and Adult Teaching and Instructing, 05.03
		Preschool, Elementary, and Secondary Teaching and Instructing, 05.02
		Purchasing, 14.05

The Relationship of High School Courses to College Majors and Work Groups

High School Course	College Majors	GOE Work Groups
Foreign Language	Advertising, African American studies, American studies, anthropology, archeology, area studies, art, art history, Asian studies, Chinese, classics, dance, drama/theater arts, early childhood education, elementary education, English, film/cinema studies, geography, history, hotel/motel and restaurant management, human resources management, humanities, industrial and labor relations, international business, international relations, Japanese, journalism and mass communications, library science, marketing, modern foreign language, music, philosophy, public administration, public relations, religion/religious studies, Russian, secondary education, social work, sociology, sports management, teaching English as a second language, urban studies, women's studies	Archival and Museum Services, 05.05 Counseling and Social Work, 10.01 Counseling, Health, and Fitness Education, 05.06 Dance, 03.08 Drama, 03.06 Human Resources Support, 04.03 Library Services, 05.04 Managerial Work, 01.01, 03.01, 04.01, 09.01 Music, 03.07 News, Broadcasting, and Public Relations, 03.03 Postsecondary and Adult Teaching and Instructing, 05.03 Preschool, Elementary, and Secondary Teaching and Instructing, 05.02 Production Precision Work, 13.06 Public Planning, 07.02 Purchasing, 14.05 Recreational Services, 09.02 Religious Work, 10.02 Social Sciences, 15.04 Sports, 09.06 Studio Art, 03.04 Writing and Editing, 03.02
French	French	News, Broadcasting, and Public Relations, 03.03 Postsecondary and Adult Teaching and Instructing, 05.03

(continued)

(continued)

The Relationship of High School Courses to College Majors and Work Groups		
High School Course	**College Majors**	**GOE Work Groups**
Geography	Environmental science, forestry, geography, international business, wildlife management	Forestry and Logging, 01.06 Life Sciences, 15.03 Managerial Work in Agriculture and Natural Resources, 04.01 Physical Sciences, 15.02 Postsecondary and Adult Teaching and Instructing, 05.03 Regulations Enforcement, 07.03 Resource Science/Engineering for Plants, Animals, and the Environment, 01.02 Resource Technologies for Plants, Animals, and the Environment, 01.03
Geometry	See Pre-Calculus	
German	German	News, Broadcasting, and Public Relations, 03.03 Postsecondary and Adult Teaching and Instructing, 05.03
History	African American studies, American studies, anthropology, archeology, area studies, art, art history, Asian studies, Chinese, classics, English, film/cinema studies, French, geography, German, Hispanic American studies, history, humanities, interior design, international relations, Japanese, law, modern foreign language, music, philosophy, political science, religion/religious studies, Russian, Spanish, urban studies, women's studies	Archival and Museum Services, 05.05 Design, 03.05 Drama, 03.06 Law Enforcement and Public Safety, 12.04 Legal Practice and Justice Administration, 12.02 Managerial Work in Arts and Communication, 03.01 Media Technology, 03.09 Music, 03.07

The Relationship of High School Courses to College Majors and Work Groups		
High School Course	**College Majors**	**GOE Work Groups**
		News, Broadcasting, and Public Relations, 03.03
		Postsecondary and Adult Teaching and Instructing, 05.03
		Public Planning, 07.02
		Religious Work, 10.02
		Social Sciences, 15.04
		Studio Art, 03.04
Industrial Arts	Business education, industrial/technology education	Postsecondary and Adult Teaching and Instructing, 05.03
		Preschool, Elementary, and Secondary Teaching and Instructing, 05.02
Keyboarding	Business education, library science	Library Services, 05.04
		Postsecondary and Adult Teaching and Instructing, 05.03
		Preschool, Elementary, and Secondary Teaching and Instructing, 05.02
		Public Administration Clerical Support, 07.04
Literature	Advertising, African American studies, American studies, area studies, art, art history, Asian studies, Chinese, classics, drama/theater arts, English, film/cinema studies, French, German, Hispanic American studies, humanities, interior design, Japanese, journalism and mass communications, photography, public relations, Russian, Spanish, women's studies	Archival and Museum Services, 05.05
		Design, 03.05
		Drama, 03.06
		General Sales, 14.03
		Managerial Work in Arts and Communication, 03.01
		Media Technology, 03.09
		Music, 03.07
		News, Broadcasting, and Public Relations, 03.03
		Postsecondary and Adult Teaching and Instructing, 05.03

(continued)

(continued)

The Relationship of High School Courses to College Majors and Work Groups

High School Course	College Majors	GOE Work Groups
		Public Administration Clerical Support, 07.04
		Social Sciences, 15.04
		Studio Art, 03.04
		Writing and Editing, 03.02
Mechanical Drawing	Graphic design/commercial art/illustration, industrial design, industrial/technology education	Design, 03.05
		Graphic Arts Production, 13.08
		Hands-On Work, Assorted Materials, 13.09
		Managerial Work in Arts and Communication, 03.01
		Media Technology, 03.09
		Postsecondary and Adult Teaching and Instructing, 05.03
		Preschool, Elementary, and Secondary Teaching and Instructing, 05.02
Music	Dance, music	Dance, 03.08
		Music, 03.07
		Postsecondary and Adult Teaching and Instructing, 05.03
Office Computer Applications	Business education, health information systems administration, hospital/health facilities administration, library science	Library Services, 05.04
		Managerial Work in Medical and Health Services, 08.01
		Medical Technology, 08.06
		Postsecondary and Adult Teaching and Instructing, 05.03
		Preschool, Elementary, and Secondary Teaching and Instructing, 05.02
		Public Administration Clerical Support, 07.04

The Relationship of High School Courses to College Majors and Work Groups

High School Course	College Majors	GOE Work Groups
Photography	Film/cinema studies, graphic design/commercial art/illustration, industrial design, photography	Design, 03.05 Drama, 03.06 Graphic Arts Production, 13.08 Hands-On Work, Assorted Materials, 13.09 Managerial Work in Arts and Communication, 03.01 Media Technology, 03.09 Postsecondary and Adult Teaching and Instructing, 05.03
Physics	Aeronautical/aerospace engineering, architecture, astronomy, biochemistry, bioengineering, biology, botany, chemical engineering, chemistry, chiropractic, civil engineering, clinical laboratory technology, computer engineering, computer science, dentistry, dietetics, earth sciences, electrical engineering, geology, industrial engineering, interior design, landscape architecture, materials science, mathematics, mechanical engineering, medicine, metallurgical engineering, meteorology, microbiology/bacteriology, occupational health and industrial hygiene, occupational therapy, oceanography, operations research, optometry, orthotics/prosthetics, petroleum engineering, pharmacy, photography, physical therapy, physics, podiatry, speech pathology and audiology, statistics, veterinary medicine, zoology	Architectural Design, 02.02 Design, 03.05 Health Specialties, 08.04 Industrial and Safety Engineering, 15.08 Managerial Work, 11.01, 15.01 Mathematics and Data Analysis, 15.06 Media Technology, 03.09 Medical Technology, 08.06 Medical Therapy, 08.07 Physical Sciences, 15.02 Postsecondary and Adult Teaching and Instructing, 05.03 Production Precision Work, 13.06 Research and Design Engineering, 15.07 Resource Science/Engineering for Plants, Animals, and the Environment, 01.02

(continued)

(continued)

The Relationship of High School Courses to College Majors and Work Groups

High School Course	College Majors	GOE Work Groups
Pre-Calculus	Actuarial science, aeronautical/aerospace engineering, agricultural engineering, architecture, astronomy, biochemistry, bioengineering, biology, botany, chemical engineering, chemistry, civil engineering, computer engineering, computer science, earth sciences, economics, electrical engineering, geology, graphic design/commercial art/illustration, health information systems administration, hospital/health facilities administration, industrial design, industrial engineering, landscape architecture, materials science, mathematics, mechanical engineering, metallurgical engineering, meteorology, microbiology/bacteriology, occupational health and industrial hygiene, oceanography, operations management, operations research, optometry, petroleum engineering, physics, statistics, transportation and logistics management	Accounting, Auditing, and Analytical Support, 04.05 Architectural Design, 02.02 Finance/Insurance Investigation and Analysis, 06.02 Industrial and Safety Engineering, 15.08 Information Technology Specialties, 11.02 Life Sciences, 15.03 Managerial Work, 02.01, 08.01, 11.01, 15.01, 16.01 Mathematics and Data Analysis, 15.06 Media Technology, 03.09 Medical Technology, 08.06 Physical Sciences, 15.02 Postsecondary and Adult Teaching and Instructing, 05.03 Research and Design Engineering, 15.07 Resource Science/Engineering for Plants, Animals, and the Environment, 01.02 Social Sciences, 15.04
Public Speaking	Advertising, African American studies, American studies, anthropology, archeology, Asian studies, business education, business management, Chinese, classics, criminal justice/law enforcement, drama/theater arts, early childhood education, elementary education, English, family and consumer sciences, French, German, Hispanic American studies, hospital/health facilities	Counseling and Social Work, 10.01 Counseling, Health, and Fitness Education, 05.06 Drama, 03.06 General Sales, 14.03 Human Resources Support, 04.03 Law Enforcement and Public Safety, 12.04

The Relationship of High School Courses to College Majors and Work Groups

High School Course	College Majors	GOE Work Groups
	administration, hotel/motel and restaurant management, human resources management, humanities, industrial and labor relations, industrial/technology education, international business, Japanese, journalism and mass communications, law, modern foreign language, physical education, public administration, public relations, recreation and parks management, religion/religious studies, Russian, secondary education, Spanish, special education, speech pathology and audiology, sports management, teaching English as a second language, women's studies	Legal Practice and Justice Administration, 12.02 Legal Support, 12.03 Library Services, 05.04 Managerial Work, 01.01, 02.01, 03.01, 04.01, 05.01, 06.01, 07.01, 08.01, 09.01, 10.01, 11.01, 12.01, 13.01, 14.01, 15.01, 16.01 Media Technology, 03.09 Medical Therapy, 08.07 Music, 03.07 News, Broadcasting, and Public Relations, 03.03 Postsecondary and Adult Teaching and Instructing, 05.03 Preschool, Elementary, and Secondary Teaching and Instructing, 05.02 Recreational Services, 09.02 Religious Work, 10.02 Social Sciences, 15.04 Sports, 09.06 Writing and Editing, 03.02
Science	Accounting, actuarial science, business education, early childhood education, elementary education, family and consumer sciences, industrial/technology education, management information systems, marketing, operations management, physical education, secondary education, special education	Counseling and Social Work, 10.01 Counseling, Health, and Fitness Education, 05.06 Design, 03.05 Engineering Technology, 15.09 Industrial and Safety Engineering, 15.08 Information Technology Specialties, 11.02 Life Sciences, 15.03 Managerial Work, 01.01, 02.01, 11.01, 13.01, 15.01, 16.01

(continued)

(continued)

The Relationship of High School Courses to College Majors and Work Groups

High School Course	College Majors	GOE Work Groups
		Mathematics and Data Analysis, 15.06
		Physical Science Laboratory Technology, 15.05
		Physical Sciences, 15.02
		Postsecondary and Adult Teaching and Instructing, 05.03
		Preschool, Elementary, and Secondary Teaching and Instructing, 05.02
		Recreational Services, 09.02
		Research and Design Engineering, 15.07
		Sports, 09.06
Social Science	Advertising, African American studies, American studies, anthropology, archeology, area studies, art history, Asian studies, Chinese, classics, criminal justice/law enforcement, dietetics, economics, English, French, geography, German, Hispanic American studies, history, humanities, industrial and labor relations, international relations, Japanese, journalism and mass communications, law, library science, modern foreign language, philosophy, political science, psychology, public administration, public relations, recreation and parks management, religion/religious studies, Russian, social work, sociology, Spanish, speech pathology and audiology, urban studies, women's studies	Archival and Museum Services, 05.05
		Counseling and Social Work, 10.01
		Finance/Insurance Investigation and Analysis, 06.02
		General Sales, 14.03
		Health Protection and Promotion, 08.09
		Human Resources Support, 04.03
		Law Enforcement and Public Safety, 12.04
		Legal Practice and Justice Administration, 12.02
		Legal Support, 12.03
		Library Services, 05.04
		Managerial Work, 03.01, 04.01, 07.01, 12.01, 14.01, 15.01
		Medical Therapy, 08.07
		News, Broadcasting, and Public Relations, 03.03
		Postsecondary and Adult Teaching and Instructing, 05.03

The Relationship of High School Courses to College Majors and Work Groups		
High School Course	**College Majors**	**GOE Work Groups**
		Public Planning, 07.02
		Recreational Services, 09.02
		Religious Work, 10.02
		Social Sciences, 15.04
		Writing and Editing, 03.02
Spanish	Hispanic American studies, Spanish	News, Broadcasting, and Public Relations, 03.03
		Postsecondary and Adult Teaching and Instructing, 05.03
Trigonometry	See Pre-Calculus	

Look over the entries that you marked in the table as most closely matching your best high school courses. Determine the majors and work groups that best fit with the high school courses you listed at the beginning of this section. Then write them in the following box. If there are many, try to find college majors and work groups that are linked to *more than one* of your best high school courses.

Similar College Majors and Work Groups
_____

Your Work-Related Values

People rarely talk about values, except occasionally when political commentators refer to "values voters." Yet values affect every decision we make. A value is something that we consider desirable to gain or keep. When we choose between two things that we have the chance to gain or keep, we base our preference on our values. Sometimes it is obvious that one choice is better aligned with all of our values than another one. But a lot of the time we have to make *trade-offs,* accepting less of one thing that we value to get something else that we value more.

For example, when choosing what to have for lunch, we make trade-offs among several values: good taste, good nutrition, reasonable price, convenient location, something different from what we had yesterday, and perhaps trying to impress our lunch date. It may be impossible to find one meal that will fit *all* of these values perfectly, but we usually can find a compromise choice that will satisfy our most important values. Note that our lunch-related values may change over time, as we might become more nutrition-conscious or short on lunch money. Most important of all, consider that there is no one "right" set of lunch-related values for all people. Some people *enjoy* having the same lunches every day, and others don't care what their lunch dates think of their choices. Lunch-related values are a matter of personal preference.

The same applies to *work-related values.* People have their own unique preferences; they often need to make trade-offs; and they may find that their values change over time. But in fact most people don't actually know consciously what their work-related values are. If you ask them, "What makes one job better than another?" they usually can name only one or two things—such as the salary or the working conditions.

This is where this section can help you: by making you more aware of your work-related values. In the following chart, look over the names and definitions of work-related values, which the U.S. Department of Labor (DOL) uses to describe jobs in its O*NET database. (The work-related values in this book are particular to the listed college majors. The DOL uses additional values that are unrelated.) When you compare the importance of two values, ask yourself, "Would I quit a job that had a lot of Value *X* if I could get a job with a lot of Value *Y?*"

Work-Related Values	
Value	**Description**
Ability Utilization	Making use of your individual abilities
Achievement	Getting a feeling of accomplishment
Advancement	Having opportunities for advancement
Authority	Giving directions and instructions to others
Autonomy	Planning your work with little supervision
Coworkers	Having coworkers who are easy to get along with
Creativity	Getting chances to try out your own ideas
Responsibility	Making decisions on your own
Security	Having steady employment
Social Service	Having work where you do things to improve other people's lives
Social Status	Being looked up to by others in your company and your community
Variety	Having something different to do every day
Working Conditions	Having good working conditions

When you've decided which three of these values are most important for you to get from your work, list them here:

Work Values for My Career
1. _____
2. _____
3. _____

In the following table, start by circling the values that you listed above as your most important. Now look in the second and third columns of the rows with circled values and circle any college majors and work groups that appeal to you. Pay special attention to college majors or work groups that appear more than once in your selected rows. At the end of this section, you can list the names of those college majors and work groups because they correspond well to your three most important work-related values. If *none* of them appears more than once in the selected rows, list some of the majors and work groups that correspond to your number-one value.

> The work-related values are related to college majors in that they characterize the occupations to which the majors are linked. They do not necessarily reflect the satisfactions that you can expect to enjoy *while in* the major.

Work-Related Values and Their Relationships to College Majors and Work Groups

Work-Related Value	College Majors	Work Groups (GOE)
Ability Utilization—making use of your individual abilities	Anthropology, architecture, art, chemistry, Chinese, classics, clinical laboratory technology, computer engineering, computer science, dance, dietetics, drama/theater arts, electrical engineering, environmental science, film/cinema studies, French, geography, German, graphic design/commercial art/illustration, industrial design, interior design, Japanese, journalism and mass communications, law, modern foreign language, music, nursing (RN training), photography, public relations, Russian, Spanish	Agriculture and Natural Resources, 01.02 Architecture and Construction, 02.02, 02.03 Arts and Communication, 03.02, 03.03, 03.05, 03.06, 03.07, 03.08, 03.09 Business and Administration, 04.05 Education and Training, 05.01, 05.03, 05.05 Finance and Insurance, 06.01 Government and Public Administration, 07.02 Health Science, 08.02, 08.04, 08.06, 08.07, 08.09 Information Technology, 11.02 Law and Public Safety, 12.02, 12.06 Manufacturing, 13.14 Scientific Research, Engineering, and Mathematics, 15.02, 15.03, 15.04, 15.06, 15.07, 15.08, 15.09 Transportation, Distribution, and Logistics, 16.02

Work-Related Values and Their Relationships to College Majors and Work Groups

Work-Related Value	College Majors	Work Groups (GOE)
Achievement—getting a feeling of accomplishment	Archeology, art, Chinese, classics, French, German, graphic design/commercial art/illustration, industrial design, Japanese, modern foreign language, music, occupational therapy, photography, physical therapy, physician assisting, Russian, Spanish, veterinary medicine	Agriculture and Natural Resources, 01.01, 01.02 Architecture and Construction, 02.02 Arts and Communication, 03.02, 03.03, 03.04, 03.05, 03.06, 03.07, 03.08, 03.09 Education and Training, 05.02, 05.03, 05.05, 05.06 Health Science, 08.02, 08.03, 08.05, 08.07 Hospitality, Tourism, and Recreation, 09.06, 09.07 Human Service, 10.01, 10.02 Law and Public Safety, 12.01, 12.06 Retail and Wholesale Sales and Service, 14.02 Scientific Research, Engineering, and Mathematics, 15.02, 15.04, 15.09
Advancement—having opportunities for advancement	Accounting, actuarial science, finance, food science, insurance, management information systems	Agriculture and Natural Resources, 01.03 Architecture and Construction, 02.06 Arts and Communication, 03.03 Business and Administration, 04.05, 04.06, 04.07 Finance and Insurance, 06.01, 06.02, 06.03, 06.04, 06.05 Government and Public Administration, 07.02, 07.03 Information Technology, 11.01, 11.02

(continued)

(continued)

Work-Related Value	College Majors	Work Groups (GOE)
Work-Related Values and Their Relationships to College Majors and Work Groups		
		Law and Public Safety, 12.03
		Manufacturing, 13.06, 13.16
		Retail and Wholesale Sales and Service, 14.03, 14.05, 14.06
		Scientific Research, Engineering, and Mathematics, 15.05, 15.06, 15.09
		Transportation, Distribution, and Logistics, 16.05, 16.07
Authority—giving directions and instructions to others	Aeronautical/aerospace engineering, African American studies, agricultural business and economics, agricultural engineering, American studies, area studies, art history, Asian studies, astronomy, bioengineering, biology, botany, business education, business management, chemical engineering, chiropractic, civil engineering, clinical laboratory technology, computer science, criminal justice/law enforcement, dance, dietetics, early childhood education, electrical engineering, elementary education, English, family and consumer sciences, film/cinema studies, finance, Hispanic American studies, history, hospital/health facilities administration, hotel/motel and restaurant management, human resources management, humanities, industrial engineering, industrial/technology education, international business, international relations, landscape architecture, library science, management information	Agriculture and Natural Resources, 01.01
		Architecture and Construction, 02.01
		Arts and Communication, 03.10
		Business and Administration, 04.01, 04.02, 04.03, 04.05
		Education and Training, 05.01, 05.02, 05.03, 05.04, 05.05, 05.06
		Finance and Insurance, 06.01
		Government and Public Administration, 07.01
		Health Science, 08.01, 08.07, 08.09
		Hospitality, Tourism, and Recreation, 09.01, 09.02, 09.06
		Human Service, 10.01, 10.03
		Information Technology, 11.01
		Law and Public Safety, 12.01, 12.04, 12.05
		Manufacturing, 13.01
		Retail and Wholesale Sales and Service, 14.01, 14.05
		Scientific Research, Engineering, and Mathematics, 15.01, 15.07, 15.08

Work-Related Values and Their Relationships to College Majors and Work Groups		
Work-Related Value	**College Majors**	**Work Groups (GOE)**
	systems, marketing, materials science, mathematics, metallurgical engineering, meteorology, occupational health and industrial hygiene, occupational therapy, operations management, orthotics/prosthetics, petroleum engineering, pharmacy, physical education, physical therapy, physician assisting, physics, political science, public administration, secondary education, sociology, special education, speech pathology and audiology, sports management, statistics, teaching English as a second language, transportation and logistics management, urban studies, veterinary medicine, women's studies, zoology	Transportation, Distribution, and Logistics, 16.01, 16.02, 16.05
Autonomy— planning your work with little supervision	Actuarial science, aeronautical/ aerospace engineering, agricultural business and economics, agricultural engineering, agronomy and crop science, animal science, anthropology, archeology, bioengineering, business management, chemical engineering, civil engineering, earth sciences, economics, environmental science, forestry, geography, geology, hotel/motel and restaurant management, industrial engineering, insurance, law, materials science, mathematics, mechanical engineering, metallurgical engineering, oceanography, operations	Agriculture and Natural Resources, 01.01, 01.02 Architecture and Construction, 02.01, 02.03 Arts and Communication, 03.01, 03.02, 03.04, 03.05, 03.07, 03.08, 03.09 Business and Administration, 04.01, 04.02 Education and Training, 05.06 Finance and Insurance, 06.02, 06.05 Government and Public Administration, 07.01, 07.02 Health Science, 08.01, 08.04

(continued)

(continued)

Work-Related Values and Their Relationships to College Majors and Work Groups		
Work-Related Value	**College Majors**	**Work Groups (GOE)**
	management, operations research, petroleum engineering, philosophy, physics, political science, psychology, public administration, recreation and parks management, religion/religious studies, social work, soil science, statistics, transportation and logistics management, urban studies, wildlife management, zoology	Hospitality, Tourism, and Recreation, 09.01, 09.06, 09.07 Human Service, 10.01, 10.02 Information Technology, 11.02 Law and Public Safety, 12.02, 12.03 Manufacturing, 13.01 Retail and Wholesale Sales and Service, 14.01, 14.02 Scientific Research, Engineering, and Mathematics, 15.01, 15.02, 15.03, 15.04, 15.06, 15.07, 15.08 Transportation, Distribution, and Logistics, 16.01, 16.05
Coworkers—having coworkers who are easy to get along with	Horticulture, nursing (RN training)	General Farming, 01.04 Safety and Security, 12.05 Studio Art, 03.04
Creativity—trying out your own ideas	Advertising, aeronautical/aerospace engineering, African American studies, agricultural business and economics, agricultural engineering, agronomy and crop science, American studies, animal science, anthropology, archeology, architecture, area studies, art, art history, Asian studies, astronomy, biochemistry, bioengineering, biology, botany, business education, business management, chemical engineering, chemistry, chiropractic, civil engineering, computer engineering, computer science, dance, drama/theater arts, early childhood education, earth sciences, electrical engineering,	Agriculture and Natural Resources, 01.01, 01.02, 01.03 Architecture and Construction, 02.01, 02.02 Arts and Communication, 03.01, 03.02, 03.03, 03.04, 03.05, 03.06, 03.07, 03.08, 03.09 Business and Administration, 04.01, 04.02 Education and Training, 05.01, 05.02, 05.03, 05.05, 05.06 Government and Public Administration, 07.01, 07.02 Health Science, 08.09 Hospitality, Tourism, and Recreation, 09.01, 09.06, 09.07

Work-Related Values and Their Relationships to College Majors and Work Groups

Work-Related Value	College Majors	Work Groups (GOE)
	elementary education, English, environmental science, family and consumer sciences, film/cinema studies, forestry, geography, geology, graphic design/commercial art/illustration, Hispanic American studies, history, hospital/health facilities administration, hotel/motel and restaurant management, humanities, industrial design, industrial engineering, industrial/technology education, interior design, journalism and mass communications, landscape architecture, management information systems, marketing, materials science, mathematics, metallurgical engineering, meteorology, microbiology/bacteriology, music, occupational health and industrial hygiene, oceanography, operations research, orthotics/prosthetics, petroleum engineering, photography, physical education, physics, political science, psychology, public administration, public relations, recreation and parks management, secondary education, sociology, soil science, special education, speech pathology and audiology, sports management, statistics, teaching English as a second language, transportation and logistics management, urban studies, veterinary medicine, wildlife management, women's studies, zoology	Human Service, 10.01, 10.02 Information Technology, 11.01, 11.02 Law and Public Safety, 12.02 Manufacturing, 13.01 Retail and Wholesale Sales and Service, 14.01, 14.02 Scientific Research, Engineering, and Mathematics, 15.01, 15.02, 15.03, 15.04, 15.07, 15.08 Transportation, Distribution, and Logistics, 16.01

(continued)

(continued)

Work-Related Values and Their Relationships to College Majors and Work Groups		
Work-Related Value	**College Majors**	**Work Groups (GOE)**
Responsibility—making decisions on your own	Agronomy and crop science, biochemistry, biology, botany, chemistry, dentistry, earth sciences, family and consumer sciences, forestry, geology, industrial and labor relations, mechanical engineering, meteorology, microbiology/bacteriology, oceanography, operations management, operations research, optometry, podiatry, soil science, wildlife management	Agriculture and Natural Resources, 01.01, 01.02 Architecture and Construction, 02.01 Arts and Communication, 03.01, 03.02 Business and Administration, 04.01, 04.02, 04.03 Education and Training, 05.02, 05.03, 05.06 Finance and Insurance, 06.02, 06.05 Government and Public Administration, 07.03 Health Science, 08.01, 08.04, 08.05 Hospitality, Tourism, and Recreation, 09.01, 09.06 Information Technology, 11.01 Law and Public Safety, 12.01 Manufacturing, 13.01, 13.07, 13.14 Retail and Wholesale Sales and Service, 14.01, 14.05 Scientific Research, Engineering, and Mathematics, 15.01, 15.02, 15.03, 15.04, 15.07, 15.08 Transportation, Distribution, and Logistics, 16.01, 16.05
Security—having steady employment	Criminal justice/law enforcement, health information systems administration	Agriculture and Natural Resources, 01.03 Arts and Communication, 03.10 Government and Public Administration, 07.01, 07.03, 07.04

Work-Related Value	College Majors	Work Groups (GOE)
		Health Science, 08.01, 08.03, 08.06, 08.08
		Human Service, 10.03
		Information Technology, 11.03
		Law and Public Safety, 12.04
		Manufacturing, 13.12, 13.14, 13.15, 13.16
		Transportation, Distribution, and Logistics, 16.04, 16.06
Social Service—doing things for other people	African American studies, American studies, area studies, art history, Asian studies, business education, Chinese, chiropractic, classics, clinical laboratory technology, dentistry, dietetics, early childhood education, elementary education, English, French, German, health information systems administration, Hispanic American studies, horticulture, hospital/health facilities administration, human resources management, humanities, industrial and labor relations, industrial/technology education, interior design, Japanese, library science, medicine, modern foreign language, nursing (RN training), occupational health and industrial hygiene, occupational therapy, optometry, orthotics/prosthetics, pharmacy, philosophy, physical education, physical therapy, physician assisting, podiatry, psychology, recreation and parks management, religion/religious studies, Russian, secondary education, social work,	Arts and Communication, 03.10 Business and Administration, 04.02, 04.03, 04.04 Education and Training, 05.02, 05.03, 05.04, 05.06 Finance and Insurance, 06.04 Government and Public Administration, 07.01, 07.04 Health Science, 08.01, 08.02, 08.03, 08.04, 08.06, 08.07, 08.08, 08.09 Hospitality, Tourism, and Recreation, 09.01, 09.02, 09.04, 09.05, 09.07 Human Service, 10.01, 10.02, 10.03, 10.04 Law and Public Safety, 12.01, 12.02, 12.03, 12.04, 12.05, 12.06 Retail and Wholesale Sales and Service, 14.03, 14.06 Scientific Research, Engineering, and Mathematics, 15.04 Transportation, Distribution, and Logistics, 16.06

(continued)

(continued)

Work-Related Value	College Majors	Work Groups (GOE)
Work-Related Values and Their Relationships to College Majors and Work Groups		
Work-Related Value	College Majors	Work Groups (GOE)
	sociology, Spanish, special education, speech pathology and audiology, sports management, teaching English as a second language, women's studies	
Social Status—being looked up to by others in your company and your community	Biochemistry, dentistry, international business, international relations, medicine, microbiology/bacteriology, optometry, pharmacy, philosophy, religion/religious studies	Architecture and Construction, 02.02, 02.03 Arts and Communication, 03.06 Business and Administration, 04.01, 04.05 Education and Training, 05.01 Health Science, 08.02, 08.03, 08.04, 08.06, 08.07 Human Service, 10.02 Law and Public Safety, 12.01, 12.06 Manufacturing, 13.10 Scientific Research, Engineering, and Mathematics, 15.03, 15.06, 15.07, 15.08 Transportation, Distribution, and Logistics, 16.02
Variety—having something different to do every day	Advertising, criminal justice/law enforcement, food science, horticulture, insurance	Agriculture and Natural Resources, 01.01, 01.02, 01.03, 01.04 Architecture and Construction, 02.01, 02.04, 02.05 Arts and Communication, 03.01, 03.03, 03.06, 03.09 Government and Public Administration, 07.02 Health Science, 08.05, 08.08, 08.09 Hospitality, Tourism, and Recreation, 09.02

Work-Related Value	College Majors	Work Groups (GOE)
		Human Service, 10.01, 10.03
		Information Technology, 11.03
		Law and Public Safety, 12.03, 12.04
		Manufacturing, 13.01, 13.12, 13.13
		Retail and Wholesale Sales and Service, 14.01, 14.02, 14.05
		Scientific Research, Engineering, and Mathematics, 15.05
		Transportation, Distribution, and Logistics, 16.01
Working Conditions—having good working conditions	Accounting, actuarial science, advertising, astronomy, computer engineering, economics, finance, food science, health information systems administration, history, human resources management, industrial and labor relations, international business, international relations, library science, mechanical engineering	Architecture and Construction, 02.03
		Arts and Communication, 03.05, 03.07
		Business and Administration, 04.01, 04.02, 04.03, 04.04, 04.05, 04.06, 04.07, 04.08
		Education and Training, 05.01, 05.02, 05.04, 05.05
		Finance and Insurance, 06.01, 06.02, 06.03, 06.04, 06.05
		Government and Public Administration, 07.02, 07.04
		Health Science, 08.06
		Human Service, 10.04
		Information Technology, 11.01, 11.02
		Law and Public Safety, 12.03
		Manufacturing, 13.15
		Retail and Wholesale Sales and Service, 14.01, 14.03, 14.05, 14.06

(continued)

(continued)

Work-Related Values and Their Relationships to College Majors and Work Groups		
Work-Related Value	**College Majors**	**Work Groups (GOE)**
		Scientific Research, Engineering, and Mathematics, 15.01, 15.06, 15.09

In the following box, write the college majors and work groups that most closely correspond to the three values you listed at the beginning of this section.

College Majors and Work Groups That Relate to My Values
_____
_____
_____
_____
_____
_____
_____
_____
_____

Your Hot List of College Majors and Careers

Now that you've done the four exercises in this part of the book, it's time for you to assemble a "Hot List" of college majors and careers that deserve your active consideration in part II.

At the end of each of the four exercises in part I—interests, skills, high school courses, and work-related values—you've created a list of the college majors and work groups that were most strongly suggested by each exercise. Look these over now and decide which of the following statements best characterizes what you see:

- **Certain majors and work groups appear at the end of all four, or three of the four, exercises.** If this is what you find, congratulations! These majors obviously correspond well to your personality, and you should write them in your Hot List on page 66.

- **Certain majors and work groups appear at the end of two of the exercises, but none appear in three or four.** This is still a meaningful finding; these majors probably belong on your Hot List. If many majors fit this description, you might ask yourself whether you feel more confident about one set of exercises than others. For example, do you feel you have a clearer notion of your interests and high school courses than of your skills and values? In that case, you might want to give greater weight to the majors you listed for your interests and high school courses.

- **There's no pattern at all—no majors or work groups appear after more than one of the exercises.** In this case, you need to decide which exercise you trust the most. Different people have different styles of thinking about themselves; for example, some have a much keener awareness of their interests than their values. Or perhaps the terms used in one exercise seem easier to understand than the terms in the others. Go with the results of the exercise that you feel most confident about. Write those majors in your Hot List.

- **One of the preceding three statements applies to you, but you have a *very* large number of majors on your Hot List.** Here's where the work groups can help you. Find the work group that appears most often in the results of the exercises for skills, high school courses, and values. Then go back to the interest exercise and see which majors are linked to that work group. These are strong candidates for your Hot List.

After you have filled in your Hot List and have started investigating these majors in part II, you can also use the Hot List as an informal way of recording your impressions:

- If a major appeals to you when you read about it, put a star next to it on your Hot List. The stars can serve to remind you which majors are the hottest of the hot!

- One of the important facts you'll read about the major is what jobs it is linked to. When you see a job that looks interesting to you, write its name next to the name of the major on the Hot List. Later you can use other resources to investigate these jobs in greater detail.

- Another important fact you'll find for each major is the *personality type* that best describes it. If the description of a major appeals to you, write the name of its personality type next to the name of the major in your Hot List. After you have done this for several majors, note whether one of the personality types dominates your Hot List and, if so, look in the appendix for majors linked to the same personality type.

My Hot List

_____

_____

_____

_____

_____

_____

_____

_____

PART II

Facts About College Majors and Careers

In this section, you get the facts about 127 college majors and the careers related to them. You will learn new things about majors that you thought you knew all about. You will also encounter majors that you have never heard of before or that you don't know well.

The Hot List you created in part I can help you choose majors to explore here. But even if you just browse at random, the facts are organized in a way that makes it easy for you to get an understanding of the major and related careers.

Here's what you'll find for each major:

- **Definition:** A brief summary of what the major covers
- **Career Snapshot:** What the subject is and what careers are related to it
- **Related Specialties in Majors and Careers:** Common areas of concentration
- **Related Job Titles, Earnings, Projected Growth, and Openings:** Specific facts about the jobs, from the U.S. Department of Labor (earnings reflect the *national* average for all workers in the occupation)
- **Typical Sequence of College Courses:** Courses often required for this major listed in the order they are most commonly taken in (each college varies)
- **Typical Sequence of High School Courses:** High school coursework that is considered good preparation
- **Personality Type:** Type of personality that best fits the related careers
- **Other Characteristics:** Aspects of the careers related to the major, including the interest areas/clusters and work groups where they belong, plus their most important skills, values, and features of the work environment
- **Related Titles in the Classification of Instructional Programs (CIP):** Code number and name of the related programs

Accounting

Prepares you to practice the profession of accounting and to perform related business functions.

Career Snapshot

Accountants maintain the financial records of organizations and supervise the recording of transactions. They provide information about the fiscal condition and trends of the organizations they serve, and figures for tax forms and financial reports. They advise management and therefore need good communication skills. A bachelor's degree is sufficient preparation for many entry-level jobs, but some employers prefer a master's degree. Accountants with diverse skills may advance to management after a few years. The job outlook is generally good.

Related Specialties in Majors and Careers

Accounting computer systems, auditing, cost accounting, financial reporting, forensic accounting, taxation.

Related Job Titles, Earnings, Projected Growth, and Openings

Job Title	Average Earnings	Projected Growth	Annual Openings
1. Accountants (O*NET-SOC Code 13-2011.01)	$57,060	17.7%	134,463
2. Auditors (O*NET-SOC Code 13-2011.02)	$57,060	17.7%	134,463
3. Budget Analysts (O*NET-SOC Code 13-2031.00)	$63,440	7.1%	6,423
4. Business Teachers, Postsecondary (O*NET-SOC Code 25-1011.00)	$64,900	22.9%	237,478
5. Credit Analysts (O*NET-SOC Code 13-2041.00)	$54,580	1.9%	3,180
6. Financial Examiners (O*NET-SOC Code 13-2061.00)	$66,670	10.7%	2,449
7. Tax Examiners, Collectors, and Revenue Agents (O*NET-SOC Code 13-2081.00)	$46,920	2.1%	4,465

Jobs 1 and 2 share 134,463 openings. Job 4 shares 237,478 openings with 35 other postsecondary teaching jobs not included in this table.

Typical Sequence of College Courses

English composition, business writing, introduction to psychology, principles of microeconomics, principles of macroeconomics, calculus for business and social sciences, statistics for business and social sciences, introduction to management information systems, introduction to accounting, legal environment of business, principles of management and organization, operations management, strategic management, business finance, introduction to marketing, cost accounting, auditing, taxation of individuals, taxation of corporations, partnerships and estates.

Typical Sequence of High School Courses

English, algebra, geometry, trigonometry, science, foreign language, computer science.

Personality Type

Conventional. These occupations frequently involve following set procedures and routines and can include working with data and details more than with ideas. Usually there is a clear line of authority to follow.

Other Characteristics

GOE—Related Interest Areas/Career Clusters: 04 Business and Administration; 05 Education and Training; 06 Finance and Insurance; 07 Government and Public Administration. **Related Work Groups:** 04.05 Accounting, Auditing, and Analytical Support; 06.02 Finance/Insurance Investigation and Analysis; 07.03 Regulations Enforcement. **Most Important Skills:** Management of financial resources, mathematics, judgment and decision making, operations analysis, systems analysis, time management. **Top Values:** Working conditions, compensation, advancement. **Work Environment:** Indoors; sitting; repetitive motions.

Related Title in the Classification of Instructional Programs (CIP)

52.0301 Accounting.

Actuarial Science

Focuses on the mathematical and statistical analysis of risk, and the application of such analysis to insurance and other business management problems.

Career Snapshot

Actuarial science is the analysis of mathematical data to predict the likelihood of certain events, such as death, accident, or disability. Insurance companies are the main employers of actuaries; actuaries determine how much the insurers charge for policies. The usual entry route is a bachelor's degree, but actuaries continue to study and sit for exams to upgrade their professional standing over the course of 5 to 10 years. Although the occupation is not expected to grow much, there will probably be many openings for those who are able to pass the series of exams.

Related Specialties in Majors and Careers

Insurance, investment.

Related Job Titles, Earnings, Projected Growth, and Openings

Job Title	Average Earnings	Projected Growth	Annual Openings
1. Actuaries (O*NET-SOC Code 15-2011.00)	$85,690	23.7%	3,245
2. Business Teachers, Postsecondary (O*NET-SOC Code 25-1011.00)	$64,900	22.9%	237,478

Job 2 shares 237,478 openings with 35 other postsecondary teaching jobs not included in this table.

Typical Sequence of College Courses

Calculus, linear algebra, advanced calculus, introduction to computer science, introduction to probability, introduction to actuarial mathematics, mathematical statistics, applied regression, actuarial models, introduction to accounting, principles of microeconomics, principles of macroeconomics, financial management, programming in C, investment analysis, price theory, income and employment theory.

Typical Sequence of High School Courses

English, algebra, geometry, trigonometry, science, pre-calculus, calculus, computer science.

Personality Type

Conventional. These occupations frequently involve following set procedures and routines and can include working with data and details more than with ideas. Usually there is a clear line of authority to follow.

Other Characteristics

GOE—Related Interest Areas/Career Clusters: 05 Education and Training; 15 Scientific Research, Engineering, and Mathematics. **Related Work Groups:** 05.03 Postsecondary and Adult Teaching and Instructing; 15.06 Mathematics and Data Analysis. **Most Important Skills:** Instructing, monitoring, mathematics, writing, learning strategies, active learning. **Top Values:** Autonomy, working conditions, advancement. **Work Environment:** Indoors; sitting; repetitive motions.

Related Title in the Classification of Instructional Programs (CIP)

52.1304 Actuarial Science.

Advertising

Focuses on the creation, execution, transmission, and evaluation of commercial messages in various media intended to promote and sell products, services, and brands and prepares individuals to function as advertising assistants, technicians, and managers.

Career Snapshot

Advertising is a combination of writing, art, and business. Graduates with bachelor's degrees in advertising often go on to jobs in advertising agencies, mostly in large cities. Competition can be keen because the industry is considered glamorous. A knowledge of how to advertise on the Internet can be an advantage.

Related Specialties in Majors and Careers

Creative process, management.

Related Job Titles, Earnings, Projected Growth, and Openings

Job Title	Average Earnings	Projected Growth	Annual Openings
1. Advertising and Promotions Managers (O*NET-SOC Code 11-2011.00)	$78,250	6.2%	2,955
2. Advertising Sales Agents (O*NET-SOC Code 41-3011.00)	$42,820	20.3%	29,233
3. Communications Teachers, Postsecondary (O*NET-SOC Code 25-1122.00)	$54,720	22.9%	237,478

Job 3 shares 237,478 openings with 35 other postsecondary teaching jobs not included in this table.

Typical Sequence of College Courses

English composition, oral communication, statistics for business and social sciences, introduction to marketing, introduction to advertising, communications theory, advertising message strategy, communication ethics, advertising media, advertising copy and layout, advertising account planning and research, advertising campaign management, mass communication law, introduction to communication research.

Typical Sequence of High School Courses

English, algebra, foreign language, art, literature, public speaking, social science.

Personality Type

Enterprising. These occupations frequently involve starting up and carrying out projects and can involve leading people and making many decisions. They sometimes require risk taking and often deal with business.

Other Characteristics

GOE—Related Interest Areas/Career Clusters: 05 Education and Training; 14 Retail and Wholesale Sales and Service. **Related Work Groups:** 05.03 Postsecondary and Adult Teaching and Instructing; 14.01 Managerial Work in Retail/Wholesale Sales and Service; 14.03 General Sales. **Most Important Skills:** Negotiation, management of financial resources, persuasion, service orientation, writing, management of personnel resources. **Top Values:** Creativity, working conditions, variety. **Work Environment:** In a vehicle or outdoors; very hot or cold; sitting; close to others.

Related Title in the Classification of Instructional Programs (CIP)

09.0903 Advertising.

Aeronautical/Aerospace Engineering

Prepares you to apply mathematical and scientific principles to the design, development, and operational evaluation of aircraft, space vehicles, and their systems.

Career Snapshot

Engineers apply scientific principles to real-world problems, finding the optimal solution that balances elegant technology with realistic cost. Aeronautical/aerospace engineers need to learn the specific principles of air flow and resistance, and the workings of various kinds of propulsion systems. Most enter the job market with a bachelor's degree. Some later move into managerial positions. Job outlook is not as good as for some other engineering fields because of cutbacks in defense spending.

Related Specialties in Majors and Careers

Airframes and aerodynamics, propulsion, spacecraft, testing.

Related Job Titles, Earnings, Projected Growth, and Openings

Job Title	Average Earnings	Projected Growth	Annual Openings
1. Aerospace Engineers (O*NET-SOC Code 17-2011.00)	$90,930	10.2%	6,498
2. Engineering Managers (O*NET-SOC Code 11-9041.00)	$111,020	7.3%	7,404
3. Engineering Teachers, Postsecondary (O*NET-SOC Code 25-1032.00)	$79,510	22.9%	237,478

Job 3 shares 237,478 openings with 35 other postsecondary teaching jobs not included in this table.

Typical Sequence of College Courses

English composition, technical writing, calculus, differential equations, introduction to computer science, general chemistry, general physics, thermodynamics, introduction to electrical circuits, introduction to aerospace engineering, statics, dynamics, materials engineering, fluid mechanics, aircraft systems and propulsion, flight control systems, aerodynamics, aircraft structural design, aircraft stability and control, experimental aerodynamics, senior design project.

Typical Sequence of High School Courses

English, algebra, geometry, trigonometry, pre-calculus, calculus, chemistry, physics, computer science.

Personality Type

Investigative. These occupations frequently involve working with ideas and require an extensive amount of thinking. They can involve searching for facts and figuring out problems mentally.

Other Characteristics

GOE—Related Interest Areas/Career Clusters: 05 Education and Training; 15 Scientific Research, Engineering, and Mathematics. **Related Work Groups:** 05.03 Postsecondary and Adult Teaching and Instructing; 15.01 Managerial Work in Scientific Research, Engineering, and Mathematics; 15.07 Research and Design Engineering. **Most Important Skills:** Science; technology design; operations analysis; management of financial resources; mathematics; judgment and decision making. **Top Values:** Authority; creativity; autonomy. **Work Environment:** Indoors; sitting; protective or safety equipment; hazardous equipment; high places; radiation; noisy.

Related Title in the Classification of Instructional Programs (CIP)

14.0201 Aerospace, Aeronautical, and Astronautical Engineering.

African American Studies

Focuses on the history, sociology, politics, culture, and economics of the North American peoples descended from the African diaspora, usually in the United States, Canada, and the Caribbean, but also including reference to Latin American elements of the diaspora.

Career Snapshot

African American studies draws on a number of disciplines, including history, sociology, literature, linguistics, and political science. Usually you can shape the program to emphasize whichever appeals most to you. Graduates frequently pursue higher degrees as a means of establishing a career in a field such as college teaching or the law.

Related Specialties in Majors and Careers

Behavioral and social inquiry, history and culture, literature, language, and the arts.

Related Job Title, Earnings, Projected Growth, and Openings

Job Title	Average Earnings	Projected Growth	Annual Openings
1. Area, Ethnic, and Cultural Studies Teachers, Postsecondary (O*NET-SOC Code 25-1062.00)	$59,150	22.9%	237,478

This job shares 237,478 openings with 35 other postsecondary teaching jobs not included in this table.

Typical Sequence of College Courses

English composition, foreign language, American history, introduction to African American studies, African American literature, African American art and culture, African American history, African Diaspora studies, research methods in African American studies, seminar (reporting on research).

Typical Sequence of High School Courses

English, algebra, foreign language, history, literature, public speaking, social science.

Personality Type

Social. These occupations frequently involve working with, communicating with, and teaching people and often involve helping or providing service to others.

Other Characteristics

GOE—Related Interest Area/Career Cluster: 05 Education and Training. **Related Work Group:** 05.03 Postsecondary and Adult Teaching and Instructing. **Most Important Skills:** Writing, critical thinking, instructing, persuasion, active learning, learning strategies. **Top Values:** Authority, social service, creativity. **Work Environment:** Indoors; sitting; disease or infections.

Related Title in the Classification of Instructional Programs (CIP)

05.0201 African-American/Black Studies.

Agricultural Business and Economics

Focuses on modern business and economic principles involved in the organization, operation, and management of agricultural enterprises.

Career Snapshot

Agriculture is a major business in the United States, and graduates of agricultural business and economics programs often work far away from farms and ranches. They may be employed by a bank that lends to farmers; by a food company that purchases large amounts of agricultural products; by a government agency that sets agricultural policies; or by a manufacturer that sells agricultural equipment, chemicals, or seed. They need to know how agricultural products are produced and how the markets for these products (increasingly global) behave. A bachelor's degree is a common entry route, although a graduate degree is useful for teaching or research positions.

Related Specialties in Majors and Careers

Agricultural economics, agricultural finance, agricultural marketing and sales, computer applications and data management, farm business management, natural resources management, public policy, ranch business management.

Related Job Titles, Earnings, Projected Growth, and Openings

Job Title	Average Earnings	Projected Growth	Annual Openings
1. Agricultural Sciences Teachers, Postsecondary (O*NET-SOC Code 25-1041.00)	$78,460	22.9%	237,478
2. Aquacultural Managers (O*NET-SOC Code 11-9011.03)	$53,720	1.1%	18,101
3. Crop and Livestock Managers (O*NET-SOC Code 11-9011.02)	$53,720	1.1%	18,101
4. Economists (O*NET-SOC Code 19-3011.00)	$80,220	7.5%	1,555
5. Farmers and Ranchers (O*NET-SOC Code 11-9012.00)	$33,360	−8.5%	129,552
6. Nursery and Greenhouse Managers (O*NET-SOC Code 11-9011.01)	$53,720	1.1%	18,101

Job 1 shares 237,478 openings with 35 other postsecondary teaching jobs not included in this table. Jobs 2, 3, and 6 share 18,101 openings.

Typical Sequence of College Courses

English composition, oral communication, business math, general biology, introduction to economics, introduction to accounting, introduction to agricultural economics and business, farm/ranch management, computer applications in agriculture, legal and social environment of agriculture, statistics for business and social sciences, microeconomic theory, macroeconomic theory, natural resource economics, agribusiness financial management, introduction to marketing, marketing and pricing agricultural products, technical writing, agricultural policy, quantitative methods in agricultural business.

Typical Sequence of High School Courses

English, algebra, geometry, trigonometry, biology, chemistry, computer science.

Personality Type

Investigative. These occupations frequently involve working with ideas and require an extensive amount of thinking. They can involve searching for facts and figuring out problems mentally.

Other Characteristics

GOE—Related Interest Areas/Career Clusters: 01 Agriculture and Natural Resources; 05 Education and Training; 15 Scientific Research, Engineering, and Mathematics. **Related Work Groups:** 01.01 Managerial Work in Agriculture and Natural Resources; 05.03 Postsecondary and Adult Teaching and Instructing; 15.04 Social Sciences. **Most Important Skills:** Management of financial resources, repairing, equipment maintenance, management of material resources, installation, operation monitoring. **Top Values:** Autonomy, creativity, authority. **Work Environment:** More often in a vehicle or outdoors than indoors; very hot or cold; hazardous equipment; extremely bright or inadequate lighting; contaminants; minor burns, cuts, bites, or stings; whole body vibration.

Related Titles in the Classification of Instructional Programs (CIP)

01.0102 Agribusiness/Agricultural Business Operations; 01.0101 Agricultural Business and Management, General; 01.0103 Agricultural Economics.

Agricultural Engineering

Prepares you to apply mathematical and scientific principles to the design, development, and operational evaluation of systems, equipment, and facilities used to produce, process, and store agricultural products.

Career Snapshot

Agricultural engineers use scientific knowledge to solve problems of growing food and fiber crops, building and maintaining agricultural equipment and structures, and processing agricultural products. A bachelor's degree is usually sufficient preparation to enter this field. Often an engineering job can be a springboard for a managerial position. Job outlook is much better than for most other engineering fields, especially in specializations related to biological engineering and environmental protection.

Related Specialties in Majors and Careers

Agricultural machinery, agricultural structures, environmental engineering, food and fiber processing, irrigation.

Related Job Titles, Earnings, Projected Growth, and Openings

Job Title	Average Earnings	Projected Growth	Annual Openings
1. Agricultural Engineers (O*NET-SOC Code 17-2021.00)	$67,710	8.6%	225
2. Engineering Managers (O*NET-SOC Code 11-9041.00)	$111,020	7.3%	7,404
3. Engineering Teachers, Postsecondary (O*NET-SOC Code 25-1032.00)	$79,510	22.9%	237,478

Job 3 shares 237,478 openings with 35 other postsecondary teaching jobs not included in this table.

Typical Sequence of College Courses

English composition, technical writing, calculus, differential equations, general biology, introduction to computer science, general chemistry, general physics, statics, dynamics, introduction to electrical circuits, thermodynamics, numerical analysis, introduction to agricultural engineering, engineering properties of biological materials, fluid mechanics, microcomputer applications, materials engineering, soil and water engineering, agricultural power and machines, biological materials processing, senior design project.

Typical Sequence of High School Courses

English, algebra, geometry, trigonometry, pre-calculus, biology, calculus, chemistry, computer science.

Personality Type

Investigative. These occupations frequently involve working with ideas and require an extensive amount of thinking. They can involve searching for facts and figuring out problems mentally.

Other Characteristics

GOE—Related Interest Areas/Career Clusters: 01 Agriculture and Natural Resources; 05 Education and Training; 15 Scientific Research, Engineering, and Mathematics. **Related Work Groups:** 01.02 Resource Science/Engineering for Plants, Animals, and the Environment; 05.03 Postsecondary and Adult Teaching and Instructing; 15.01 Managerial Work in Scientific Research, Engineering, and Mathematics. **Most Important Skills:** Science, technology design, operations analysis, management of financial resources, installation, mathematics. **Top Values:** Authority, creativity, autonomy. **Work Environment:** More often indoors than in a vehicle; protective or safety equipment; sitting; hazardous equipment; extremely bright or inadequate lighting; high places; noisy.

Related Title in the Classification of Instructional Programs (CIP)

14.0301 Agricultural/Biological Engineering and Bioengineering.

Agronomy and Crop Science

Focuses on the chemical, physical, and biological relationships of crops and the soils nurturing them.

Career Snapshot

Agronomists and crop scientists look for ways to improve the production and quality of food, feed, and fiber crops. They need to understand the chemical requirements of soils and growing plants and the genetic basis of plant development—especially now that genetic engineering is growing in importance. Those with a bachelor's degree may work in applied research, but a graduate degree is useful to do basic research. Because agriculture is a vital U.S. industry supported by agricultural extension programs, a large number of agronomists and crop scientists work for federal, state, and local governments.

Related Specialties in Majors and Careers

Agro-industry, soil and crop management, turfgrass management.

Related Job Titles, Earnings, Projected Growth, and Openings

Job Title	Average Earnings	Projected Growth	Annual Openings
1. Agricultural Sciences Teachers, Postsecondary (O*NET-SOC Code 25-1041.00)	$78,460	22.9%	237,478
2. Crop and Livestock Managers (O*NET-SOC Code 11-9011.02)	$53,720	1.1%	18,101
3. Farmers and Ranchers (O*NET-SOC Code 11-9012.00)	$33,360	−8.5%	129,552
4. First-Line Supervisors/Managers of Agricultural Crop and Horticultural Workers (O*NET-SOC Code 45-1011.07)	$38,510	−0.4%	11,898
5. Soil and Plant Scientists (O*NET-SOC Code 19-1013.00)	$58,000	8.4%	850

Job 1 shares 237,478 openings with 35 other postsecondary teaching jobs not included in this table. Job 2 shares 18,101 openings with two other jobs not included in this table. Job 4 shares 11,898 openings with four other jobs not included in this table.

Typical Sequence of College Courses

English composition, college algebra, general biology, general chemistry, organic chemistry, genetics, introduction to agricultural economics and business, introduction to soil science, botany, computer applications in agriculture, plant pathology, seed production, crop production, soil fertility, plant nutrition and fertilizers, plant breeding, general entomology, weed control.

Typical Sequence of High School Courses

Biology, chemistry, algebra, geometry, trigonometry, computer science, English, public speaking.

Personality Type

Investigative. These occupations frequently involve working with ideas and require an extensive amount of thinking. They can involve searching for facts and figuring out problems mentally.

Other Characteristics

GOE—Related Interest Areas/Career Clusters: 01 Agriculture and Natural Resources; 05 Education and Training. **Related Work Groups:** 01.01 Managerial Work in Agriculture and Natural Resources; 01.02 Resource Science/Engineering for Plants, Animals, and the Environment; 05.03 Postsecondary and Adult Teaching and Instructing. **Most Important Skills:** Management of financial resources, repairing, management of material resources, equipment maintenance, installation, troubleshooting. **Top Values:** Autonomy, creativity, responsibility. **Work Environment:** More often in a vehicle than outdoors or indoors; very hot or cold; hazardous equipment; extremely bright or inadequate lighting; contaminants; minor burns, cuts, bites, or stings; whole body vibration.

Related Title in the Classification of Instructional Programs (CIP)

01.1102 Agronomy and Crop Science.

American Studies

Focuses on the history, society, politics, culture, and economics of the United States and its pre-Columbian and colonial predecessors, including the flow of immigrants from other societies.

Career Snapshot

American studies is an interdisciplinary major that allows you to concentrate on the aspect of American culture that is of greatest interest to you. Many, perhaps most, graduates use this major as a springboard to postgraduate or professional training to prepare for a career in college teaching, business, law, the arts, politics, or some other field.

Related Specialties in Majors and Careers

History and political science, literature, language, popular culture, the arts.

Related Job Title, Earnings, Projected Growth, and Openings

Job Title	Average Earnings	Projected Growth	Annual Openings
1. Area, Ethnic, and Cultural Studies Teachers, Postsecondary (O*NET-SOC Code 25-1062.00)	$59,150	22.9%	237,478

This job shares 237,478 openings with 35 other postsecondary teaching jobs not included in this table.

Typical Sequence of College Courses

English composition, American history, American government, American literature, American popular culture, seminar (reporting on research).

Typical Sequence of High School Courses

English, algebra, foreign language, history, literature, public speaking, social science.

Personality Type

Social. These occupations frequently involve working with, communicating with, and teaching people and often involve helping or providing service to others.

Other Characteristics

GOE—Related Interest Area/Career Cluster: 05 Education and Training.
Related Work Group: 05.03 Postsecondary and Adult Teaching and Instructing.
Most Important Skills: Writing, critical thinking, instructing, persuasion, active learning, learning strategies. **Top Values:** Authority, social service, creativity. **Work Environment:** Indoors; sitting.

Related Title in the Classification of Instructional Programs (CIP)

05.0102 American/United States Studies/Civilization.

Animal Science

Focuses on the scientific principles that underlie the breeding and raising of agricultural animals, and the production, processing, and distribution of agricultural animal products.

Career Snapshot

Animal science graduates may work directly for farms and ranches that raise animals, or they may work in research, marketing, or sales for pharmaceutical or feed companies that supply farmers, ranchers, and veterinarians. About one-third go on to veterinary school, medical school, or another postgraduate scientific field.

Related Specialties in Majors and Careers

Production, veterinary research.

Related Job Title, Earnings, Projected Growth, and Openings

Job Title	Average Earnings	Projected Growth	Annual Openings
1. Animal Scientists (O*NET-SOC Code 19-1011.00)	$48,360	9.8%	299

Typical Sequence of College Courses

English composition, college algebra, statistics, general biology, general chemistry, organic chemistry, genetics, introduction to agricultural economics and business, introduction to animal science, meats and other animal products, plant physiology, anatomy and physiology of farm animals, animal nutrition and nutritional diseases, feeds and feeding, reproduction of farm animals, animal breeding, marking and grading of livestock and meats.

Typical Sequence of High School Courses

Biology, chemistry, algebra, geometry, trigonometry, computer science, English, public speaking.

Personality Type

Investigative. These occupations frequently involve working with ideas and require an extensive amount of thinking. They can involve searching for facts and figuring out problems mentally.

Other Characteristics

GOE—Related Interest Area/Career Cluster: 01 Agriculture and Natural Resources. **Related Work Group:** 01.02 Resource Science/Engineering for Plants, Animals, and the Environment. **Most Important Skills:** Science, management of financial resources, systems analysis, programming, writing, complex problem solving. **Top Values:** Autonomy, creativity, independence. **Work Environment:** More outdoors or in a vehicle than indoors; very hot or cold temperatures; exposed to hazardous equipment; extremely bright or inadequate lighting; contaminants; minor burns, cuts, bites, or stings; whole body vibration.

Related Title in the Classification of Instructional Programs (CIP)

01.0901 Animal Sciences, General.

Anthropology

Studies human beings, their antecedents and related primates, and their cultural behavior and institutions in comparative perspective.

Career Snapshot

Some anthropologists study the social and cultural behavior of people. They investigate communities throughout the world, focusing on those communities' arts, religions, and economic and social institutions. A graduate degree is usually needed to do research or college teaching in this field, but some graduates with bachelor's degrees find their skills useful in business, such as in marketing research. Other anthropologists specialize in human physical characteristics and may study human remains to understand history or evolution, or to provide evidence in criminal investigations. A graduate degree is usually required for this specialization.

Related Specialties in Majors and Careers

Archaeology, biological/forensic, cultural.

Related Job Titles, Earnings, Projected Growth, and Openings

Job Title	Average Earnings	Projected Growth	Annual Openings
1. Anthropologists (O*NET-SOC Code 19-3091.01)	$53,080	15.0%	446
2. Anthropology and Archeology Teachers, Postsecondary (O*NET-SOC Code 25-1061.00)	$64,530	22.9%	237,478

Job 1 shares 446 openings with another job not included in this table. Job 2 shares 237,478 openings with 35 other postsecondary teaching jobs not included in this table.

Typical Sequence of College Courses

English composition, general biology, statistics for business and social sciences, human growth and development, introduction to sociology, foreign language, cultural anthropology, physical anthropology, introduction to archeology, language and culture, history of anthropological theory, research methods in anthropology, current issues in anthropology.

Typical Sequence of High School Courses

Algebra, English, foreign language, social science, history, biology, public speaking, chemistry.

Personality Type

Social. These occupations frequently involve working with, communicating with, and teaching people and often involve helping or providing service to others.

Other Characteristics

GOE—Related Interest Areas/Career Clusters: 05 Education and Training; 15 Scientific Research, Engineering, and Mathematics. **Related Work Groups:** 05.03 Postsecondary and Adult Teaching and Instructing; 15.04 Social Sciences. **Most Important Skills:** Writing, science, reading comprehension, critical thinking, active learning, complex problem solving. **Top Values:** Creativity, autonomy, ability utilization. **Work Environment:** More often indoors than outdoors; sitting.

Related Title in the Classification of Instructional Programs (CIP)

45.0201 Anthropology.

Archeology

Focuses on the systematic study of extinct societies, and the past of living societies, via the excavation, analysis and interpretation of their artifactual, human, and associated remains.

Career Snapshot

Archeology (also spelled archaeology) is the study of prehistoric and historic cultures through the discovery, preservation, and interpretation of their material remains. As a major, it is sometimes offered as a specialization within anthropology or classics. Students work with languages as well as physical objects, so they develop a number of skills that are appreciated in the business world. They may also get higher degrees in archeology in order to do museum work, field work, or college teaching.

Related Specialties in Majors and Careers

Ancient civilizations, field work, prehistoric archeology, preservation.

Related Job Titles, Earnings, Projected Growth, and Openings

Job Title	Average Earnings	Projected Growth	Annual Openings
1. Anthropology and Archeology Teachers, Postsecondary (O*NET-SOC Code 25-1061.00)	$64,530	22.9%	237,478
2. Archeologists (O*NET-SOC Code 19-3091.02)	$53,080	15.0%	446

Job 1 shares 237,478 openings with 35 other postsecondary teaching jobs not included in this table. Job 2 shares 446 openings with another job not included in this table.

Typical Sequence of College Courses

English composition, statistics for business and social sciences, foreign language, introduction to archeology, world prehistory, ancient literate civilizations, field methods in archeology, new world archeology, seminar (reporting on research).

Typical Sequence of High School Courses

Algebra, English, foreign language, social science, history, biology, public speaking.

Personality Type

Social. These occupations frequently involve working with, communicating with, and teaching people and often involve helping or providing service to others.

Other Characteristics

GOE—Related Interest Areas/Career Clusters: 05 Education and Training; 15 Scientific Research, Engineering, and Mathematics. **Related Work Groups:** 05.03 Postsecondary and Adult Teaching and Instructing; 15.04 Social Sciences. **Most Important Skills:** Science, writing, management of financial resources, reading comprehension, critical thinking, active learning. **Top Values:** Creativity, autonomy, achievement. **Work Environment:** More often indoors than outdoors; sitting.

Related Title in the Classification of Instructional Programs (CIP)

45.0301 Archeology.

Architecture

Prepares you for the independent professional practice of architecture and to conduct research in various aspects of the field.

Career Snapshot

Architects design buildings and the spaces between them. They must have a combination of artistic, technical, and business skills. In order to be licensed, they must obtain a professional degree in architecture (sometimes a five-year bachelor's degree, sometimes a master's degree after a bachelor's in another field), get some on-the-job training, and pass a licensing exam. About one-third are self-employed, and most architectural firms are quite small. Computer skills can be a big advantage for new graduates.

Related Specialties in Majors and Careers

Architectural engineering, design, history, theory and criticism, urban studies.

Related Job Titles, Earnings, Projected Growth, and Openings

Job Title	Average Earnings	Projected Growth	Annual Openings
1. Architects, Except Landscape and Naval (O*NET-SOC Code 17-1011.00)	$67,620	17.7%	11,324
2. Architecture Teachers, Postsecondary (O*NET-SOC Code 25-1031.00)	$68,540	22.9%	237,478
3. Engineering Managers (O*NET-SOC Code 11-9041.00)	$111,020	7.3%	7,404

Job 2 shares 237,478 openings with 35 other postsecondary teaching jobs not included in this table.

Typical Sequence of College Courses

English composition, basic drawing, art history: Renaissance to modern, calculus, introduction to computer science, general physics, history of architecture, structures, building science, visual analysis of architecture, architectural graphics, architectural design, architectural computer graphics, site analysis, introduction to urban planning.

Typical Sequence of High School Courses

English, algebra, geometry, trigonometry, pre-calculus, calculus, physics, computer science, art.

Personality Type

Enterprising. These occupations frequently involve starting up and carrying out projects and can involve leading people and making many decisions. They sometimes require risk taking and often deal with business.

Other Characteristics

GOE—Related Interest Areas/Career Clusters: 02 Architecture and Construction; 05 Education and Training; 15 Scientific Research, Engineering, and Mathematics. **Related Work Groups:** 02.02 Architectural Design; 05.03 Postsecondary and Adult Teaching and Instructing; 15.01 Managerial Work in Scientific Research, Engineering, and Mathematics. **Most Important Skills:** Operations analysis, management of financial resources, technology design, science, complex problem solving, quality control analysis. **Top Values:** Creativity, recognition, ability utilization. **Work Environment:** More often indoors than in a vehicle; sitting; extremely bright or inadequate lighting; protective or safety equipment; high places; hazardous equipment.

Related Title in the Classification of Instructional Programs (CIP)

04.0201 Architecture (BArch, BA/BS, MArch, MA/MS, PhD).

Area Studies

Focuses on the history, society, politics, culture, and economics of a defined group of people or geographic region.

Career Snapshot

Certain very popular area studies—African American studies, American studies, Asian studies, Hispanic American studies, and women's studies—are described elsewhere in this book. But many colleges offer other area studies majors, usually defined in terms of a region of the world: Middle Eastern studies, European studies, Latin American studies, and so on. These are interdisciplinary majors that may involve some combination of linguistics, literature, history, sociology, political science, economic development, or other disciplines. Usually you can emphasize whichever aspects interest you most. Graduates of area studies may go into business or government careers where knowledge of a specific culture is an advantage. Many get higher degrees to prepare for a career in law or college teaching.

Related Specialties in Majors and Careers

Economics and trade, history and culture, language and literature, political science.

Related Job Title, Earnings, Projected Growth, and Openings

Job Title	Average Earnings	Projected Growth	Annual Openings
1. Area, Ethnic, and Cultural Studies Teachers, Postsecondary (O*NET-SOC Code 25-1062.00)	$59,150	22.9%	237,478

This job shares 237,478 openings with 35 other postsecondary teaching jobs not included in this table.

Typical Sequence of College Courses

English composition, foreign language, foreign literature and culture, comparative governments, introduction to economics, international economics, seminar (reporting on research).

Typical Sequence of High School Courses

English, foreign language, history, literature, social science, algebra.

Personality Type

Social. These occupations frequently involve working with, communicating with, and teaching people and often involve helping or providing service to others.

Other Characteristics

GOE—Related Interest Area/Career Cluster: 05 Education and Training. **Related Work Group:** 05.03 Postsecondary and Adult Teaching and Instructing. **Most Important Skills:** Writing, critical thinking, instructing, persuasion, active learning, learning strategies. **Top Values:** Authority, social service, creativity. **Work Environment:** Indoors; sitting; disease or infections.

Related Titles in the Classification of Instructional Programs (CIP)

05.0115 Canadian Studies; 05.0105 Central/Middle and Eastern European Studies; 05.0104 East Asian Studies; 05.0106 European Studies/Civilization; 05.0107 Latin American Studies; 05.0108 Near and Middle Eastern Studies; 05.0109 Pacific Area/Pacific Rim Studies; 05.0110 Russian Studies; 05.0111 Scandinavian Studies.

Art

Prepares you to function as a creative artist in the visual and plastic media.

Career Snapshot

Only a few highly talented and motivated artists are able to support themselves by producing and selling their artwork. But many other graduates of art programs find work in education—as private instructors, school teachers, and university instructors of art and art history. Some apply their artistic skills to crafts or to commercial applications such as illustration or cartooning.

Related Specialties in Majors and Careers

Art education, ceramics, painting, screenprinting, sculpture, studio art.

Related Job Titles, Earnings, Projected Growth, and Openings

Job Title	Average Earnings	Projected Growth	Annual Openings
1. Art, Drama, and Music Teachers, Postsecondary (O*NET-SOC Code 25-1121.00)	$55,190	22.9%	237,478
2. Fine Artists, Including Painters, Sculptors, and Illustrators (O*NET-SOC Code 27-1013.00)	$42,070	9.9%	3,830

Job 1 shares 237,478 openings with 35 other postsecondary teaching jobs not included in this table.

Typical Sequence of College Courses

English composition, foreign language, art and culture, basic drawing, color and design, two-dimensional design, three-dimensional design, art history: prehistoric to Renaissance, art history: Renaissance to modern, figure drawing, a medium (e.g., painting, sculpture, ceramics), art practicum.

Typical Sequence of High School Courses

English, foreign language, literature, history, art.

Personality Type

Artistic. These occupations frequently involve working with forms, designs, and patterns. They often require self-expression, and the work can be done without following a clear set of rules.

Other Characteristics

GOE—Related Interest Areas/Career Clusters: 03 Arts and Communication; 05 Education and Training. **Related Work Groups:** 03.04 Studio Art; 05.03 Postsecondary and Adult Teaching and Instructing. **Most Important Skills:** Instructing, speaking, social perceptiveness, persuasion, active listening, learning strategies. **Top Values:** Creativity, ability utilization, achievement. **Work Environment:** Indoors; sitting; specialized protective or safety equipment.

Related Title in the Classification of Instructional Programs (CIP)

50.0702 Fine/Studio Arts, General.

Art History

Focuses on the historical development of art, the analysis of works of art, and art conservation.

Career Snapshot

Art has been important to humans since we first painted on cave walls, and art history majors learn how art forms, techniques, and traditions have developed since then within their historical and cultural contexts. Study abroad is often part of the curriculum. Graduates of art history programs with bachelor's degrees may work for museums, auction houses, or publishers. With additional education or training, they may work as restorers or college teachers.

Related Specialties in Majors and Careers

A historical period (such as Renaissance), a particular artistic medium, a region of the world, criticism.

Related Job Titles, Earnings, Projected Growth, and Openings

Job Title	Average Earnings	Projected Growth	Annual Openings
1. Archivists (O*NET-SOC Code 25-4011.00)	$43,110	14.4%	795
2. Art, Drama, and Music Teachers, Postsecondary (O*NET-SOC Code 25-1121.00)	$55,190	22.9%	237,478
3. Curators (O*NET-SOC Code 25-4012.00)	$46,000	23.3%	1,416
4. Museum Technicians and Conservators (O*NET-SOC Code 25-4013.00)	$35,350	15.9%	1,341

Job 2 shares 237,478 openings with 35 other postsecondary teaching jobs not included in this table.

Typical Sequence of College Courses

English composition, foreign language, art and culture, studio art, world history to the early modern era, world history in the modern era, art history: prehistoric to Renaissance, art history: Renaissance to modern, non-Western art, critical study of visual art.

Typical Sequence of High School Courses

English, art, foreign language, history, literature, social science.

Personality Type

Artistic. These occupations frequently involve working with forms, designs, and patterns. They often require self-expression, and the work can be done without following a clear set of rules.

Other Characteristics

GOE—Related Interest Area/Career Cluster: 05 Education and Training. **Related Work Groups:** 05.03 Postsecondary and Adult Teaching and Instructing; 05.05 Archival and Museum Services. **Most Important Skills:** Instructing, speaking, persuasion, active listening, social perceptiveness, critical thinking. **Top Values:** Authority, creativity, social service. **Work Environment:** Indoors; sitting; close to others.

Related Title in the Classification of Instructional Programs (CIP)

50.0703 Art History, Criticism, and Conservation.

Asian Studies

Focuses on the history, society, politics, culture, and economics of one or more of the peoples of the Asian continent, including the study of the Asian diasporas overseas.

Career Snapshot

Asia has long seemed mysterious to many Americans, but as it gains in economic, political, and military power the mystery is fading. Asia also is a major source of new American citizens. A bachelor's in Asian Studies can prepare you for a career in business or government, perhaps in combination with an advanced degree in business or law. A graduate degree is needed if you want to teach the subject in college.

Related Specialties in Majors and Careers

An Asian country or language, economics and trade, history and culture, sociology.

Related Job Title, Earnings, Projected Growth, and Openings

Job Title	Average Earnings	Projected Growth	Annual Openings
1. Area, Ethnic, and Cultural Studies Teachers, Post-secondary (O*NET-SOC Code 25-1062.00)	$59,150	22.9%	237,478

This job shares 237,478 openings with 35 other postsecondary teaching jobs not included in this table.

Typical Sequence of College Courses

English composition, an Asian language, introduction to Asian studies, Asian history, Asian politics, Asian literature, Asian art, Asian culture, research methods in Asian studies, study abroad, seminar (reporting on research).

Typical Sequence of High School Courses

English, algebra, foreign language, history, literature, public speaking, social science.

Personality Type

Social. These occupations frequently involve working with, communicating with, and teaching people and often involve helping or providing service to others.

Other Characteristics

GOE—Related Interest Area/Career Cluster: 05 Education and Training.
Related Work Group: 05.03 Postsecondary and Adult Teaching and Instructing.
Most Important Skills: Writing, critical thinking, instructing, persuasion, active learning, learning strategies. **Top Values:** Authority, social service, creativity. **Work Environment:** Indoors; sitting; disease or infections.

Related Title in the Classification of Instructional Programs (CIP)

05.0103 Asian Studies/Civilization.

Astronomy

Focuses on the planetary, galactic, and stellar phenomena occurring in outer space.

Career Snapshot

Almost every year, astronomers make important discoveries that challenge existing theories about the planets, stars, and galaxies and the forces that formed them. Astronomers typically spend only a small fraction of their time actually observing, and much more time analyzing data and comparing it to theoretical models. Many are college faculty members with teaching responsibilities. A Ph.D. is the usual requirement for astronomers, and many new Ph.D.s find a postdoctoral research appointment helpful for future employment. Competition in this field is expected to remain intense for the foreseeable future.

Related Specialties in Majors and Careers

Astrophysics, cosmology.

Related Job Titles, Earnings, Projected Growth, and Openings

Job Title	Average Earnings	Projected Growth	Annual Openings
1. Astronomers (O*NET-SOC Code 19-2011.00)	$99,020	5.6%	128
2. Atmospheric, Earth, Marine, and Space Sciences Teachers, Postsecondary (O*NET-SOC Code 25-1051.00)	$73,280	22.9%	237,478
3. Natural Sciences Managers (O*NET-SOC Code 11-9121.00)	$104,040	11.4%	3,661

Job 2 shares 237,478 openings with 35 other postsecondary teaching jobs not included in this table.

Typical Sequence of College Courses

English composition, introduction to computer science, calculus, differential equations, general chemistry, general physics, mechanics, electricity and magnetism, thermal physics, introduction to astrophysics, astrophysical processes, quantum and atomic physics, observational astronomy.

Typical Sequence of High School Courses

English, algebra, geometry, trigonometry, chemistry, physics, pre-calculus, computer science, calculus.

Personality Type

Investigative. These occupations frequently involve working with ideas and require an extensive amount of thinking. They can involve searching for facts and figuring out problems mentally.

Other Characteristics

GOE—Related Interest Areas/Career Clusters: 05 Education and Training; 15 Scientific Research, Engineering, and Mathematics. **Related Work Groups:** 05.03 Postsecondary and Adult Teaching and Instructing; 15.01 Managerial Work in Scientific Research, Engineering, and Mathematics; 15.02 Physical Sciences. **Most Important Skills:** Science, mathematics, management of personnel resources, active learning, reading comprehension, complex problem solving. **Top Values:** Authority, creativity, working conditions. **Work Environment:** More often indoors than outdoors; hazardous conditions; sitting; protective or safety equipment; climbing; specialized protective or safety equipment.

Related Title in the Classification of Instructional Programs (CIP)

40.0201 Astronomy.

Biochemistry

Focuses on the scientific study of the chemistry of living systems, their fundamental chemical substances and reactions, and their chemical pathways and information transfer systems, with particular reference to carbohydrates, proteins, lipids, and nucleic acids.

Career Snapshot

Biochemistry studies the fundamental chemical processes that support life. The recent growth of the pharmaceutical industry and of genetic engineering technology has fueled the demand for biochemistry majors, especially at the graduate level. Those with bachelor's degrees may find work in nonresearch jobs such as clinical laboratory testing.

Related Specialties in Majors and Careers

Forensic chemistry, pharmacological chemistry, recombinant DNA, research.

Related Job Titles, Earnings, Projected Growth, and Openings

Job Title	Average Earnings	Projected Growth	Annual Openings
1. Biochemists and Biophysicists (O*NET-SOC Code 19-1021.00)	$79,270	15.9%	1,637
2. Biological Science Teachers, Postsecondary (O*NET-SOC Code 25-1042.00)	$71,780	22.9%	237,478
3. Medical Scientists, Except Epidemiologists (O*NET-SOC Code 19-1042.00)	$64,200	20.2%	10,596
4. Natural Sciences Managers (O*NET-SOC Code 11-9121.00)	$104,040	11.4%	3,661

Job 2 shares 237,478 openings with 35 other postsecondary teaching jobs not included in this table.

Typical Sequence of College Courses

English composition, calculus, introduction to computer science, general chemistry, general biology, organic chemistry, general physics, analytical chemistry, general microbiology, introduction to biochemistry, cell biology, molecular biology, physical chemistry, genetics.

Typical Sequence of High School Courses

English, algebra, trigonometry, biology, geometry, chemistry, physics, computer science, pre-calculus, calculus.

Personality Type

Investigative. These occupations frequently involve working with ideas and require an extensive amount of thinking. They can involve searching for facts and figuring out problems mentally.

Other Characteristics

GOE—Related Interest Areas/Career Clusters: 05 Education and Training; 15 Scientific Research, Engineering, and Mathematics. **Related Work Groups:** 05.03 Postsecondary and Adult Teaching and Instructing; 15.01 Managerial Work in Scientific Research, Engineering, and Mathematics; 15.03 Life Sciences. **Most Important Skills:** Science, writing, reading comprehension, complex problem solving, active learning, management of financial resources. **Top Values:** Creativity, social status, responsibility. **Work Environment:** Indoors; disease or infections; sitting; hazardous conditions; radiation; specialized protective or safety equipment.

Related Title in the Classification of Instructional Programs (CIP)

26.0202 Biochemistry.

Bioengineering

Prepares you to apply mathematical and scientific principles to the design, development, and operational evaluation of systems, equipment, and facilities used to produce, process, and store products derived from or serving living organisms.

Career Snapshot

Bioengineering uses engineering principles of analysis and design to solve problems in medicine and biology. It finds ways to improve health care, agriculture, and industrial processes. Many graduates get an advanced degree to enter the industry at a higher professional level or to prepare for a career in research or college teaching. Others go on to medical school. This is one of the fastest-moving fields in engineering, so people in this field need to learn continuously to keep up with new technologies.

Related Specialties in Majors and Careers

Biomechanics, biomedical engineering, computational bioengineering, controlled drug delivery, engineered biomaterials, medical imaging, molecular bioengineering, prosthetics and artificial organs.

Related Job Titles, Earnings, Projected Growth, and Openings

Job Title	Average Earnings	Projected Growth	Annual Openings
1. Biomedical Engineers (O*NET-SOC Code 17-2031.00)	$75,440	21.1%	1,804
2. Engineering Managers (O*NET-SOC Code 11-9041.00)	$111,020	7.3%	7,404
3. Engineering Teachers, Postsecondary (O*NET-SOC Code 25-1032.00)	$79,510	22.9%	237,478

Job 3 shares 237,478 openings with 35 other postsecondary teaching jobs not included in this table.

Typical Sequence of College Courses

English composition, technical writing, calculus, differential equations, general chemistry, introduction to computer science, general physics, introduction to electrical circuits, general biology, mechanics, introduction to bioengineering, bioinstrumentation, biomaterials, biomechanics, business information processing.

Typical Sequence of High School Courses

English, algebra, geometry, trigonometry, pre-calculus, calculus, chemistry, biology, physics, computer science.

Personality Type

Investigative. These occupations frequently involve working with ideas and require an extensive amount of thinking. They can involve searching for facts and figuring out problems mentally.

Other Characteristics

GOE—Related Interest Areas/Career Clusters: 05 Education and Training; 15 Scientific Research, Engineering, and Mathematics. **Related Work Groups:** 05.03 Postsecondary and Adult Teaching and Instructing; 15.01 Managerial Work in Scientific Research, Engineering, and Mathematics. **Most Important Skills:** Science, technology design, operations analysis, installation, management of financial resources, mathematics. **Top Values:** Authority, autonomy, creativity. **Work Environment:** More often indoors than in a vehicle; protective or safety equipment; sitting; hazardous equipment; extremely bright or inadequate lighting; high places; noisy.

Related Title in the Classification of Instructional Programs (CIP)

14.0501 Biomedical/Medical Engineering.

Biology

Focuses on the scientific study of living organisms, habitats, and ecosystem relations.

Career Snapshot

Although it is often possible to study a specialization—such as botany, zoology, or biochemistry—many colleges offer a major in the general field of biology. With a bachelor's degree in biology, you may work as a technician or entry-level researcher in a medical, pharmaceutical, or governmental regulatory setting, or as a sales representative in a technical field such as pharmaceuticals. Teaching biology in high school or middle school almost always requires additional coursework (perhaps a master's) in teaching theory and methods, plus supervised classroom experience. A large number of biology majors go on to pursue graduate or professional degrees and thus prepare for careers as researchers, college teachers, physicians, dentists, and veterinarians.

Related Specialties in Majors and Careers

Biochemistry, botany, cell biology, ecology, genetics, microbiology, zoology.

Related Job Titles, Earnings, Projected Growth, and Openings

Job Title	Average Earnings	Projected Growth	Annual Openings
1. Biological Science Teachers, Postsecondary (O*NET-SOC Code 25-1042.00)	$71,780	22.9%	237,478
2. Natural Sciences Managers (O*NET-SOC Code 11-9121.00)	$104,040	11.4%	3,661

Job 1 shares 237,478 openings with 35 other postsecondary teaching jobs not included in this table.

Typical Sequence of College Courses

English composition, calculus, introduction to computer science, general chemistry, statistics, general biology, organic chemistry, genetics, general physics, cell biology, introduction to biochemistry, general microbiology, ecology, organisms and populations, animal anatomy and physiology, plant anatomy.

Typical Sequence of High School Courses

Algebra, English, biology, geometry, trigonometry, chemistry, physics, pre-calculus, computer science, calculus.

Personality Type

Investigative. These occupations frequently involve working with ideas and require an extensive amount of thinking. They can involve searching for facts and figuring out problems mentally.

Other Characteristics

GOE—Related Interest Areas/Career Clusters: 05 Education and Training; 15 Scientific Research, Engineering, and Mathematics. **Related Work Groups:** 05.03 Postsecondary and Adult Teaching and Instructing; 15.01 Managerial Work in Scientific Research, Engineering, and Mathematics. **Most Important Skills:** Science, writing, reading comprehension, active learning, mathematics, critical thinking. **Top Values:** Authority, creativity, responsibility. **Work Environment:** More often indoors than in a vehicle; hazardous conditions; sitting; disease or infections.

Related Title in the Classification of Instructional Programs (CIP)

26.0101 Biology/Biological Sciences, General.

Botany

Focuses on the scientific study of plants, related microbial organisms, and plant habitats and ecosystem relations.

Career Snapshot

Botany is the science of plants. Since all of our food resources and the very air we breathe ultimately depend on the growth of plants, botany is a vital field of knowledge. A bachelor's degree in this field prepares you for some nonresearch jobs in industry, agriculture, forestry, and environmental protection. Best opportunities are in agricultural research, where a graduate degree is expected.

Related Specialties in Majors and Careers

Forestry, phytopathology (plant disease), plant genetics.

Related Job Titles, Earnings, Projected Growth, and Openings

Job Title	Average Earnings	Projected Growth	Annual Openings
1. Biological Science Teachers, Postsecondary (O*NET-SOC Code 25-1042.00)	$71,780	22.9%	237,478
2. Natural Sciences Managers (O*NET-SOC Code 11-9121.00)	$104,040	11.4%	3,661

Job 1 shares 237,478 openings with 35 other postsecondary teaching jobs not included in this table.

Typical Sequence of College Courses

English composition, calculus, introduction to computer science, general chemistry, statistics, general biology, organic chemistry, genetics, general physics, cell biology, introduction to biochemistry, general microbiology, taxonomy of flowering plants, ecology, plant anatomy, plant physiology.

Typical Sequence of High School Courses

English, algebra, biology, geometry, trigonometry, chemistry, physics, pre-calculus, computer science, calculus.

Personality Type

Investigative. These occupations frequently involve working with ideas and require an extensive amount of thinking. They can involve searching for facts and figuring out problems mentally.

Other Characteristics

GOE—Related Interest Areas/Career Clusters: 05 Education and Training; 15 Scientific Research, Engineering, and Mathematics. **Related Work Groups:** 05.03 Postsecondary and Adult Teaching and Instructing; 15.01 Managerial Work in Scientific Research, Engineering, and Mathematics. **Most Important Skills:** Science, writing, reading comprehension, active learning, mathematics, critical thinking. **Top Values:** Authority, creativity, responsibility. **Work Environment:** More often indoors than in a vehicle; hazardous conditions; sitting; disease or infections.

Related Title in the Classification of Instructional Programs (CIP)

26.0301 Botany/Plant Biology.

Business Education

Prepares you to teach vocational business programs at various educational levels.

Career Snapshot

Business educators teach secondary school students the skills and knowledge they will need to succeed in the business world. Therefore, they must know about one or more specific business fields—such as bookkeeping, retailing, or office computer applications—as well as about techniques for teaching and for managing the classroom. A bachelor's degree is often an entry route to the first teaching job, but job security and pay raises often require a master's degree.

Related Specialties in Majors and Careers

Distributive education, office skills.

Related Job Titles, Earnings, Projected Growth, and Openings

Job Title	Average Earnings	Projected Growth	Annual Openings
1. Business Teachers, Postsecondary (O*NET-SOC Code 25-1011.00)	$64,900	22.9%	237,478
2. Education Teachers, Postsecondary (O*NET-SOC Code 25-1081.00)	$54,220	22.9%	237,478
3. Secondary School Teachers, Except Special and Vocational Education (O*NET-SOC Code 25-2031.00)	$49,420	5.6%	93,166
4. Vocational Education Teachers, Postsecondary (O*NET-SOC Code 25-1194.00)	$45,850	22.9%	237,478

Jobs 1, 2, and 4 share 237,478 openings with each other and with 33 other postsecondary teaching jobs not included in this table.

Typical Sequence of College Courses

Introduction to psychology, English composition, oral communication, history and philosophy of education, human growth and development, introduction to accounting, legal environment of business, introduction to business management, business math, business information processing, keyboarding, statistics, business reports and communication, introduction to marketing, methods of teaching business subjects, student teaching.

Typical Sequence of High School Courses

English, algebra, geometry, trigonometry, science, foreign language, industrial arts, keyboarding, office computer applications, public speaking.

Personality Type

Social. These occupations frequently involve working with, communicating with, and teaching people and often involve helping or providing service to others.

Other Characteristics

GOE—Related Interest Area/Career Cluster: 05 Education and Training. **Related Work Groups:** 05.02 Preschool, Elementary, and Secondary Teaching and Instructing; 05.03 Postsecondary and Adult Teaching and Instructing. **Most Important Skills:** Learning strategies, instructing, social perceptiveness, persuasion, monitoring, time management. **Top Values:** Social service, authority, creativity. **Work Environment:** Indoors; standing; close to others.

Related Title in the Classification of Instructional Programs (CIP)

13.1303 Business Teacher Education.

Business Management

Prepares you to plan, organize, direct, and control the functions and processes of a firm or organization.

Career Snapshot

Students learn about the principles of economics, the legal and social environment in which business operates, and quantitative methods for measuring and projecting business activity. Graduates may enter the business world directly or pursue a master's degree. Some get a bachelor's degree in a nonbusiness field and enter a master's of business administration program after getting some entry-level work experience.

Related Specialties in Majors and Careers

International business, management, marketing, operations.

Related Job Titles, Earnings, Projected Growth, and Openings

Job Title	Average Earnings	Projected Growth	Annual Openings
1. Administrative Services Managers (O*NET-SOC Code 11-3011.00)	$70,990	11.7%	19,513
2. Chief Executives (O*NET-SOC Code 11-1011.00)	$145,600+	2.0%	21,209
3. Construction Managers (O*NET-SOC Code 11-9021.00)	$76,230	15.7%	44,158
4. Cost Estimators (O*NET-SOC Code 13-1051.00)	$54,920	18.5%	38,379
5. Industrial Production Managers (O*NET-SOC Code 11-3051.00)	$80,560	−5.9%	14,889
6. Management Analysts (O*NET-SOC Code 13-1111.00)	$71,150	21.9%	125,669
7. Sales Managers (O*NET-SOC Code 11-2022.00)	$94,910	10.2%	36,392
8. Social and Community Service Managers (O*NET-SOC Code 11-9151.00)	$54,530	24.7%	23,788
9. Storage and Distribution Managers (O*NET-SOC Code 11-3071.02)	$76,310	8.3%	6,994
10. Transportation Managers (O*NET-SOC Code 11-3071.01)	$76,310	8.3%	6,994
11. General and Operations Managers (O*NET-SOC Code 11-1021.00)	$88,700	1.5%	112,072
12. Business Teachers, Postsecondary (O*NET-SOC Code 25-1011.00)	$64,900	22.9%	237,478

Jobs 9 and 10 share 6,994 openings. Job 12 shares 237,478 openings with 35 other postsecondary teaching jobs not included in this table.

Typical Sequence of College Courses

English composition, business writing, introduction to psychology, principles of microeconomics, principles of macroeconomics, calculus for business and social sciences, statistics for business and social sciences, introduction to management information systems, introduction to accounting, legal environment of business, principles of management and organization, operations management, strategic management, business finance, introduction to marketing, organizational behavior, human resource management, international management, organizational theory.

Typical Sequence of High School Courses

English, algebra, geometry, trigonometry, science, foreign language, computer science, public speaking.

Personality Type

Enterprising. These occupations frequently involve starting up and carrying out projects and can involve leading people and making many decisions. They sometimes require risk taking and often deal with business.

Other Characteristics

GOE—Related Interest Areas/Career Clusters: 02 Architecture and Construction; 04 Business and Administration; 05 Education and Training; 06 Finance and Insurance; 07 Government and Public Administration; 13 Manufacturing; 14 Retail and Wholesale Sales and Service; 16 Transportation, Distribution, and Logistics. **Related Work Groups:** 02.01 Managerial Work in Architecture and Construction; 04.01 Managerial Work in General Business; 04.02 Managerial Work in Business Detail; 04.05 Accounting, Auditing, and Analytical Support; 05.03 Postsecondary and Adult Teaching and Instructing; 06.02 Finance/Insurance Investigation and Analysis; 07.01 Managerial Work in Government and Public Administration; 13.01 Managerial Work in Manufacturing; 14.01 Managerial Work in Retail/Wholesale Sales and Service; 16.01 Managerial Work in Transportation. **Most Important Skills:** Management of financial resources, management of personnel resources, management of material resources, negotiation, monitoring, judgment and decision making. **Top Values:** Authority, creativity, autonomy. **Work Environment:** More often indoors than in a vehicle; sitting.

Related Title in the Classification of Instructional Programs (CIP)

52.0201 Business Administration and Management, General.

Chemical Engineering

Prepares you to apply mathematical and scientific principles to the design, development, and operational evaluation of systems employing chemical processes and to the analysis of chemistry-related problems.

Career Snapshot

Chemical engineers apply principles of chemistry to solve engineering problems, such as how to prepare large batches of chemical compounds economically and with uniform consistency and quality. A bachelor's degree is the usual entry route for this field. Keen competition is expected for entry-level jobs, with best opportunities in the manufacture of specialty chemicals, plastics, pharmaceuticals, and electronics, plus in some nonmanufacturing industries. Engineers often move on to managerial jobs.

Related Specialties in Majors and Careers

Bioengineering, nuclear engineering, pharmaceuticals, quality control.

Related Job Titles, Earnings, Projected Growth, and Openings

Job Title	Average Earnings	Projected Growth	Annual Openings
1. Chemical Engineers (O*NET-SOC Code 17-2041.00)	$81,500	7.9%	2,111
2. Engineering Managers (O*NET-SOC Code 11-9041.00)	$111,020	7.3%	7,404
3. Engineering Teachers, Postsecondary (O*NET-SOC Code 25-1032.00)	$79,510	22.9%	237,478

Job 3 shares 237,478 openings with 35 other postsecondary teaching jobs not included in this table.

Typical Sequence of College Courses

English composition, technical writing, calculus, differential equations, general chemistry, general physics, introduction to computer science, introduction to electrical circuits, organic chemistry, introduction to chemical engineering, thermodynamics, numerical analysis, materials engineering, chemical engineering thermodynamics, kinetics and reactor design, mass transfer operations, plant design, process dynamics and controls, process design and optimization, senior design project.

Typical Sequence of High School Courses

English, algebra, geometry, trigonometry, pre-calculus, calculus, chemistry, physics, computer science.

Personality Type

Investigative. These occupations frequently involve working with ideas and require an extensive amount of thinking. They can involve searching for facts and figuring out problems mentally.

Other Characteristics

GOE—Related Interest Areas/Career Clusters: 05 Education and Training; 15 Scientific Research, Engineering, and Mathematics. **Related Work Groups:** 05.03 Postsecondary and Adult Teaching and Instructing; 15.01 Managerial Work in Scientific Research, Engineering, and Mathematics; 15.07 Research and Design Engineering. **Most Important Skills:** Science, technology design, operations analysis, installation, management of financial resources, mathematics. **Top Values:** Authority, creativity, autonomy. **Work Environment:** More often indoors than in a vehicle; protective or safety equipment; sitting; hazardous equipment; hazardous conditions; extremely bright or inadequate lighting; noisy.

Related Title in the Classification of Instructional Programs (CIP)

14.0701 Chemical Engineering.

Chemistry

Focuses on the scientific study of the composition and behavior of matter, including its micro- and macro-structure, the processes of chemical change, and the theoretical description and laboratory simulation of these phenomena.

Career Snapshot

Everything around us and within us is composed of chemicals, and chemists search for and put to use new knowledge about the nature and properties of matter. Chemists develop new fibers, paints, pharmaceuticals, solvents, fuels, and countless other materials that are used in industry and the home. A bachelor's degree is usually required for entry to this field, but a Ph.D. is often needed for research or college teaching. Job opportunities are good, especially in companies that manufacture pharmaceuticals or do chemical testing.

Related Specialties in Majors and Careers

Forensic chemistry, geological/ocean chemistry, quality control, research.

Related Job Titles, Earnings, Projected Growth, and Openings

Job Title	Average Earnings	Projected Growth	Annual Openings
1. Chemistry Teachers, Postsecondary (O*NET-SOC Code 25-1052.00)	$63,870	22.9%	237,478
2. Chemists (O*NET-SOC Code 19-2031.00)	$63,490	9.1%	9,024
3. Natural Sciences Managers (O*NET-SOC Code 11-9121.00)	$104,040	11.4%	3,661

Job 1 shares 237,478 openings with 35 other postsecondary teaching jobs not included in this table.

Typical Sequence of College Courses

English composition, calculus, introduction to computer science, general chemistry, molecular structure and bonding, organic chemistry, qualitative analysis, quantitative analysis, general physics, statistics, physical chemistry, inorganic chemistry, undergraduate research project.

Typical Sequence of High School Courses

English, algebra, geometry, trigonometry, pre-calculus, calculus, chemistry, physics, computer science.

Personality Type

Investigative. These occupations frequently involve working with ideas and require an extensive amount of thinking. They can involve searching for facts and figuring out problems mentally.

Other Characteristics

GOE—Related Interest Areas/Career Clusters: 05 Education and Training; 15 Scientific Research, Engineering, and Mathematics. **Related Work Groups:** 05.03 Postsecondary and Adult Teaching and Instructing; 15.01 Managerial Work in Scientific Research, Engineering, and Mathematics; 15.02 Physical Sciences. **Most Important Skills:** Science, quality control analysis, technology design, mathematics, management of financial resources, reading comprehension. **Top Values:** Creativity, ability utilization, responsibility. **Work Environment:** Indoors; sitting; hazardous conditions; protective or safety equipment; contaminants; specialized protective or safety equipment; radiation.

Related Title in the Classification of Instructional Programs (CIP)

40.0501 Chemistry, General.

 **Chinese**

Focuses on the Chinese language and its associated dialects and literature.

Career Snapshot

Chinese (Mandarin) is spoken by more people than any other language. Now that U.S. trade with China is constantly increasing, there is a growing need for Americans with knowledge of the Chinese language and culture. A bachelor's degree in Chinese, perhaps with additional education in business or law, may lead to an Asia-centered career in business or government. A graduate degree is good preparation for translation or college teaching.

Related Specialties in Majors and Careers

History and culture, language education, literature, translation.

Related Job Titles, Earnings, Projected Growth, and Openings

Job Title	Average Earnings	Projected Growth	Annual Openings
1. Foreign Language and Literature Teachers, Post-secondary (O*NET-SOC Code 25-1124.00)	$53,610	22.9%	237,478
2. Interpreters and Translators (O*NET-SOC Code 27-3091.00)	$37,490	23.6%	6,630

Job 1 shares 237,478 openings with 35 other postsecondary teaching jobs not included in this table.

Typical Sequence of College Courses

Chinese language, conversation, composition, linguistics, Chinese literature, East Asian literature, East Asian studies, grammar, phonetics, study abroad.

Typical Sequence of High School Courses

English, public speaking, foreign language, history, literature, social science.

Personality Type

Artistic. These occupations frequently involve working with forms, designs, and patterns. They often require self-expression, and the work can be done without following a clear set of rules.

Other Characteristics

GOE—Related Interest Areas/Career Clusters: 03 Arts and Communication; 05 Education and Training. **Related Work Groups:** 03.03 News, Broadcasting, and Public Relations; 05.03 Postsecondary and Adult Teaching and Instructing. **Most Important Skills:** Social perceptiveness, speaking, writing, active listening, reading comprehension, learning strategies. **Top Values:** Social service, ability utilization, achievement. **Work Environment:** Indoors; sitting; close to others.

Related Title in the Classification of Instructional Programs (CIP)

16.0301 Chinese Language and Literature.

Chiropractic

Prepares you for the independent professional practice of chiropractic, a health-care and healing system based on the application of noninvasive treatments and spinal adjustments to alleviate health problems caused by vertebral misalignments affecting bodily function as derived from the philosophy of Daniel Palmer.

Career Snapshot

Chiropractors are health practitioners who specialize in health problems associated with the muscular, nervous, and skeletal systems, especially the spine. They learn a variety of specialized diagnostic and treatment techniques but also tend to emphasize the patient's overall health and wellness, recommending changes in diet and lifestyle that can help the body's own healing powers. The educational program includes not only theory and laboratory work, but also a lot of supervised clinical work with patients. With the aging of the population and increased acceptance of chiropractic medicine, job opportunities for graduates are expected to be good.

Related Specialties in Majors and Careers

Diagnostic imaging, orthopedics, sports medicine.

Related Job Titles, Earnings, Projected Growth, and Openings

Job Title	Average Earnings	Projected Growth	Annual Openings
1. Chiropractors (O*NET-SOC Code 29-1011.00)	$65,890	14.4%	3,179
2. Health Specialties Teachers, Postsecondary (O*NET-SOC Code 25-1071.00)	$80,700	22.9%	237,478

Job 2 shares 237,478 openings with 35 other postsecondary teaching jobs not included in this table.

Typical Sequence of College Courses

English composition, introduction to psychology, college algebra, calculus, introduction to sociology, oral communication, general chemistry, general biology, introduction to computer science, organic chemistry, human anatomy and physiology, general microbiology, genetics, introduction to biochemistry, veterinary gross anatomy, spinal anatomy, histology, biomechanics, physical diagnosis, neuroanatomy, neurophysiology, radiographic anatomy, emergency care, nutrition, neuromusculoskeletal diagnosis and treatment, chiropractic manipulative therapeutics, pathology, public health, patient examination and evaluation, pharmacology, minor surgery, clinical experience in obstetrics/gynecology, clinical experience in pediatrics, clinical experience in geriatrics, mental health, ethics in health care, professional practice management.

Typical Sequence of High School Courses

English, algebra, geometry, trigonometry, biology, computer science, public speaking, chemistry, foreign language, physics, pre-calculus.

Personality Type

Investigative. These occupations frequently involve working with ideas and require an extensive amount of thinking. They can involve searching for facts and figuring out problems mentally.

Other Characteristics

GOE—Related Interest Areas/Career Clusters: 05 Education and Training; 08 Health Science. **Related Work Groups:** 05.03 Postsecondary and Adult Teaching and Instructing; 08.04 Health Specialties. **Most Important Skills:** Science, writing, instructing, reading comprehension, critical thinking, learning strategies. **Top Values:** Social service, authority, creativity. **Work Environment:** Indoors; sitting; disease or infections; radiation; close to others.

Related Title in the Classification of Instructional Programs (CIP)

51.0101 Chiropractic (DC).

Civil Engineering

Prepares you to apply mathematical and scientific principles to environmental safety measures and the design, development, and operational evaluation of structural, load-bearing, material moving, transportation, water resource, and material control systems.

Career Snapshot

Civil engineers design and supervise construction of roads, buildings, bridges, dams, airports, water-supply systems, and many other projects that affect the quality of our environment. They apply principles of physics and other sciences to devise engineering solutions that are technically effective, as well as being economically and environmentally sound. A bachelor's degree is the usual way to enter the field. Engineering is also a good way to prepare for a later position in management. Employment opportunities tend to rise and fall with the economy.

Related Specialties in Majors and Careers

Environmental engineering, geotechnical engineering, structural engineering, transportation engineering, water resources.

Related Job Titles, Earnings, Projected Growth, and Openings

Job Title	Average Earnings	Projected Growth	Annual Openings
1. Civil Engineers (O*NET-SOC Code 17-2051.00)	$71,710	18.0%	15,979
2. Engineering Managers (O*NET-SOC Code 11-9041.00)	$111,020	7.3%	7,404
3. Engineering Teachers, Postsecondary (O*NET-SOC Code 25-1032.00)	$79,510	22.9%	237,478

Job 3 shares 237,478 openings with 35 other postsecondary teaching jobs not included in this table.

Typical Sequence of College Courses

English composition, technical writing, calculus, differential equations, general chemistry, introduction to computer science, general physics, introduction to electrical circuits, engineering graphics, statics, dynamics, materials engineering, introduction to civil engineering, numerical analysis, fluid mechanics, engineering surveying and measurement, environmental engineering and design, soil mechanics, engineering economics, analysis of structures, highway and transportation engineering, reinforced concrete design, steel design, water resources and hydraulic engineering, senior design project.

Typical Sequence of High School Courses

English, algebra, geometry, trigonometry, pre-calculus, calculus, chemistry, physics, computer science.

Personality Type

Investigative. These occupations frequently involve working with ideas and require an extensive amount of thinking. They can involve searching for facts and figuring out problems mentally.

Other Characteristics

GOE—Related Interest Areas/Career Clusters: 05 Education and Training; 15 Scientific Research, Engineering, and Mathematics. **Related Work Groups:** 05.03 Postsecondary and Adult Teaching and Instructing; 15.01 Managerial Work in Scientific Research, Engineering, and Mathematics; 15.07 Research and Design Engineering. **Most Important Skills:** Science, operations analysis, technology design, mathematics, installation, negotiation. **Top Values:** Authority, creativity, autonomy. **Work Environment:** More often indoors than in a vehicle or outdoors; sitting; hazardous equipment; very hot or cold; radiation; protective or safety equipment; contaminants.

Related Title in the Classification of Instructional Programs (CIP)

14.0801 Civil Engineering, General.

Classics

Focuses on the literary culture of the ancient Graeco-Roman world and the Greek and Latin languages and literatures and their development prior to the fall of the Roman Empire.

Career Snapshot

The classical languages—Latin and Ancient Greek—may be dead, but students who study them often end up in very lively careers. The mental discipline and critical-thinking skills learned in the classics can be first-rate preparation for law school and medical school, and business recruiters report that classics graduates have an exceptional breadth of view. The demand for Latin teachers in secondary schools is strong. A classics major is also a good first step to graduate training in archeology, history, or theology.

Related Specialties in Majors and Careers

Archeology, classical civilization, classical linguistics, classical literature/mythology, Greek, Latin.

Related Job Titles, Earnings, Projected Growth, and Openings

Job Title	Average Earnings	Projected Growth	Annual Openings
1. Archeologists (O*NET-SOC Code 19-3091.02)	$53,080	15.0%	446
2. Foreign Language and Literature Teachers, Post-secondary (O*NET-SOC Code 25-1124.00)	$53,610	22.9%	237,478
3. Interpreters and Translators (O*NET-SOC Code 27-3091.00)	$37,490	23.6%	6,630
4. Social Sciences Teachers, Postsecondary, All Other (O*NET-SOC Code 25-1069.99)	$61,190	22.9%	237,478

Jobs 2 and 4 share 237,478 openings with each other and with 34 other postsecondary teaching jobs not included in this table.

Typical Sequence of College Courses

Latin, Greek, grammar, linguistics, literature of the Roman Empire, literature in Ancient Greek, history of the ancient world.

Typical Sequence of High School Courses

English, public speaking, foreign language, history, literature, social science.

Personality Type

Artistic. These occupations frequently involve working with forms, designs, and patterns. They often require self-expression, and the work can be done without following a clear set of rules.

Other Characteristics

GOE—Related Interest Areas/Career Clusters: 03 Arts and Communication; 05 Education and Training; 15 Scientific Research, Engineering, and Mathematics. **Related Work Groups:** 03.03 News, Broadcasting, and Public Relations; 05.03 Postsecondary and Adult Teaching and Instructing; 15.04 Social Sciences. **Most Important Skills:** Speaking, social perceptiveness, writing, reading comprehension, active listening, critical thinking. **Top Values:** Social service, ability utilization, achievement. **Work Environment:** Indoors; sitting; close to others.

Related Title in the Classification of Instructional Programs (CIP)

16.1200 Classics and Classical Languages, Literatures, and Linguistics, General.

Clinical Laboratory Technology

Prepares you to conduct and supervise complex medical tests, clinical trials, and research experiments; manage clinical laboratories; and consult with physicians and clinical researchers on diagnoses, disease causation and spread, and research outcomes.

Career Snapshot

The detection, diagnosis, and prevention of disease depend heavily on various kinds of medical tests—of blood, urine, tissue samples, and so on. Medical technologists, also called clinical laboratory scientists, are trained to perform these tests after studying the principles of chemistry, microbiology, and other basic sciences, plus laboratory techniques that sometimes involve complex and sophisticated equipment. A bachelor's degree is the usual preparation. Job outlook is generally good, with best opportunities for those who have skills in multiple specializations.

Related Specialties in Majors and Careers

Blood banking, body fluid analysis, clinical chemistry, clinical microbiology, hematology, immunology.

Related Job Titles, Earnings, Projected Growth, and Openings

Job Title	Average Earnings	Projected Growth	Annual Openings
1. Health Specialties Teachers, Postsecondary (O*NET-SOC Code 25-1071.00)	$80,700	22.9%	237,478
2. Medical and Clinical Laboratory Technologists (O*NET-SOC Code 29-2011.00)	$51,720	12.4%	11,457

Job 1 shares 237,478 openings with 35 other postsecondary teaching jobs not included in this table.

Typical Sequence of College Courses

English composition, general biology, general chemistry, organic chemistry, human anatomy and physiology, general microbiology, introduction to biochemistry, college algebra, introduction to computer science, statistics, body fluid analysis, parasitology, clinical chemistry, hematology and coagulation, clinical microbiology, immunohematology, clinical immunology and serology, medical technology education, medical technology management and supervision.

Typical Sequence of High School Courses

Algebra, biology, chemistry, computer science, English, physics, geometry, trigonometry.

Personality Type

Investigative. These occupations frequently involve working with ideas and require an extensive amount of thinking. They can involve searching for facts and figuring out problems mentally.

Other Characteristics

GOE—Related Interest Areas/Career Clusters: 05 Education and Training; 08 Health Science. **Related Work Groups:** 05.03 Postsecondary and Adult Teaching and Instructing; 08.06 Medical Technology. **Most Important Skills:** Science, quality control analysis, operation monitoring, equipment maintenance, instructing, critical thinking. **Top Values:** Ability utilization, social service, authority. **Work Environment:** Indoors; disease or infections; hazardous conditions; protective or safety equipment; sitting; contaminants; repetitive motions; radiation; specialized protective or safety equipment.

Related Title in the Classification of Instructional Programs (CIP)

51.1005 Clinical Laboratory Science/Medical Technology/Technologist.

Computer Engineering

Prepares you to apply mathematical and scientific principles to the design, development, and operational evaluation of computer hardware and software systems and related equipment and facilities; and the analysis of specific problems of computer applications for various tasks.

Career Snapshot

Computer engineers use their knowledge of scientific principles to design computers, networks of computers, and systems (such as telecommunications) that include computers. They need to understand both hardware and software, and they might build prototypes of new systems. The usual entry route is via a bachelor's degree. Opportunities for employment are excellent, as there seems to be no end to the boom in computer use. Some engineers go into management, and the computer industry provides many opportunities for creative and motivated engineers to become entrepreneurs.

Related Specialties in Majors and Careers

Business communications, speech/rhetoric.

Related Job Titles, Earnings, Projected Growth, and Openings

Job Title	Average Earnings	Projected Growth	Annual Openings
1. Computer Hardware Engineers (O*NET-SOC Code 17-2061.00)	$91,860	4.6%	3,572
2. Computer Software Engineers, Applications (O*NET-SOC Code 15-1031.00)	$83,130	44.6%	58,690
3. Computer Software Engineers, Systems Software (O*NET-SOC Code 15-1032.00)	$89,070	28.2%	33,139
4. Computer Systems Engineers/Architects (O*NET-SOC Code 15-1099.02)	$71,510	15.1%	14,374
5. Engineering Managers (O*NET-SOC Code 11-9041.00)	$111,020	7.3%	7,404
6. Engineering Teachers, Postsecondary (O*NET-SOC Code 25-1032.00)	$79,510	22.9%	237,478
7. Network Designers (O*NET-SOC Code 15-1099.03)	$71,510	15.1%	14,374
8. Software Quality Assurance Engineers and Testers (O*NET-SOC Code 15-1099.01)	$71,510	15.1%	14,374

Job Title	Average Earnings	Projected Growth	Annual Openings
9. Web Administrators (O*NET-SOC Code 15-1099.05)	$71,510	15.1%	14,374
10. Web Developers (O*NET-SOC Code 15-1099.04)	$71,510	15.1%	14,374

Jobs 4, 7, 8, 9, and 10 share 14,374 openings. Job 6 shares 237,478 openings with 35 other postsecondary teaching jobs not included in this table.

Typical Sequence of College Courses

English composition, technical writing, calculus, differential equations, general chemistry, introduction to computer science, general physics, introduction to engineering, introduction to electrical circuits, engineering circuit analysis, numerical analysis, electrical networks, electronics, computer architecture, algorithms and data structures, digital system design, software engineering, operating systems, microcomputer systems, senior design project.

Typical Sequence of High School Courses

English, algebra, geometry, trigonometry, pre-calculus, calculus, chemistry, physics, computer science.

Personality Type

Investigative. These occupations frequently involve working with ideas and require an extensive amount of thinking. They can involve searching for facts and figuring out problems mentally.

Other Characteristics

GOE—Related Interest Areas/Career Clusters: 05 Education and Training; 11 Information Technology; 15 Scientific Research, Engineering, and Mathematics. **Related Work Groups:** 05.03 Postsecondary and Adult Teaching and Instructing; 11.02 Information Technology Specialties; 15.01 Managerial Work in Scientific Research, Engineering, and Mathematics; 15.07 Research and Design Engineering. **Most Important Skills:** Programming, technology design, troubleshooting, systems analysis, operations analysis, quality control analysis. **Top Values:** Creativity, ability utilization, working conditions. **Work Environment:** Indoors; sitting; repetitive motions.

Related Title in the Classification of Instructional Programs (CIP)

14.0901 Computer Engineering, General.

Computer Science

Focuses on computers, computing problems and solutions, and the design of computer systems and user interfaces from a scientific perspective.

Career Snapshot

Computer science is among the hottest fields now, especially with the explosion of Internet sites, and it is likely to continue to offer many job openings. The major teaches you not only specific languages, but the principles by which languages are created, the structures used to store data, and the logical structures by which programs solve problems. You may want to concentrate more on business or scientific programming needs and procedures.

Related Specialties in Majors and Careers

Hardware design, software/systems design, systems analysis.

Related Job Titles, Earnings, Projected Growth, and Openings

Job Title	Average Earnings	Projected Growth	Annual Openings
1. Computer and Information Systems Managers (O*NET-SOC Code 11-3021.00)	$108,070	16.4%	30,887
2. Computer Science Teachers, Postsecondary (O*NET-SOC Code 25-1021.00)	$62,020	22.9%	237,478
3. Computer Software Engineers, Applications (O*NET-SOC Code 15-1031.00)	$83,130	44.6%	58,690
4. Computer Software Engineers, Systems Software (O*NET-SOC Code 15-1032.00)	$89,070	28.2%	33,139
5. Computer Systems Engineers/Architects (O*NET-SOC Code 15-1099.02)	$71,510	15.1%	14,374
6. Network Designers (O*NET-SOC Code 15-1099.03)	$71,510	15.1%	14,374
7. Software Quality Assurance Engineers and Testers (O*NET-SOC Code 15-1099.01)	$71,510	15.1%	14,374
8. Web Administrators (O*NET-SOC Code 15-1099.05)	$71,510	15.1%	14,374
9. Web Developers (O*NET-SOC Code 15-1099.04)	$71,510	15.1%	14,374

Job 2 shares 237,478 openings with 35 other postsecondary teaching jobs not included in this table. Jobs 5, 6, 7, 8, and 9 share 14,374 with each other and with another job not included in this table.

Typical Sequence of College Courses

English composition, calculus, introduction to economics, statistics for business and social sciences, introduction to computer science, programming in a language (e.g., C++, Pascal, Visual Basic), algorithms and data structures, software engineering, operating systems, database systems, theory of computer languages, computer architecture, artificial intelligence.

Typical Sequence of High School Courses

English, algebra, geometry, trigonometry, pre-calculus, calculus, chemistry, physics, computer science.

Personality Type

Investigative. These occupations frequently involve working with ideas and require an extensive amount of thinking. They can involve searching for facts and figuring out problems mentally.

Other Characteristics

GOE—Related Interest Areas/Career Clusters: 05 Education and Training; 11 Information Technology. **Related Work Groups:** 05.03 Postsecondary and Adult Teaching and Instructing; 11.01 Managerial Work in Information Technology; 11.02 Information Technology Specialties. **Most Important Skills:** Programming, systems analysis, technology design, troubleshooting, operations analysis, quality control analysis. **Top Values:** Creativity, ability utilization, authority. **Work Environment:** Indoors; sitting; repetitive motions.

Related Title in the Classification of Instructional Programs (CIP)

11.0701 Computer Science.

Criminal Justice/Law Enforcement

Prepares you to perform the duties of police and public security officers, including patrol and investigative activities, traffic control, crowd control and public relations, witness interviewing, evidence collection and management, basic crime prevention methods, weapon and equipment operation and maintenance, report preparation, and other routine law enforcement responsibilities.

Career Snapshot

We live in a society that is governed by laws at the municipal, state, and federal levels. These laws are enforced by people who understand the laws themselves; the workings of the agencies that are empowered to enforce them; and the techniques for detecting violation of the laws, arresting violators, and processing them through the court system. Public concern about crime has created many job opportunities in this field, especially at the local level.

Related Specialties in Majors and Careers

Business security, homeland security, police administration, police work.

Related Job Titles, Earnings, Projected Growth, and Openings

Job Title	Average Earnings	Projected Growth	Annual Openings
1. Bailiffs (O*NET-SOC Code 33-3011.00)	$36,900	11.2%	2,223
2. Criminal Investigators and Special Agents (O*NET-SOC Code 33-3021.03)	$59,930	17.3%	14,746
3. Criminal Justice and Law Enforcement Teachers, Postsecondary (O*NET-SOC Code 25-1111.00)	$51,060	22.9%	237,478
4. Immigration and Customs Inspectors (O*NET-SOC Code 33-3021.05)	$59,930	17.3%	14,746
5. Police Detectives (O*NET-SOC Code 33-3021.01)	$59,930	17.3%	14,746
6. Police Identification and Records Officers (O*NET-SOC Code 33-3021.02)	$59,930	17.3%	14,746
7. Police Patrol Officers (O*NET-SOC Code 33-3051.01)	$49,630	10.8%	37,842
8. Private Detectives and Investigators (O*NET-SOC Code 33-9021.00)	$37,640	18.2%	7,329

Job Title	Average Earnings	Projected Growth	Annual Openings
9. Sheriffs and Deputy Sheriffs (O*NET-SOC Code 33-3051.03)	$49,630	10.8%	37,842

Jobs 2, 4, 5, and 6 share 14,746 openings. Job 3 shares 237,478 openings with 35 other postsecondary teaching jobs not included in this table. Jobs 7 and 9 share 37,842 openings.

Typical Sequence of College Courses

Technical writing, introduction to criminal justice, introduction to psychology, American government, criminal law, criminal investigation, introduction to sociology, police organization and administration, criminal procedures, police-community relations, ethics, diversity and conflict, seminar (reporting on research).

Typical Sequence of High School Courses

Algebra, English, foreign language, social science, history, public speaking, computer science.

Personality Type

Social. These occupations frequently involve working with, communicating with, and teaching people and often involve helping or providing service to others.

Other Characteristics

GOE—Related Interest Areas/Career Clusters: 05 Education and Training; 07 Government and Public Administration; 12 Law and Public Safety. **Related Work Groups:** 05.03 Postsecondary and Adult Teaching and Instructing; 07.03 Regulations Enforcement; 12.04 Law Enforcement and Public Safety; 12.05 Safety and Security. **Most Important Skills:** Persuasion, negotiation, social perceptiveness, judgment and decision making, service orientation, complex problem solving. **Top Values:** Security, variety, authority. **Work Environment:** More often in a vehicle than indoors or outdoors; disease or infections; specialized protective or safety equipment; very hot or cold; extremely bright or inadequate lighting; hazardous equipment; contaminants.

Related Title in the Classification of Instructional Programs (CIP)

43.0107 Criminal Justice/Police Science.

Dance

A general program that prepares individuals to express ideas, feelings, and/or inner visions through the performance of one or more of the dance disciplines, including but not limited to ballet, modern, jazz, ethnic, and folk dance, and that focuses on the study and analysis of dance as a cultural phenomenon.

Career Snapshot

Dance is one of the most basic arts of all because the medium is the dancer's own body. This means that dance is also a physical discipline as demanding as any sport. Most dancers start training at very early ages and often must give up performing as their bodies age. However, many find continuing satisfaction and employment in dance instruction and choreography. This is a very competitive field, and only the most talented find regular employment as dancers or choreographers. Job opportunities are better for dance teachers.

Related Specialties in Majors and Careers

Ballet, ballroom dance, composite dance, dance education, folk dance, modern dance.

Related Job Titles, Earnings, Projected Growth, and Openings

Job Title	Average Earnings	Projected Growth	Annual Openings
1. Art, Drama, and Music Teachers, Postsecondary (O*NET-SOC Code 25-1121.00)	$55,190	22.9%	237,478
2. Choreographers (O*NET-SOC Code 27-2032.00)	$35,580	2.4%	1,316
3. Dancers (O*NET-SOC Code 27-2031.00)	No data available	9.5%	1,455

Job 1 shares 237,478 openings with 35 other postsecondary teaching jobs not included in this table.

Typical Sequence of College Courses

Introduction to music, anatomy and kinesiology for dance, history of dance, dance improvisation, methods of teaching dance, dance composition, dance notation, dance technique (e.g., ballet, tap, modern).

Typical Sequence of High School Courses

Biology, foreign language, dance, music.

Personality Type

Artistic. These occupations frequently involve working with forms, designs, and patterns. They often require self-expression, and the work can be done without following a clear set of rules.

Other Characteristics

GOE—Related Interest Areas/Career Clusters: 03 Arts and Communication; 05 Education and Training. **Related Work Groups:** 03.08 Dance; 05.03 Postsecondary and Adult Teaching and Instructing. **Most Important Skills:** Instructing, social perceptiveness, persuasion, speaking, active listening, monitoring. **Top Values:** Creativity, authority, ability utilization. **Work Environment:** Indoors; standing; keeping or regaining balance; close to others; repetitive motions; kneeling or crouching; bending or twisting the body; extremely bright or inadequate lighting.

Related Title in the Classification of Instructional Programs (CIP)

50.0301 Dance, General.

Dentistry

Prepares you for the professional practice of dentistry/dental medicine, encompassing the evaluation, diagnosis, prevention, and treatment of diseases, disorders, and conditions of the oral cavity, maxillofacial area, and adjacent structures and their impact on the human body and health.

Career Snapshot

Dentists generally get at least eight years of education beyond high school. Those who want to teach or do research usually must get additional education. Besides academic ability, students of dentistry need good eye-hand coordination and communication skills. Although it seems unlikely that a vaccine against decay germs will be developed anytime soon, tooth sealants and fluoridation have reduced the incidence of tooth decay among young people, which means that dentistry's emphasis has shifted to prevention and maintenance.

Related Specialties in Majors and Careers

Endodontics, oral and maxillofacial surgery, oral pathology, orthodontics, periodontics, public health dentistry.

Related Job Titles, Earnings, Projected Growth, and Openings

Job Title	Average Earnings	Projected Growth	Annual Openings
1. Dentists, General (O*NET-SOC Code 29-1021.00)	$137,630	9.2%	7,106
2. Health Specialties Teachers, Postsecondary (O*NET-SOC Code 25-1071.00)	$80,700	22.9%	237,478

Job 2 shares 237,478 openings with 35 other postsecondary teaching jobs not included in this table.

Typical Sequence of College Courses

English composition, introduction to psychology, college algebra, introduction to business management, introduction to sociology, oral communication, general chemistry, general biology, organic chemistry, nutrition, introduction to accounting, introduction to biochemistry, dental morphology and function, occlusion, dental materials, ethics in health care, head and neck anatomy, oral radiology, assessment and treatment planning, dental anesthesia, pharmacology, prosthodontics (fixed/removable, partial/complete), community dentistry programs, endodontics, oral pathology, pediatric dentistry, dental emergency diagnosis and treatment, chronic orofacial pain, oral implantology, professional practice management, clinical experience in dentistry.

Typical Sequence of High School Courses

English, algebra, geometry, trigonometry, biology, computer science, public speaking, chemistry, foreign language, physics, pre-calculus.

Personality Type

Investigative. These occupations frequently involve working with ideas and require an extensive amount of thinking. They can involve searching for facts and figuring out problems mentally.

Other Characteristics

GOE—Related Interest Areas/Career Clusters: 05 Education and Training; 08 Health Science. **Related Work Groups:** 05.03 Postsecondary and Adult Teaching and Instructing; 08.03 Dentistry. **Most Important Skills:** Science, complex problem solving, reading comprehension, management of financial resources, instructing, management of material resources. **Top Values:** Social service, social status, responsibility. **Work Environment:** Indoors; disease or infections; radiation; hazardous conditions; protective or safety equipment; close to others; contaminants.

Related Title in the Classification of Instructional Programs (CIP)

51.0401 Dentistry (DDS, DMD).

Dietetics

Prepares you to integrate and apply the principles of the food and nutrition sciences, human behavior, and the biomedical sciences to design and manage effective nutrition programs in a variety of settings.

Career Snapshot

Dietitians plan food and nutrition programs and supervise the preparation and serving of food. They are concerned with creating diets that are healthful, appetizing, and within budget. They need to know about human nutritional needs in sickness and health, cultural preferences for foods, the nutritional properties of various foods and how they are affected by preparation techniques, and the business or health-care environment in which food is prepared and served. A bachelor's degree is good preparation for entering this field; for research, teaching, advanced management, or public health, a graduate degree is helpful or required.

Related Specialties in Majors and Careers

Clinical dietetics, community dietetics, dietetics education, food service management, research dietetics.

Related Job Titles, Earnings, Projected Growth, and Openings

Job Title	Average Earnings	Projected Growth	Annual Openings
1. Dietetic Technicians (O*NET-SOC Code 29-2051.00)	$24,750	14.8%	4,062
2. Dietitians and Nutritionists (O*NET-SOC Code 29-1031.00)	$49,010	8.6%	4,996

Typical Sequence of College Courses

English composition, college algebra, general biology, general chemistry, organic chemistry, oral communication, statistics, introduction to computer science, microbiology, introduction to economics, introduction to business management, introduction to biochemistry, introduction to food science and technology, human anatomy, human physiology, nutrition through life, food service operational management, diet therapy, menu management, community nutrition.

Typical Sequence of High School Courses

English, algebra, social science, biology, trigonometry, chemistry, physics, geometry.

Personality Type

Investigative. These occupations frequently involve working with ideas and require an extensive amount of thinking. They can involve searching for facts and figuring out problems mentally.

Other Characteristics

GOE—Related Interest Area/Career Cluster: 08 Health Science. **Related Work Group:** 08.09 Health Protection and Promotion. **Most Important Skills:** Social perceptiveness, reading comprehension, writing, science, instructing, service orientation. **Top Values:** Social service, authority, ability utilization. **Work Environment:** Indoors; sitting; disease or infections; minor burns, cuts, bites, or stings; standing; protective or safety equipment.

Related Title in the Classification of Instructional Programs (CIP)

51.3101 Dietetics/Dietitian (RD).

Drama/Theater Arts

Focuses on the general study of dramatic works and their performance.

Career Snapshot

Drama is one of the most ancient art forms and continues to entertain audiences today. As in all performing arts, there are better opportunities for teachers than for performers. The technical aspects of theater—set design, lighting, costume design, and makeup—also offer jobs for nonperformers. Academic programs includes many opportunities to learn through student performances.

Related Specialties in Majors and Careers

Acting, design and technology, directing.

Related Job Titles, Earnings, Projected Growth, and Openings

Job Title	Average Earnings	Projected Growth	Annual Openings
1. Actors (O*NET-SOC Code 27-2011.00)	No data available	11.6%	20,895
2. Art, Drama, and Music Teachers, Postsecondary (O*NET-SOC Code 25-1121.00)	$55,190	22.9%	237,478
3. Directors—Stage, Motion Pictures, Television, and Radio (O*NET-SOC Code 27-2012.02)	$61,090	11.1%	8,992
4. Producers (O*NET-SOC Code 27-2012.01)	$61,090	11.1%	8,992
5. Program Directors (O*NET-SOC Code 27-2012.03)	$61,090	11.1%	8,992
6. Talent Directors (O*NET-SOC Code 27-2012.04)	$61,090	11.1%	8,992
7. Technical Directors/Managers (O*NET-SOC Code 27-2012.05)	$61,090	11.1%	8,992

Job 2 shares 237,478 openings with 35 other postsecondary teaching jobs not included in this table. Jobs 3, 4, 5, 6, and 7 share 8,992 openings.

Typical Sequence of College Courses

English composition, foreign language, history of theater, acting technique, dramatic literature, performance techniques, theater technology (e.g., set, costume, lighting), theater practicum.

Typical Sequence of High School Courses

English, foreign language, literature, public speaking.

Personality Type

Artistic. These occupations frequently involve working with forms, designs, and patterns. They often require self-expression, and the work can be done without following a clear set of rules.

Other Characteristics

GOE—Related Interest Areas/Career Clusters: 03 Arts and Communication; 05 Education and Training. **Related Work Groups:** 03.01 Managerial Work in Arts and Communication; 03.06 Drama; 03.07 Music; 05.03 Postsecondary and Adult Teaching and Instructing. **Most Important Skills:** Speaking, social perceptiveness, active listening, persuasion, management of personnel resources, time management. **Top Values:** Creativity, ability utilization, recognition. **Work Environment:** Indoors; sitting; close to others; extremely bright or inadequate lighting.

Related Title in the Classification of Instructional Programs (CIP)

50.0501 Drama and Dramatics/Theatre Arts, General.

Early Childhood Education

Prepares you to teach students ranging in age from infancy through nine years (grade three), depending on the school system or state regulations.

Career Snapshot

Because very young children do not think exactly the same way as adults do, an important part of an early childhood education major is learning effective educational techniques for this age group. As in any other teaching major, a bachelor's degree is the minimum requirement for employment, and a master's degree is often needed for job security and pay raises. Although enrollments of very young students are expected to decline for some time, jobs will open to replace teachers who are retiring.

Related Specialties in Majors and Careers

Art education, bilingual education, music education, reading readiness.

Related Job Titles, Earnings, Projected Growth, and Openings

Job Title	Average Earnings	Projected Growth	Annual Openings
1. Kindergarten Teachers, Except Special Education (O*NET-SOC Code 25-2012.00)	$45,120	16.3%	27,603
2. Preschool Teachers, Except Special Education (O*NET-SOC Code 25-2011.00)	$23,130	26.3%	78,172

Typical Sequence of College Courses

Introduction to psychology, English composition, oral communication, history and philosophy of education, human growth and development, teaching methods, educational alternatives for exceptional students, educational psychology, reading assessment and teaching, mathematics education, art education, music education, physical education, health education, science education, children's literature, student teaching.

Typical Sequence of High School Courses

English, algebra, geometry, trigonometry, science, foreign language, public speaking.

Personality Type

Social. These occupations frequently involve working with, communicating with, and teaching people and often involve helping or providing service to others.

Other Characteristics

GOE—Related Interest Area/Career Cluster: 05 Education and Training. **Related Work Group:** 05.02 Preschool, Elementary, and Secondary Teaching and Instructing. **Most Important Skills:** Learning strategies, social perceptiveness, writing, monitoring, instructing, negotiation. **Top Values:** Social service, authority, creativity. **Work Environment:** More often indoors than outdoors; standing; disease or infections; close to others; kneeling or crouching; bending or twisting the body; walking and running.

Related Title in the Classification of Instructional Programs (CIP)

13.1210 Early Childhood Education and Teaching.

Earth Sciences

Focuses on the scientific study of the earth; the forces acting upon it; and the behavior of the solids, liquids, and gases comprising it.

Career Snapshot

The earth sciences major combines the disciplines of geology, oceanography, meteorology, and environmental science. Some graduates with bachelor's degrees go to work in environmental planning for consulting companies or government agencies, or find employment with mining or petroleum companies. Others go into secondary school teaching, with the addition of coursework (or perhaps a master's degree) in education. A higher degree in the field can lead to a career in college teaching or research.

Related Specialties in Majors and Careers

Climatology, earth science education, marine science, meteorology, watersheds and water resources.

Related Job Titles, Earnings, Projected Growth, and Openings

Job Title	Average Earnings	Projected Growth	Annual Openings
1. Atmospheric, Earth, Marine, and Space Sciences Teachers, Postsecondary (O*NET-SOC Code 25-1051.00)	$73,280	22.9%	237,478
2. Geoscientists, Except Hydrologists and Geographers (O*NET-SOC Code 19-2042.00)	$75,800	21.9%	2,471
3. Hydrologists (O*NET-SOC Code 19-2043.00)	$68,140	24.3%	687
4. Natural Sciences Managers (O*NET-SOC Code 11-9121.00)	$104,040	11.4%	3,661

Job 1 shares 237,478 openings with 35 other postsecondary teaching jobs not included in this table.

Typical Sequence of College Courses

English composition, calculus, general chemistry, general physics, introduction to computer science, introduction to environmental science, introduction to geology, geological oceanography, introduction to ground water/hydrology, mineralogy, structural geology, stratigraphy, summer field geology.

Typical Sequence of High School Courses

English, algebra, geometry, trigonometry, chemistry, physics, pre-calculus, computer science, calculus.

Personality Type

Investigative. These occupations frequently involve working with ideas and require an extensive amount of thinking. They can involve searching for facts and figuring out problems mentally.

Other Characteristics

GOE—Related Interest Areas/Career Clusters: 05 Education and Training; 15 Scientific Research, Engineering, and Mathematics. **Related Work Groups:** 05.03 Postsecondary and Adult Teaching and Instructing; 15.01 Managerial Work in Scientific Research, Engineering, and Mathematics; 15.02 Physical Sciences. **Most Important Skills:** Science, mathematics, management of financial resources, management of personnel resources, active learning, writing. **Top Values:** Creativity, responsibility, autonomy. **Work Environment:** More often indoors than outdoors or in a vehicle; sitting; hazardous conditions; hazardous equipment; radiation; extremely bright or inadequate lighting; specialized protective or safety equipment.

Related Title in the Classification of Instructional Programs (CIP)

40.0601 Geology/Earth Science, General.

Economics

Focuses on the systematic study of the production, conservation, and allocation of resources in conditions of scarcity, together with the organizational frameworks related to these processes.

Career Snapshot

Economics at its most basic is the study of human needs and how they are satisfied. Therefore, it looks at how goods and services are produced, distributed, and consumed; how markets for these goods and services are created and behave; and how the actions of individuals, businesses, and governments affect these markets. Graduates of economics programs may work for business, government, or universities. The best job opportunities should be in the private sector for those with graduate degrees.

Related Specialties in Majors and Careers

Applied economics, econometrics, economic theory.

Related Job Titles, Earnings, Projected Growth, and Openings

Job Title	Average Earnings	Projected Growth	Annual Openings
1. Economics Teachers, Postsecondary (O*NET-SOC Code 25-1063.00)	$75,300	22.9%	237,478
2. Economists (O*NET-SOC Code 19-3011.00)	$80,220	7.5%	1,555
3. Market Research Analysts (O*NET-SOC Code 19-3021.00)	$60,300	20.1%	45,015
4. Survey Researchers (O*NET-SOC Code 19-3022.00)	$36,820	15.9%	4,959

Job 1 shares 237,478 openings with 35 other postsecondary teaching jobs not included in this table.

Typical Sequence of College Courses

English composition, introduction to psychology, introduction to sociology, American government, foreign language, statistics, calculus, introduction to economics, statistics for business and social sciences, introduction to computer science, microeconomic theory, macroeconomic theory, mathematical methods in economics, econometrics.

Typical Sequence of High School Courses
Algebra, English, foreign language, social science, trigonometry, pre-calculus.

Personality Type
Social. These occupations frequently involve working with, communicating with, and teaching people and often involve helping or providing service to others.

Other Characteristics
GOE—Related Interest Areas/Career Clusters: 05 Education and Training; 06 Finance and Insurance; 15 Scientific Research, Engineering, and Mathematics. **Related Work Groups:** 05.03 Postsecondary and Adult Teaching and Instructing; 06.02 Finance/Insurance Investigation and Analysis; 15.04 Social Sciences. **Most Important Skills:** Writing, persuasion, judgment and decision making, management of financial resources, negotiation, reading comprehension. **Top Values:** Autonomy, working conditions, recognition. **Work Environment:** Indoors; sitting.

Related Title in the Classification of Instructional Programs (CIP)
45.0601 Economics, General.

Electrical Engineering

Prepares you to apply mathematical and scientific principles to the design, development, and operational evaluation of electrical, electronic, and related systems and their components, including electrical power generation systems; and the analysis of problems such as superconduction, wave propagation, energy storage and retrieval, and reception and amplification.

Career Snapshot

Electrical engineers apply principles of physics, chemistry, and materials science to the generation, transmission, and use of electric power. They may develop huge dynamos or tiny chips. Usually a graduate enters the field with a bachelor's degree. Management may be an option later in their careers. Electricity is not likely to be replaced as a power source anytime soon, and new electronic devices are being developed constantly, so the job outlook for electrical engineers is expected to be good.

Related Specialties in Majors and Careers

Aerospace applications, broadcasting, communications, computers, controls, power generation/transmission.

Related Job Titles, Earnings, Projected Growth, and Openings

Job Title	Average Earnings	Projected Growth	Annual Openings
1. Electrical Engineers (O*NET-SOC Code 17-2071.00)	$79,240	6.3%	6,806
2. Electronics Engineers, Except Computer (O*NET-SOC Code 17-2072.00)	$83,340	3.7%	5,699
3. Engineering Managers (O*NET-SOC Code 11-9041.00)	$111,020	7.3%	7,404
4. Engineering Teachers, Postsecondary (O*NET-SOC Code 25-1032.00)	$79,510	22.9%	237,478

Job 4 shares 237,478 openings with 35 other postsecondary teaching jobs not included in this table.

Typical Sequence of College Courses

English composition, technical writing, calculus, differential equations, introduction to computer science, general chemistry, general physics, introduction to engineering, introduction to electrical circuits, engineering circuit analysis, signals and systems, semiconductor devices, digital systems, logic design, electromagnetic fields, communication systems, control systems, senior design project.

Typical Sequence of High School Courses

English, algebra, geometry, trigonometry, pre-calculus, calculus, chemistry, physics, computer science.

Personality Type

Investigative. These occupations frequently involve working with ideas and require an extensive amount of thinking. They can involve searching for facts and figuring out problems mentally.

Other Characteristics

GOE—Related Interest Areas/Career Clusters: 05 Education and Training; 15 Scientific Research, Engineering, and Mathematics. **Related Work Groups:** 05.03 Postsecondary and Adult Teaching and Instructing; 15.01 Managerial Work in Scientific Research, Engineering, and Mathematics; 15.07 Research and Design Engineering. **Most Important Skills:** Technology design, science, operations analysis, installation, troubleshooting, mathematics. **Top Values:** Creativity, ability utilization, authority. **Work Environment:** Indoors; sitting; protective or safety equipment.

Related Title in the Classification of Instructional Programs (CIP)

14.1001 Electrical, Electronics and Communications Engineering.

Elementary Education

Prepares you to teach students in the elementary grades, which may include kindergarten through grade eight, depending on the school system or state regulations.

Career Snapshot

In elementary education, it is usually possible to specialize in a particular subject, such as reading or science, or to get a general background. Everyone in this field needs to learn general principles of how young people develop physically and mentally, as well as the teaching and classroom-management techniques that work best with children of this age. A bachelor's degree is often sufficient to enter this career, but in many school districts it is expected that you will continue your education as far as a master's degree. Enrollments in elementary schools are expected to decline for some time, but there will be job openings to replace teachers who retire.

Related Specialties in Majors and Careers

Art education, bilingual education, mathematics education, music education, reading, science education.

Related Job Title, Earnings, Projected Growth, and Openings

Job Title	Average Earnings	Projected Growth	Annual Openings
1. Elementary School Teachers, Except Special Education (O*NET-SOC Code 25-2021.00)	$47,330	13.6%	181,612

Typical Sequence of College Courses

Introduction to psychology, English composition, oral communication, history and philosophy of education, human growth and development, teaching methods, educational alternatives for exceptional students, educational psychology, reading assessment and teaching, mathematics education, art education, physical education, social studies education, health education, science education, language arts and literature, student teaching.

Typical Sequence of High School Courses

English, algebra, geometry, trigonometry, science, foreign language, public speaking.

Personality Type

Social. These occupations frequently involve working with, communicating with, and teaching people and often involve helping or providing service to others.

Other Characteristics

GOE—Related Interest Area/Career Cluster: 05 Education and Training. **Related Work Group:** 05.02 Preschool, Elementary, and Secondary Teaching and Instructing. **Most Important Skills:** Instructing, learning strategies, monitoring, social perceptiveness, speaking, persuasion. **Top Values:** Authority, social service, creativity. **Work Environment:** Indoors; standing; disease or infections; close to others; kneeling or crouching; walking and running.

Related Title in the Classification of Instructional Programs (CIP)

13.1202 Elementary Education and Teaching.

English

Focuses on the English language, including its history, structure, and related communications skills, and the literature and culture of English-speaking peoples.

Career Snapshot

English majors not only learn about a great literary tradition, but they also develop first-rate writing and critical-thinking skills that can be valuable in a variety of careers. Besides teaching, many of them go into business, law, and library science. They are said to make excellent trainees in computer programming. In a wide range of careers, their humanistic skills often allow them to advance higher than those who prepare through more specifically career-oriented curricula.

Related Specialties in Majors and Careers

Creative writing, English education, language, literature.

Related Job Title, Earnings, Projected Growth, and Openings

Job Title	Average Earnings	Projected Growth	Annual Openings
1. English Language and Literature Teachers, Post-secondary (O*NET-SOC Code 25-1123.00)	$54,000	22.9%	237,478

This job shares 237,478 openings with 35 other postsecondary teaching jobs not included in this table.

Typical Sequence of College Courses

English composition, introduction to literary study, foreign language, survey of British literature, survey of American literature, a major writer (e.g., Shakespeare, James Joyce, William Blake), a genre (e.g., drama, short story, poetry), creative writing, history of the English language, comparative literature.

Typical Sequence of High School Courses

English, foreign language, literature, history, public speaking, social science.

Personality Type

Artistic. These occupations frequently involve working with forms, designs, and patterns. They often require self-expression, and the work can be done without following a clear set of rules.

Other Characteristics

GOE—Related Interest Area/Career Cluster: 05 Education and Training.
Related Work Group: 05.03 Postsecondary and Adult Teaching and Instructing.
Most Important Skills: Instructing, writing, learning strategies, social perceptiveness, persuasion, reading comprehension. **Top Values:** Authority, social service, creativity. **Work Environment:** Indoors; sitting; close to others.

Related Title in the Classification of Instructional Programs (CIP)

23.0101 English Language and Literature, General.

Environmental Science

Focuses on the application of biological, chemical, and physical principles to the study of the physical environment and the solution of environmental problems, including subjects such as abating or controlling environmental pollution and degradation, the interaction between human society and the natural environment, and natural resources management.

Career Snapshot

Environmental science/studies is a multidisciplinary subject that involves a number of sciences such as biology, geology, and chemistry, as well as social sciences such as economics and geography. It also touches on urban/regional planning and on law and public policy. Those with bachelor's degrees may work for an environmental consulting business or a government planning agency or go on to get a graduate or professional degree in one of the following related fields.

Related Specialties in Majors and Careers

Environmental education, environmental policy, environmental technology, land resources, natural history.

Related Job Titles, Earnings, Projected Growth, and Openings

Job Title	Average Earnings	Projected Growth	Annual Openings
1. Environmental Science and Protection Technicians, Including Health (O*NET-SOC Code 19-4091.00)	$39,370	28.0%	8,404
2. Environmental Scientists and Specialists, Including Health (O*NET-SOC Code 19-2041.00)	$58,380	25.1%	6,961

Typical Sequence of College Courses

English composition, college algebra, general biology, general chemistry, organic chemistry, oral communication, statistics, introduction to computer science, introduction to geology, ecology, introduction to environmental science, natural resource management and water quality, microbiology, introduction to economics, introduction to ground water/hydrology, regional planning and environmental protection, environmental impact assessment, environmental economics, environmental law, environmental chemistry.

Typical Sequence of High School Courses

Biology, chemistry, algebra, geometry, trigonometry, computer science, English, public speaking, geography.

Personality Type

Investigative. These occupations frequently involve working with ideas and require an extensive amount of thinking. They can involve searching for facts and figuring out problems mentally.

Other Characteristics

GOE—Related Interest Areas/Career Clusters: 01 Agriculture and Natural Resources; 15 Scientific Research, Engineering, and Mathematics. **Related Work Groups:** 01.03 Resource Technologies for Plants, Animals, and the Environment; 15.03 Life Sciences. **Most Important Skills:** Science, reading comprehension, mathematics, negotiation, complex problem solving, operations analysis. **Top Values:** Creativity, autonomy, ability utilization. **Work Environment:** More often outdoors or in a vehicle than indoors; sitting; very hot or cold; extremely bright or inadequate lighting; minor burns, cuts, bites, or stings; disease or infections; keeping or regaining balance.

Related Titles in the Classification of Instructional Programs (CIP)

03.0104 Environmental Science; 03.0103 Environmental Studies.

Family and Consumer Sciences

Prepares you to teach vocational home economics programs at various educational levels.

Career Snapshot

Family and consumer sciences, formerly known as home economics, is a combination of several concerns related to families and their economic needs and behaviors. Family and consumer sciences educators study subjects related to these concerns, perhaps specializing in one or more. They must also master the techniques of education, including teaching strategies and classroom management. With a graduate degree, a family and consumer sciences educator may work for the federal government as a cooperative extension agent.

Related Specialties in Majors and Careers

Child care and family life, clothing and textiles, consumer merchandising, consumer services and advocacy, family financial management, foods and nutrition, human sciences communication.

Related Job Titles, Earnings, Projected Growth, and Openings

Job Title	Average Earnings	Projected Growth	Annual Openings
1. Education Teachers, Postsecondary (O*NET-SOC Code 25-1081.00)	$54,220	22.9%	237,478
2. Farm and Home Management Advisors (O*NET-SOC Code 25-9021.00)	$41,830	5.1%	2,037
3. Fashion Designers (O*NET-SOC Code 27-1022.00)	$62,810	5.0%	1,968
4. First-Line Supervisors/Managers of Retail Sales Workers (O*NET-SOC Code 41-1011.00)	$34,470	4.2%	221,241
5. Home Economics Teachers, Postsecondary (O*NET-SOC Code 25-1192.00)	$58,170	22.9%	237,478
6. Marketing Managers (O*NET-SOC Code 11-2021.00)	$104,400	14.4%	20,189
7. Middle School Teachers, Except Special and Vocational Education (O*NET-SOC Code 25-2022.00)	$47,900	11.2%	75,270
8. Sales Managers (O*NET-SOC Code 11-2022.00)	$94,910	10.2%	36,392
9. Secondary School Teachers, Except Special and Vocational Education (O*NET-SOC Code 25-2031.00)	$49,420	5.6%	93,166

Job Title	Average Earnings	Projected Growth	Annual Openings
10. Wholesale and Retail Buyers, Except Farm Products (O*NET-SOC 13-1022.00)	$46,960	–0.1%	19,847

Jobs 1 and 5 share 237,478 openings with 34 other postsecondary teaching jobs not included in this table.

Typical Sequence of College Courses

English composition, introduction to psychology, oral communication, history and philosophy of education, human growth and development, consumer economics, housing, introduction to interior design, introduction to nutrition, foods, marriage and the family, clothing and fashion, textiles, student teaching.

Typical Sequence of High School Courses

English, algebra, geometry, trigonometry, science, foreign language, public speaking, family and consumer sciences.

Personality Type

Social. These occupations frequently involve working with, communicating with, and teaching people and often involve helping or providing service to others.

Other Characteristics

GOE—Related Interest Areas/Career Clusters: 03 Arts and Communication; 05 Education and Training; 14 Retail and Wholesale Sales and Service. **Related Work Groups:** 03.05 Design; 05.02 Preschool, Elementary, and Secondary Teaching and Instructing; 05.03 Postsecondary and Adult Teaching and Instructing; 14.01 Managerial Work in Retail/Wholesale Sales and Service; 14.05 Purchasing. **Most Important Skills:** Persuasion, management of personnel resources, monitoring, social perceptiveness, instructing, negotiation. **Top Values:** Authority, creativity, responsibility. **Work Environment:** Indoors; standing; disease or infections; close to others; noisy; walking and running.

Related Titles in the Classification of Instructional Programs (CIP)

19.0702 Adult Development and Aging; 19.0905 Apparel and Textile Marketing Management; 19.0901 Apparel and Textiles, General; 19.0706 Child Development; 19.0203 Consumer Merchandising/Retailing Management; 19.0707 Family and Community Services; 13.1308 Family and Consumer Sciences/Home Economics Teacher Education; 19.0101 Family and Consumer Sciences/Human Sciences, General; 19.9999 Family and Consumer Sciences/Human Sciences, Other; 19.0906 Fashion and Fabric Consultant; 19.0701 Human Development and Family Studies, General.

Film/Cinema Studies

Focuses on the study of the history, development, theory, and criticism of the film/video arts, as well as the basic principles of film making and film production.

Career Snapshot

Film is a new art form and still straddles the borderline between popular culture and high art. The American film and video industry continues to grow as it increasingly dominates the world market, but there is keen competition for creative jobs in this field. Some graduates of film programs become critics or work in industrial or educational film production. Students can usually tailor their academic programs to emphasize the aspects of film that interest them; therefore, they may do anything from a lot of writing about film to a lot of hands-on work producing film.

Related Specialties in Majors and Careers

Criticism, directing/producing, editing, screenwriting.

Related Job Titles, Earnings, Projected Growth, and Openings

Job Title	Average Earnings	Projected Growth	Annual Openings
1. Art, Drama, and Music Teachers, Postsecondary (O*NET-SOC Code 25-1121.00)	$55,190	22.9%	237,478
2. Camera Operators, Television, Video, and Motion Picture (O*NET-SOC Code 27-4031.00)	$41,850	11.5%	3,496
3. Directors—Stage, Motion Pictures, Television, and Radio (O*NET-SOC Code 27-2012.02)	$61,090	11.1%	8,992
4. Film and Video Editors (O*NET-SOC Code 27-4032.00)	$47,870	12.7%	2,707
5. Producers (O*NET-SOC Code 27-2012.01)	$61,090	11.1%	8,992
6. Program Directors (O*NET-SOC Code 27-2012.03)	$61,090	11.1%	8,992
7. Talent Directors (O*NET-SOC Code 27-2012.04)	$61,090	11.1%	8,992
8. Technical Directors/Managers (O*NET-SOC Code 27-2012.05)	$61,090	11.1%	8,992

Job 1 shares 237,478 openings with 35 other postsecondary teaching jobs not included in this table. Jobs 5, 6, 7, and 8 share 8,992 openings.

Typical Sequence of College Courses

English composition, foreign language, world history in the modern era, introduction to psychology, film as a narrative art, history of film, film styles and genres, major film directors, literature and media, film theory and criticism, gender and film, seminar (reporting on research).

Typical Sequence of High School Courses

English, foreign language, literature, history, photography.

Personality Type

Artistic. These occupations frequently involve working with forms, designs, and patterns. They often require self-expression, and the work can be done without following a clear set of rules.

Other Characteristics

GOE—Related Interest Areas/Career Clusters: 03 Arts and Communication; 05 Education and Training. **Related Work Groups:** 03.01 Managerial Work in Arts and Communication; 03.06 Drama; 03.07 Music; 03.09 Media Technology; 05.03 Postsecondary and Adult Teaching and Instructing. **Most Important Skills:** Speaking, management of personnel resources, active listening, time management, persuasion, social perceptiveness. **Top Values:** Authority, creativity, ability utilization. **Work Environment:** More often indoors than outdoors; sitting.

Related Titles in the Classification of Instructional Programs (CIP)

50.0602 Cinematography and Film/Video Production; 50.0601 Film/Cinema Studies.

Finance

Prepares you to plan, manage, and analyze the financial and monetary aspects and performance of business enterprises, banking institutions, or other organizations.

Career Snapshot

Finance is the study of how organizations acquire funds and use them in ways that maximize their values. The banking and insurance industries, as well as investment service companies, employ graduates in this field. A bachelor's degree is good preparation for an entry-level job.

Related Specialties in Majors and Careers

Corporate finance, public finance, securities analysis.

Related Job Titles, Earnings, Projected Growth, and Openings

Job Title	Average Earnings	Projected Growth	Annual Openings
1. Budget Analysts (O*NET-SOC Code 13-2031.00)	$63,440	7.1%	6,423
2. Business Teachers, Postsecondary (O*NET-SOC Code 25-1011.00)	$64,900	22.9%	237,478
3. Credit Analysts (O*NET-SOC Code 13-2041.00)	$54,580	1.9%	3,180
4. Financial Analysts (O*NET-SOC Code 13-2051.00)	$70,400	33.8%	29,317
5. Financial Managers, Branch or Department (O*NET-SOC Code 11-3031.02)	$95,310	12.6%	57,589
6. Loan Officers (O*NET-SOC Code 13-2072.00)	$53,000	11.5%	54,237
7. Personal Financial Advisors (O*NET-SOC Code 13-2052.00)	$67,660	41.0%	17,114
8. Treasurers and Controllers (O*NET-SOC Code 11-3031.01)	$95,310	12.6%	57,589

Job 2 shares 237,478 openings with 35 other postsecondary teaching jobs not included in this table. Jobs 5 and 8 share 57,589 openings.

Typical Sequence of College Courses

English composition, business writing, introduction to psychology, principles of microeconomics, principles of macroeconomics, calculus for business and social

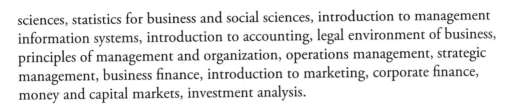

sciences, statistics for business and social sciences, introduction to management information systems, introduction to accounting, legal environment of business, principles of management and organization, operations management, strategic management, business finance, introduction to marketing, corporate finance, money and capital markets, investment analysis.

Typical Sequence of High School Courses

English, algebra, geometry, trigonometry, science, foreign language, computer science.

Personality Type

Enterprising. These occupations frequently involve starting up and carrying out projects and can involve leading people and making many decisions. They sometimes require risk taking and often deal with business.

Other Characteristics

GOE—Related Interest Areas/Career Clusters: 04 Business and Administration; 05 Education and Training; 06 Finance and Insurance. **Related Work Groups:** 04.05 Accounting, Auditing, and Analytical Support; 06.01 Managerial Work in Finance and Insurance; 06.02 Finance/Insurance Investigation and Analysis; 06.05 Finance/Insurance Sales and Support. **Most Important Skills:** Management of financial resources, persuasion, judgment and decision making, negotiation, management of personnel resources, complex problem solving. **Top Values:** Working conditions, authority, advancement. **Work Environment:** Indoors; sitting.

Related Title in the Classification of Instructional Programs (CIP)

52.0801 Finance, General.

Food Science

Focuses on the application of biological, chemical, and physical principles to the study of converting raw agricultural products into processed forms suitable for direct human consumption, and the storage of such products.

Career Snapshot

A glance at the label on a package of food will tell you that the science of making, packaging, and ensuring the quality of foods involves both biology and chemistry. Food science graduates work in research, product development, and quality control. A bachelor's degree is usually sufficient for an entry-level job in quality control. But for advancement and for research jobs, a graduate degree helps.

Related Specialties in Majors and Careers

Food quality assurance, food research, management of food processing, product development.

Related Job Titles, Earnings, Projected Growth, and Openings

Job Title	Average Earnings	Projected Growth	Annual Openings
1. Agricultural Sciences Teachers, Postsecondary (O*NET-SOC Code 25-1041.00)	$78,460	22.9%	237,478
2. Agricultural Technicians (O*NET-SOC Code 19-4011.01)	$33,630	6.6%	4,049
3. Chemical Technicians (O*NET-SOC Code 19-4031.00)	$40,740	5.8%	4,010
4. Food Science Technicians (O*NET-SOC Code 19-4011.02)	$33,630	6.6%	4,049
5. Food Scientists and Technologists (O*NET-SOC Code 19-1012.00)	$57,870	10.3%	663

Job 1 shares 237,478 openings with 35 other postsecondary teaching jobs not included in this table. Jobs 2 and 4 share 4,049 openings.

Typical Sequence of College Courses

English composition, college algebra, general biology, general chemistry, organic chemistry, oral communication, statistics, introduction to computer science, microbiology, introduction to economics, general physics, introduction to biochemistry, introduction to food science and technology, food analysis, food chemistry, food processing, food bacteriology, nutrition, food plant engineering.

Typical Sequence of High School Courses

Biology, chemistry, algebra, geometry, trigonometry, computer science, English, public speaking.

Personality Type

Investigative. These occupations frequently involve working with ideas and require an extensive amount of thinking. They can involve searching for facts and figuring out problems mentally.

Other Characteristics

GOE—Related Interest Areas/Career Clusters: 01 Agriculture and Natural Resources; 05 Education and Training; 15 Scientific Research, Engineering, and Mathematics. **Related Work Groups:** 01.03 Resource Technologies for Plants, Animals, and the Environment; 05.03 Postsecondary and Adult Teaching and Instructing; 15.05 Physical Science Laboratory Technology. **Most Important Skills:** Science, operation monitoring, quality control analysis, equipment maintenance, mathematics, troubleshooting. **Top Values:** Variety, advancement, working conditions. **Work Environment:** Indoors; standing; hazardous conditions; protective or safety equipment; contaminants; noisy; hazardous equipment; radiation.

Related Title in the Classification of Instructional Programs (CIP)

01.1001 Food Science.

Forestry

Prepares you to manage and develop forest areas for economic, recreational, and ecological purposes.

Career Snapshot

Foresters manage wooded land. Most of them work for governments, concerned with conservation and fire prevention. Some work for logging companies and plan the harvesting of timber with attention to economics, safety, and environmental laws. Foresters also help plant and grow trees to regenerate forests. A bachelor's degree is usually a good preparation for this field, and the job outlook is good because of increasing interest in preserving the environment.

Related Specialties in Majors and Careers

Forest management, forest product production, forest restoration, urban forestry.

Related Job Titles, Earnings, Projected Growth, and Openings

Job Title	Average Earnings	Projected Growth	Annual Openings
1. Forest and Conservation Workers (O*NET-SOC Code 45-4011.00)	$20,510	5.5%	1,862
2. Foresters (O*NET-SOC Code 19-1032.00)	$52,440	5.1%	772
3. Forest and Conservation Technicians (O*NET-SOC Code 19-4093.00)	$33,520	–2.0%	5,946
4. Park Naturalists (O*NET-SOC Code 19-1031.03)	$56,150	5.3%	1,161
5. Range Managers (O*NET-SOC Code 19-1031.02)	$56,150	5.3%	1,161
6. Soil and Water Conservationists (O*NET-SOC Code 19-1031.01)	$56,150	5.3%	1,161

Jobs 4, 5, and 6 share 1,161 openings.

Typical Sequence of College Courses

English composition, calculus, general biology, general chemistry, organic chemistry, introduction to geology, oral communication, statistics, computer applications in agriculture, introduction to soil science, ecology, introduction to forestry, dendrology, forest ecology, silviculture, forest resources policy, forest inventory and growth, forest surveying and mapping, tree pests and diseases, wood properties and utilization, forest economics and valuation, forest watershed management, timber harvesting, introduction to wildlife conservation, remote sensing.

Typical Sequence of High School Courses

Biology, chemistry, algebra, geometry, trigonometry, computer science, English, public speaking, geography.

Personality Type

Realistic. These occupations frequently involve work activities that include practical, hands-on problems and solutions. They often deal with plants; animals; and real-world materials such as wood, tools, and machinery. Many of the occupations require working outside and do not involve a lot of paperwork or working closely with others.

Other Characteristics

GOE—Related Interest Area/Career Cluster: 01 Agriculture and Natural Resources. **Related Work Groups:** 01.01 Managerial Work in Agriculture and Natural Resources; 01.02 Resource Science/Engineering for Plants, Animals, and the Environment; 01.06 Forestry and Logging. **Most Important Skills:** Science, management of financial resources, management of personnel resources, operations analysis, equipment selection, mathematics. **Top Values:** Autonomy, responsibility, creativity. **Work Environment:** More often in a vehicle than outdoors; minor burns, cuts, bites, or stings; very hot or cold; whole body vibration; hazardous equipment; specialized protective or safety equipment; protective or safety equipment.

Related Title in the Classification of Instructional Programs (CIP)

03.0501 Forestry, General.

French

Focuses on the French language, its literature, and its related dialects and may include applications in business, science/technology, and other settings.

Career Snapshot

French is a native tongue in several regions on several continents and is prominently spoken in parts of the United States. It also has a rich cultural heritage associated with the arts and literature. French majors may go into careers in international business, travel, or teaching.

Related Specialties in Majors and Careers

History and culture, language education, literature, translation.

Related Job Titles, Earnings, Projected Growth, and Openings

Job Title	Average Earnings	Projected Growth	Annual Openings
1. Foreign Language and Literature Teachers, Postsecondary (O*NET-SOC Code 25-1124.00)	$53,610	22.9%	237,478
2. Interpreters and Translators (O*NET-SOC Code 27-3091.00)	$37,490	23.6%	6,630

Job 1 shares 237,478 openings with 35 other postsecondary teaching jobs not included in this table.

Typical Sequence of College Courses

French language, conversation, composition, linguistics, French literature, French history and civilization, European history and civilization, grammar, phonetics, study abroad.

Typical Sequence of High School Courses

English, public speaking, French, history, literature, social science.

Personality Type

Artistic. These occupations frequently involve working with forms, designs, and patterns. They often require self-expression, and the work can be done without following a clear set of rules.

Other Characteristics

GOE—Related Interest Areas/Career Clusters: 03 Arts and Communication; 05 Education and Training. **Related Work Groups:** 03.03 News, Broadcasting, and Public Relations; 05.03 Postsecondary and Adult Teaching and Instructing. **Most Important Skills:** Social perceptiveness, speaking, writing, active listening, reading comprehension, learning strategies. **Top Values:** Social service, ability utilization, achievement. **Work Environment:** Indoors; sitting; close to others.

Related Title in the Classification of Instructional Programs (CIP)

16.0901 French Language and Literature.

Geography

Focuses on the systematic study of the spatial distribution and interrelationships of people, natural resources, and plant and animal life.

Career Snapshot

Geographers study how people and their environments relate to one another. They analyze the human habitat spatially and record information about it in various forms, with an increasing emphasis on databases. Geographers work for governments, public-interest organizations, and businesses. They help with site planning, environmental impact studies, market research, competitive intelligence, and military intelligence.

Related Specialties in Majors and Careers

Development, environmental science, geographic information systems, management and policy, urban planning.

Related Job Titles, Earnings, Projected Growth, and Openings

Job Title	Average Earnings	Projected Growth	Annual Openings
1. Geographers (O*NET-SOC Code 19-3092.00)	$65,690	6.1%	75
2. Geography Teachers, Postsecondary (O*NET-SOC Code 25-1064.00)	$61,310	22.9%	237,478

Job 2 shares 237,478 openings with 35 other postsecondary teaching jobs not included in this table.

Typical Sequence of College Courses

English composition, American history, foreign language, introduction to economics, introduction to sociology, statistics, introduction to computer science, introduction to geology, introduction to human geography, economic geography, world history in the modern era, thematic cartography, geography of a region, physical geography, field geography, research techniques in geography, quantitative methods in geography, remote sensing, geographic information systems (GIS).

Typical Sequence of High School Courses

Art, English, social science, foreign language, trigonometry, history, geography, computer science.

Personality Type

Investigative. These occupations frequently involve working with ideas and require an extensive amount of thinking. They can involve searching for facts and figuring out problems mentally.

Other Characteristics

GOE—Related Interest Areas/Career Clusters: 05 Education and Training; 15 Scientific Research, Engineering, and Mathematics. **Related Work Groups:** 05.03 Postsecondary and Adult Teaching and Instructing; 15.02 Physical Sciences. **Most Important Skills:** Science, writing, instructing, reading comprehension, learning strategies, complex problem solving. **Top Values:** Autonomy, creativity, ability utilization. **Work Environment:** More often indoors than outdoors; sitting.

Related Title in the Classification of Instructional Programs (CIP)

45.0701 Geography.

Geology

Focuses on the scientific study of the earth; the forces acting upon it; and the behavior of the solids, liquids, and gases comprising it.

Career Snapshot

Geology is the study of the physical makeup, processes, and history of the earth. Geologists use knowledge of this field to locate water, mineral, and petroleum resources; to protect the environment; and to offer advice on construction and land-use projects. A bachelor's degree opens the door for many entry-level jobs, but a master's degree helps for advancement. Many research jobs in universities and the government require a Ph.D. Some field research requires going to remote places, but it is also possible to specialize in laboratory sciences.

Related Specialties in Majors and Careers

Atmospheric physics, environmental geophysics, geomagnetism, paleomagnetism, physical oceanography, remote sensing, seismology, volcanology.

Related Job Titles, Earnings, Projected Growth, and Openings

Job Title	Average Earnings	Projected Growth	Annual Openings
1. Atmospheric, Earth, Marine, and Space Sciences Teachers, Postsecondary (O*NET-SOC Code 25-1051.00)	$73,280	22.9%	237,478
2. Geoscientists, Except Hydrologists and Geographers (O*NET-SOC Code 19-2042.00)	$75,800	21.9%	2,471
3. Hydrologists (O*NET-SOC Code 19-2043.00)	$68,140	24.3%	687
4. Natural Sciences Managers (O*NET-SOC Code 11-9121.00)	$104,040	11.4%	3,661

Job 1 shares 237,478 openings with 35 other postsecondary teaching jobs not included in this table.

Typical Sequence of College Courses

English composition, calculus, introduction to computer science, general chemistry, general physics, introduction to geology, invertebrate paleontology, summer field geology, structural geology, mineralogy, optical mineralogy, igneous and metamorphic petrology, sedimentary petrology, stratigraphy.

Typical Sequence of High School Courses

English, algebra, geometry, trigonometry, chemistry, physics, pre-calculus, computer science, calculus.

Personality Type

Investigative. These occupations frequently involve working with ideas and require an extensive amount of thinking. They can involve searching for facts and figuring out problems mentally.

Other Characteristics

GOE—Related Interest Areas/Career Clusters: 05 Education and Training; 15 Scientific Research, Engineering, and Mathematics. **Related Work Groups:** 05.03 Postsecondary and Adult Teaching and Instructing; 15.01 Managerial Work in Scientific Research, Engineering, and Mathematics; 15.02 Physical Sciences. **Most Important Skills:** Science, mathematics, management of financial resources, management of personnel resources, active learning, writing. **Top Values:** Creativity, responsibility, autonomy. **Work Environment:** More often indoors than in a vehicle or outdoors; sitting; hazardous conditions; hazardous equipment; radiation; extremely bright or inadequate lighting; specialized protective or safety equipment.

Related Title in the Classification of Instructional Programs (CIP)

40.0601 Geology/Earth Science, General.

German

Focuses on the German language, its literature, and its related dialects, and may include applications in business, science/technology, and other settings.

Career Snapshot

United once again, Germany is a major economic and cultural force in Europe and the world. A degree in German can open many doors in international business, travel, and law. Many employers are looking for graduates with an understanding of a second language and culture. Those with a graduate degree in German may go into translation or college teaching.

Related Specialties in Majors and Careers

History and culture, language education, literature, translation.

Related Job Titles, Earnings, Projected Growth, and Openings

Job Title	Average Earnings	Projected Growth	Annual Openings
1. Foreign Language and Literature Teachers, Postsecondary (O*NET-SOC Code 25-1124.00)	$53,610	22.9%	237,478
2. Interpreters and Translators (O*NET-SOC Code 27-3091.00)	$37,490	23.6%	6,630

Job 1 shares 237,478 openings with 35 other postsecondary teaching jobs not included in this table.

Typical Sequence of College Courses

German language, conversation, composition, linguistics, German literature, German history and civilization, European history and civilization, grammar, phonetics, study abroad.

Typical Sequence of High School Courses

English, public speaking, German, history, literature, social science.

Personality Type

Artistic. These occupations frequently involve working with forms, designs, and patterns. They often require self-expression, and the work can be done without following a clear set of rules.

Other Characteristics

GOE—Related Interest Areas/Career Clusters: 03 Arts and Communication; 05 Education and Training. **Related Work Groups:** 03.03 News, Broadcasting, and Public Relations; 05.03 Postsecondary and Adult Teaching and Instructing. **Most Important Skills:** Social perceptiveness, speaking, writing, active listening, reading comprehension, learning strategies. **Top Values:** Social service, ability utilization, achievement. **Work Environment:** Indoors; sitting; close to others.

Related Title in the Classification of Instructional Programs (CIP)

16.0501 German Language and Literature.

Graphic Design, Commercial Art, and Illustration

Prepares you to use artistic techniques to effectively communicate ideas and information to business and consumer audiences via illustrations and other forms of digital or printed media.

Career Snapshot

Many consumer goods, such as books, magazines, and Web pages, consist primarily of graphic elements—illustrations and text. Other goods, such as cereal boxes, use graphic elements conspicuously. Graphic design teaches you how to represent ideas graphically and give maximum visual appeal to text and pictures. These programs involve considerable studio time, and an important goal is creating a good portfolio of work. The ability to work with computers is becoming vital in this field. Many graduates with associate or bachelor's degrees work for publishers and design firms while some freelance.

Related Specialties in Majors and Careers

Cartooning, illustration, letterform, typography, Web page design.

Related Job Titles, Earnings, Projected Growth, and Openings

Job Title	Average Earnings	Projected Growth	Annual Openings
1. Art Directors (O*NET-SOC Code 27-1011.00)	$72,320	9.0%	9,719
2. Art, Drama, and Music Teachers, Postsecondary (O*NET-SOC Code 25-1121.00)	$55,190	22.9%	237,478
3. Commercial and Industrial Designers (O*NET-SOC Code 27-1021.00)	$56,550	7.2%	4,777
4. Graphic Designers (O*NET-SOC Code 27-1024.00)	$41,280	9.8%	26,968
5. Multi-Media Artists and Animators (O*NET-SOC Code 27-1014.00)	$54,550	25.8%	13,182
6. Painting, Coating, and Decorating Workers (O*NET-SOC Code 51-9123.00)	$23,180	3.6%	1,672
7. Prepress Technicians and Workers (O*NET-SOC Code 51-5022.00)	$33,990	–21.1%	10,002

Job Title	Average Earnings	Projected Growth	Annual Openings
8. Set and Exhibit Designers (O*NET-SOC Code 27-1027.00)	$43,220	17.8%	1,402

Job 2 shares 237,478 openings with 35 other postsecondary teaching jobs not included in this table.

Typical Sequence of College Courses

English composition, college algebra, basic drawing, oral communication, art history: prehistoric to Renaissance, art history: Renaissance to modern, introduction to graphic design, visual thinking and problem solving, presentation graphics, history of graphic design, letterform, two-dimensional design, three-dimensional design, visual communication, typography, computer applications in graphic design, senior design project.

Typical Sequence of High School Courses

Algebra, geometry, trigonometry, pre-calculus, English, public speaking, art, computer science, mechanical drawing, photography.

Personality Type

Artistic. These occupations frequently involve working with forms, designs, and patterns. They often require self-expression, and the work can be done without following a clear set of rules.

Other Characteristics

GOE—Related Interest Areas/Career Clusters: 03 Arts and Communication; 05 Education and Training; 13 Manufacturing. **Related Work Groups:** 03.03 News, Broadcasting, and Public Relations; 03.05 Design; 05.03 Postsecondary and Adult Teaching and Instructing; 13.08 Graphic Arts Production; 13.09 Hands-On Work, Assorted Materials. **Most Important Skills:** Operations analysis, persuasion, time management, technology design, equipment selection, complex problem solving. **Top Values:** Creativity, ability utilization, achievement. **Work Environment:** Indoors; sitting; repetitive motions; using hands on objects, tools, or controls.

Related Titles in the Classification of Instructional Programs (CIP)

50.0402 Commercial and Advertising Art; 50.0409 Graphic Design; 50.0410 Illustration.

Health Information Systems Administration

Prepares you to plan, design, and manage systems, processes, and facilities used to collect, store, secure, retrieve, analyze, and transmit medical records and other health information used by clinical professionals and health-care organizations.

Career Snapshot

Health information systems are needed for much more than billing patients or their HMOs. Many medical discoveries have been made when researchers have examined large collections of health information. Therefore, health information systems administrators must know about the health-care system, about various kinds of diseases and vital statistics, about the latest database technologies, and about how researchers compile data to test hypotheses. Some people enter this field with bachelor's degrees, whereas others get bachelor's degrees in other fields (perhaps related to health, information systems, or management) and complete postgraduate certification programs.

Related Specialties in Majors and Careers

Information technology, management.

Related Job Titles, Earnings, Projected Growth, and Openings

Job Title	Average Earnings	Projected Growth	Annual Openings
1. Medical and Health Services Managers (O*NET-SOC Code 11-9111.00)	$76,990	16.4%	31,877
2. Medical Records and Health Information Technicians (O*NET-SOC Code 29-2071.00)	$29,290	17.8%	39,048

Typical Sequence of College Courses

English composition, introduction to computer science, college algebra, oral communication, introduction to psychology, accounting, introduction to business management, statistics for business and social sciences, epidemiology, introduction to medical terminology, financial management of health care, human resource management in health-care facilities, legal aspects of health care, American health-care systems, introduction to health records, health data and analysis, clinical classification systems, fundamentals of medical science, health data research, seminar (reporting on research).

Typical Sequence of High School Courses

Algebra, English, geometry, trigonometry, pre-calculus, biology, chemistry, computer science, office computer applications, public speaking, foreign language, social science.

Personality Type

Enterprising. These occupations frequently involve starting up and carrying out projects and can involve leading people and making many decisions. They sometimes require risk taking and often deal with business.

Other Characteristics

GOE—Related Interest Area/Career Cluster: 08 Health Science. **Related Work Group:** 08.01 Managerial Work in Medical and Health Services. **Most Important Skills:** Systems evaluation, management of personnel resources, management of material resources, service orientation, monitoring, critical thinking. **Top Values:** Working conditions, social service, security. **Work Environment:** Indoors; sitting; disease or infections; radiation; specialized protective or safety equipment; walking and running; protective or safety equipment; close to others.

Related Titles in the Classification of Instructional Programs (CIP)

51.0706 Health Information/Medical Records Administration/Administrator; 51.0707 Health Information/Medical Records Technology/Technician.

Hispanic American Studies

Focuses on the history, sociology, politics, culture, and economics of one or more of the Hispanic American immigrant populations within the United States and Canada, including Mexican American Studies, Cuban American Studies, Puerto Rican Studies, and others.

Career Snapshot

Hispanics are now the largest U.S. minority group, but they come from many different cultures. Therefore, this major sometimes is offered with a focus on one Hispanic group, such as Chicano Studies or Puerto Rican Studies. At the bachelor's level, this major may prepare you for a career in business, law, or advocacy, especially if you gain additional graduate or professional credentials. Study at the graduate level can lead to a career in college teaching.

Related Specialties in Majors and Careers

Heritage from country of origin, history, role in American culture, sociology.

Related Job Title, Earnings, Projected Growth, and Openings

Job Title	Average Earnings	Projected Growth	Annual Openings
1. Area, Ethnic, and Cultural Studies Teachers, Post-secondary (O*NET-SOC Code 25-1062.00)	$59,150	22.9%	237,478

This job shares 237,478 openings with 35 other postsecondary teaching jobs not included in this table.

Typical Sequence of College Courses

English composition, Spanish, American history, introduction to Hispanic American studies, Hispanic American literature, Hispanic American art and culture, Hispanic American history, history of a country of origin, research methods in Hispanic American studies, seminar (reporting on research).

Typical Sequence of High School Courses

English, algebra, Spanish, history, literature, public speaking, social science.

Personality Type

Social. These occupations frequently involve working with, communicating with, and teaching people and often involve helping or providing service to others.

Other Characteristics

GOE—Related Interest Area/Career Cluster: 05 Education and Training. **Related Work Group:** 05.03 Postsecondary and Adult Teaching and Instructing. **Most Important Skills:** Writing, critical thinking, instructing, persuasion, active learning, learning strategies. **Top Values:** Authority, social service, creativity. **Work Environment:** Indoors; sitting.

Related Title in the Classification of Instructional Programs (CIP)

05.0203 Hispanic-American, Puerto Rican, and Mexican-American/Chicano Studies.

 # History

Focuses on the general study and interpretation of the past, including the gathering, recording, synthesizing, and criticizing of evidence and theories about past events.

Career Snapshot

Historians study past civilizations in order to understand the present, preserve our heritage, and appreciate the richness of human accomplishment. Almost every field—whether it be in the field of arts, science, or health—includes some study of its past. Therefore, many job opportunities in this field are in teaching. Other historians may work as archivists, genealogists, or curators. Some graduates use the critical-thinking skills they develop from history to go into administration or law.

Related Specialties in Majors and Careers

Applied history, genealogy, history education.

Related Job Titles, Earnings, Projected Growth, and Openings

Job Title	Average Earnings	Projected Growth	Annual Openings
1. Archivists (O*NET-SOC Code 25-4011.00)	$43,110	14.4%	795
2. Curators (O*NET-SOC Code 25-4012.00)	$46,000	23.3%	1,416
3. Historians (O*NET-SOC Code 19-3093.00)	$50,790	7.8%	245
4. History Teachers, Postsecondary (O*NET-SOC Code 25-1125.00)	$59,160	22.9%	237,478

Job 4 shares 237,478 openings with 35 other postsecondary teaching jobs not included in this table.

Typical Sequence of College Courses

English composition, foreign language, introduction to philosophy, introduction to political science, world history to the early modern era, world history in the modern era, American history, theory and practice of history, introduction to international relations, seminar (reporting on research).

Typical Sequence of High School Courses

Algebra, English, foreign language, social science, trigonometry, history.

Personality Type

Social. These occupations frequently involve working with, communicating with, and teaching people and often involve helping or providing service to others.

Other Characteristics

GOE—Related Interest Areas/Career Clusters: 05 Education and Training; 15 Scientific Research, Engineering, and Mathematics. **Related Work Groups:** 05.03 Postsecondary and Adult Teaching and Instructing; 05.05 Archival and Museum Services; 15.04 Social Sciences. **Most Important Skills:** Writing, reading comprehension, persuasion, speaking, management of personnel resources, critical thinking. **Top Values:** Authority, creativity, working conditions. **Work Environment:** Indoors; sitting.

Related Title in the Classification of Instructional Programs (CIP)

54.0101 History, General.

Horticulture

Focuses on the general production and processing of domesticated plants, shrubs, flowers, foliage, trees, groundcovers, and related plant materials; the management of technical and business operations connected with horticultural services; and the scientific principles needed to understand plants and their management and care.

Career Snapshot

Lawn grasses, shrubs, and indoor plants have commercial value just as farm crops do. Golf courses and vineyards depend on healthy plant growth. Horticulturalists start up or work for businesses that establish, maintain, and market these plantings. A bachelor's degree program is a good way to learn the necessary green-thumb skills and business know-how.

Related Specialties in Majors and Careers

Crop production, landscape maintenance, ornamental, research, sales, turf management, viticulture.

Related Job Titles, Earnings, Projected Growth, and Openings

Job Title	Average Earnings	Projected Growth	Annual Openings
1. Agricultural Sciences Teachers, Postsecondary (O*NET-SOC Code 25-1041.00)	$78,460	22.9%	237,478
2. Farmers and Ranchers (O*NET-SOC Code 11-9012.00)	$33,360	–8.5%	129,552
3. Farmworkers, Farm and Ranch Animals (O*NET-SOC Code 45-2093.00)	$20,350	2.7%	26,707
4. First-Line Supervisors/Managers of Landscaping, Lawn Service, and Groundskeeping Workers (O*NET-SOC Code 37-1012.00)	$38,720	17.6%	18,956
5. First-Line Supervisors/Managers of Retail Sales Workers (O*NET-SOC Code 41-1011.00)	$34,470	4.2%	221,241
6. Floral Designers (O*NET-SOC Code 27-1023.00)	$22,540	–8.9%	7,408
7. Landscaping and Groundskeeping Workers (O*NET-SOC Code 37-3011.00)	$22,240	18.1%	307,138
8. Nursery and Greenhouse Managers (O*NET-SOC Code 11-9011.01)	$53,720	1.1%	18,101
9. Pesticide Handlers, Sprayers, and Applicators, Vegetation (O*NET-SOC Code 37-3012.00)	$28,560	14.0%	7,443

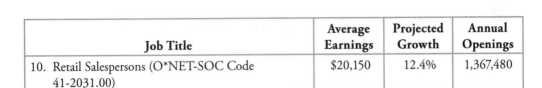

Job Title	Average Earnings	Projected Growth	Annual Openings
10. Retail Salespersons (O*NET-SOC Code 41-2031.00)	$20,150	12.4%	1,367,480

Job 1 shares 237,478 openings with 35 other postsecondary teaching jobs not included in this table. Job 8 shares 18,101 openings with two other jobs not included in this table.

Typical Sequence of College Courses

English composition, oral communication, business math, general biology, general chemistry, introduction to economics, introduction to accounting, principles of soil science, computer applications in agriculture, plant materials, turfgrass management, landscape design, greenhouse/nursery management, plant propagation, introductory plant pathology, weed and pest management, vegetable crops.

Typical Sequence of High School Courses

English, algebra, geometry, trigonometry, biology, chemistry, computer science.

Personality Type

Enterprising. These occupations frequently involve starting up and carrying out projects and can involve leading people and making many decisions. They sometimes require risk taking and often deal with business.

Other Characteristics

GOE—Related Interest Areas/Career Clusters: 01 Agriculture and Natural Resources; 03 Arts and Communication; 05 Education and Training; 14 Retail and Wholesale Sales and Service. **Related Work Groups:** 01.01 Managerial Work in Agriculture and Natural Resources; 01.04 General Farming; 01.05 Nursery, Groundskeeping, and Pest Control; 03.05 Design; 05.03 Postsecondary and Adult Teaching and Instructing; 14.01 Managerial Work in Retail/Wholesale Sales and Service; 14.03 General Sales. **Most Important Skills:** Management of personnel resources, repairing. **Top Values:** Variety, coworkers, social service. **Work Environment:** More often outdoors than in a vehicle or indoors; more often sitting than standing.

Related Titles in the Classification of Instructional Programs (CIP)

01.0601 Applied Horticulture/Horticulture Operations, General; 01.0608 Floriculture/Floristry Operations and Management; 01.0604 Greenhouse Operations and Management; 01.0605 Landscaping and Groundskeeping; 01.0603 Ornamental Horticulture; 01.0606 Plant Nursery Operations and Management; 01.0607 Turf and Turfgrass Management.

Hospital/Health Facilities Administration

Prepares you to apply managerial principles to the administration of hospitals, clinics, nursing homes, and other health-care facilities.

Career Snapshot

Hospital and health facilities administrators need to combine standard business management skills with an understanding of the American health-care system and its current issues and trends. They may be generalists who manage an entire facility, or they may specialize in running a department or some specific service of the facility. A generalist is usually expected to have a master's degree, especially in large facilities; whereas specialists or those seeking employment in small facilities may enter with a bachelor's degree. Best employment prospects are in home health agencies, residential care facilities, and practitioners' offices and clinics.

Related Specialties in Majors and Careers

Health policy, hospital management, long-term care management.

Related Job Title, Earnings, Projected Growth, and Openings

Job Title	Average Earnings	Projected Growth	Annual Openings
1. Medical and Health Services Managers (O*NET-SOC Code 11-9111.00)	$76,990	16.4%	31,877

Typical Sequence of College Courses

English composition, introduction to economics, college algebra, oral communication, introduction to psychology, accounting, introduction to business management, statistics for business and social sciences, American health-care systems, introduction to medical terminology, introduction to management information systems, financial management of health care, human resource management in health-care facilities, strategy and planning for health care, legal aspects of health care, health care and politics.

Typical Sequence of High School Courses

Algebra, English, geometry, trigonometry, pre-calculus, biology, chemistry, computer science, office computer applications, public speaking, social science, foreign language.

Personality Type

Enterprising. These occupations frequently involve starting up and carrying out projects and can involve leading people and making many decisions. They sometimes require risk taking and often deal with business.

Other Characteristics

GOE—Related Interest Area/Career Cluster: 08 Health Science. **Related Work Group:** 08.01 Managerial Work in Medical and Health Services. **Most Important Skills:** Management of personnel resources, management of material resources, systems evaluation, management of financial resources, persuasion, service orientation. **Top Values:** Authority, social service, creativity. **Work Environment:** Indoors; sitting; disease or infections; radiation; specialized protective or safety equipment; walking and running; protective or safety equipment; close to others.

Related Titles in the Classification of Instructional Programs (CIP)

51.0701 Health/Health Care Administration/Management; 51.0702 Hospital and Health Care Facilities Administration/Management.

Hotel/Motel and Restaurant Management

Prepares you to plan, manage, and market restaurants, food services in hospitality establishments, food service chains and franchise networks, restaurant supply operations, and lodging services for the traveling public.

Career Snapshot

Students of hotel/motel and restaurant management learn many skills required in any management program—economics, accounting, human resources, finance—plus the specialized skills needed for the hospitality industry. Some enter the field with an associate degree, but opportunities are better with a bachelor's degree. Usually new hires enter an on-the-job training program where they learn all aspects of the business. The outlook for employment is mostly good, especially in restaurants.

Related Specialties in Majors and Careers

Hotels/motels, resorts and theme parks, restaurants.

Related Job Titles, Earnings, Projected Growth, and Openings

Job Title	Average Earnings	Projected Growth	Annual Openings
1. Food Service Managers (O*NET-SOC Code 11-9051.00)	$44,570	5.0%	59,302
2. Lodging Managers (O*NET-SOC Code 11-9081.00)	$44,240	12.2%	5,529
3. Residential Advisors (O*NET-SOC Code 39-9041.00)	$23,050	18.5%	8,053

Typical Sequence of College Courses

English composition, business writing, introduction to psychology, principles of microeconomics, principles of macroeconomics, calculus for business and social sciences, statistics for business and social sciences, introduction to management information systems, introduction to accounting, legal environment of business, principles of management and organization, operations management, strategic management, business finance, introduction to marketing, introduction to the hospitality industry, food and beverage production and management, food service and lodging operations, law and the hospitality industry, hotel financial management, marketing hospitality and leisure services, hospitality human resource management, hospitality technology applications, field experience/internship.

Typical Sequence of High School Courses

English, algebra, geometry, trigonometry, science, foreign language, computer science, public speaking.

Personality Type

Enterprising. These occupations frequently involve starting up and carrying out projects and can involve leading people and making many decisions. They sometimes require risk taking and often deal with business.

Other Characteristics

GOE—Related Interest Areas/Career Clusters: 09 Hospitality, Tourism, and Recreation; 10 Human Service. **Related Work Groups:** 09.01 Managerial Work in Hospitality and Tourism; 10.01 Counseling and Social Work. **Most Important Skills:** Management of personnel resources, management of financial resources, management of material resources, monitoring, speaking, social perceptiveness. **Top Values:** Authority, creativity, autonomy. **Work Environment:** Indoors; standing; walking and running; very hot or cold; minor burns, cuts, bites, or stings; close to others; protective or safety equipment.

Related Titles in the Classification of Instructional Programs (CIP)

52.0904 Hotel/Motel Administration/Management; 52.0905 Restaurant/Food Services Management.

Human Resources Management

Prepares you to manage the development of human capital in organizations and to provide related services to individuals and groups.

Career Snapshot

Human resource managers are responsible for attracting the right employees for an organization, training them, keeping them productively employed, and sometimes severing the relationship through outplacement or retirement. Generalists often enter the field with a bachelor's degree, although specialists may find a master's degree (or perhaps a law degree) advantageous. Generalists most often find entry-level work with small organizations. There is a trend toward outsourcing many specialized functions, such as outplacement, to specialized service firms.

Related Specialties in Majors and Careers

Compensation/benefits, job analysis, labor relations, training.

Related Job Titles, Earnings, Projected Growth, and Openings

Job Title	Average Earnings	Projected Growth	Annual Openings
1. Business Teachers, Postsecondary (O*NET-SOC Code 25-1011.00)	$64,900	22.9%	237,478
2. Compensation and Benefits Managers (O*NET-SOC Code 11-3041.00)	$81,410	12.0%	6,121
3. Compensation, Benefits, and Job Analysis Specialists (O*NET-SOC Code 13-1072.00)	$52,180	18.4%	18,761
4. Employment Interviewers (O*NET-SOC Code 13-1071.01)	$44,380	18.4%	33,588
5. Personnel Recruiters (O*NET-SOC Code 13-1071.02)	$44,380	18.4%	33,588
6. Training and Development Managers (O*NET-SOC Code 11-3042.00)	$84,340	15.6%	3,759
7. Training and Development Specialists (O*NET-SOC Code 13-1073.00)	$49,630	18.3%	35,862

Job 1 shares 237,478 openings with 35 other postsecondary teaching jobs not included in this table. Jobs 4 and 5 share 33,588 openings.

Typical Sequence of College Courses

English composition, business writing, introduction to psychology, principles of microeconomics, principles of macroeconomics, calculus for business and social sciences, statistics for business and social sciences, introduction to management information systems, introduction to accounting, legal environment of business, principles of management and organization, operations management, strategic management, business finance, introduction to marketing, organizational theory, human resource management, compensation and benefits administration, training and development, employment law, industrial relations and labor management.

Typical Sequence of High School Courses

English, algebra, geometry, trigonometry, science, foreign language, computer science, public speaking.

Personality Type

Social. These occupations frequently involve working with, communicating with, and teaching people and often involve helping or providing service to others.

Other Characteristics

GOE—Related Interest Areas/Career Clusters: 04 Business and Administration; 05 Education and Training. **Related Work Groups:** 04.01 Managerial Work in General Business; 04.03 Human Resources Support; 05.03 Postsecondary and Adult Teaching and Instructing. **Most Important Skills:** Persuasion, writing, service orientation, social perceptiveness, management of personnel resources, speaking. **Top Values:** Social service, working conditions, authority. **Work Environment:** Indoors; sitting; repetitive motions.

Related Title in the Classification of Instructional Programs (CIP)

52.1001 Human Resources Management/Personnel Administration, General.

Humanities

Focuses on combined studies and research into human constructs and concerns as distinguished from the social and physical sciences, emphasizing languages, literatures, art, music, philosophy, and religion.

Career Snapshot

Humanities (sometimes called liberal arts) is an interdisciplinary major that covers a wide range of the arts and other nonscientific modes of thought, such as history, philosophy, religious studies, and language. Graduates of this major usually have strong skills for communicating and critical thinking, and they often advance further in the business world than those who hold more business-focused degrees. Some pursue careers in teaching, media, or the arts. Others get professional degrees in law or medicine.

Related Specialties in Majors and Careers

History, language, literature, peace and justice studies, philosophy, religion, the arts.

Related Job Titles, Earnings, Projected Growth, and Openings

Job Title	Average Earnings	Projected Growth	Annual Openings
1. Anthropology and Archeology Teachers, Postsecondary (O*NET-SOC Code 25-1061.00)	$64,530	22.9%	237,478
2. Area, Ethnic, and Cultural Studies Teachers, Postsecondary (O*NET-SOC Code 25-1062.00)	$59,150	22.9%	237,478
3. Art, Drama, and Music Teachers, Postsecondary (O*NET-SOC Code 25-1121.00)	$55,190	22.9%	237,478
4. Communications Teachers, Postsecondary (O*NET-SOC Code 25-1122.00)	$54,720	22.9%	237,478
5. Economics Teachers, Postsecondary (O*NET-SOC Code 25-1063.00)	$75,300	22.9%	237,478
6. Education Teachers, Postsecondary (O*NET-SOC Code 25-1081.00)	$54,220	22.9%	237,478
7. English Language and Literature Teachers, Postsecondary (O*NET-SOC Code 25-1123.00)	$54,000	22.9%	237,478
8. Foreign Language and Literature Teachers, Postsecondary (O*NET-SOC Code 25-1124.00)	$53,610	22.9%	237,478
9. Geography Teachers, Postsecondary (O*NET-SOC Code 25-1064.00)	$61,310	22.9%	237,478

Job Title	Average Earnings	Projected Growth	Annual Openings
10. Graduate Teaching Assistants (O*NET-SOC Code 25-1191.00)	$28,060	22.9%	237,478
11. History Teachers, Postsecondary (O*NET-SOC Code 25-1125.00)	$59,160	22.9%	237,478
12. Library Science Teachers, Postsecondary (O*NET-SOC Code 25-1082.00)	$56,810	22.9%	237,478
13. Philosophy and Religion Teachers, Postsecondary (O*NET-SOC Code 25-1126.00)	$56,380	22.9%	237,478
14. Political Science Teachers, Postsecondary (O*NET-SOC Code 25-1065.00)	$63,100	22.9%	237,478
15. Psychology Teachers, Postsecondary (O*NET-SOC Code 25-1066.00)	$60,610	22.9%	237,478

All of these jobs share 237,478 openings with each other and with 21 other postsecondary teaching jobs not included in this table.

Typical Sequence of College Courses

Foreign language, major thinkers and issues in philosophy, literature, art and culture, European history and civilization, writing, seminar (reporting on research).

Typical Sequence of High School Courses

English, algebra, foreign language, history, literature, public speaking, social science.

Personality Type

Social. These occupations frequently involve working with, communicating with, and teaching people and often involve helping or providing service to others.

Other Characteristics

GOE—Related Interest Area/Career Cluster: 05 Education and Training. **Related Work Group:** 05.03 Postsecondary and Adult Teaching and Instructing. **Most Important Skills:** Instructing, learning strategies, writing, social perceptiveness, speaking, reading comprehension. **Top Values:** Authority, social service, creativity. **Work Environment:** Indoors; sitting.

Related Title in the Classification of Instructional Programs (CIP)

24.0103 Humanities/Humanistic Studies.

Industrial and Labor Relations

Focuses on employee-management interactions and the management of issues and disputes regarding working conditions and worker benefit packages; may prepare you to function as a labor or personnel relations specialist.

Career Snapshot

Although labor unions are not as widespread as they once were, they still play an important role in American business. The "just in time" strategy that is popular in the manufacturing and transportation industries means that a strike lasting only a few hours can seriously disrupt business. Employers are eager to settle labor disputes before they start, and this creates job opportunities for labor relations specialists working for either the employer or the union. Other job openings are found in government agencies that deal with labor. Many of these specialists hold bachelor's degrees, but a master's degree or law degree can be helpful for jobs involving contract negotiations and mediation.

Related Specialties in Majors and Careers

Arbitration, labor law, mediation, worker compensation.

Related Job Titles, Earnings, Projected Growth, and Openings

Job Title	Average Earnings	Projected Growth	Annual Openings
1. Business Teachers, Postsecondary (O*NET-SOC Code 25-1011.00)	$64,900	22.9%	237,478
2. Compensation and Benefits Managers (O*NET-SOC Code 11-3041.00)	$81,410	12.0%	6,121
3. Compensation, Benefits, and Job Analysis Specialists (O*NET-SOC Code 13-1072.00)	$52,180	18.4%	18,761
4. Employment Interviewers (O*NET-SOC Code 13-1071.01)	$44,380	18.4%	33,588
5. Personnel Recruiters (O*NET-SOC Code 13-1071.02)	$44,380	18.4%	33,588

Job 1 shares 237,478 openings with 35 other postsecondary teaching jobs not included in this table. Jobs 4 and 5 share 33,588 openings.

Typical Sequence of College Courses

English composition, business writing, introduction to psychology, principles of microeconomics, principles of macroeconomics, calculus for business and social sciences, statistics for business and social sciences, introduction to management information systems, introduction to accounting, legal environment of business, business finance, introduction to marketing, organizational behavior, human resource management, industrial relations and labor management, employment law, training and development, systems of conflict resolution.

Typical Sequence of High School Courses

English, algebra, geometry, trigonometry, foreign language, computer science, public speaking, social science.

Personality Type

Enterprising. These occupations frequently involve starting up and carrying out projects and can involve leading people and making many decisions. They sometimes require risk taking and often deal with business.

Other Characteristics

GOE—Related Interest Areas/Career Clusters: 04 Business and Administration; 05 Education and Training. **Related Work Groups:** 04.01 Managerial Work in General Business; 04.03 Human Resources Support; 05.03 Postsecondary and Adult Teaching and Instructing. **Most Important Skills:** Management of personnel resources, persuasion, negotiation, management of financial resources, service orientation, social perceptiveness. **Top Values:** Working conditions, social service, responsibility. **Work Environment:** Indoors; sitting; repetitive motions.

Related Title in the Classification of Instructional Programs (CIP)

52.1002 Labor and Industrial Relations.

Industrial Design

Prepares you to use artistic techniques to effectively communicate ideas and information to business and consumer audiences via the creation of effective forms, shapes, and packaging for manufactured products.

Career Snapshot

Industrial designers develop every conceivable kind of manufactured product, from cars to computers to children's toys. They need to understand the technology that will make the product work and the human context in which the product will be used—such as the way it will be held in the hand—as well as the marketplace in which the product will compete. Therefore, this field requires students to learn a combination of technical, creative, and business skills. Demand for graduates is expected to be good.

Related Specialties in Majors and Careers

Computer modeling, product design.

Related Job Titles, Earnings, Projected Growth, and Openings

Job Title	Average Earnings	Projected Growth	Annual Openings
1. Art, Drama, and Music Teachers, Postsecondary (O*NET-SOC Code 25-1121.00)	$55,190	22.9%	237,478
2. Commercial and Industrial Designers (O*NET-SOC Code 27-1021.00)	$56,550	7.2%	4,777
3. Graphic Designers (O*NET-SOC Code 27-1024.00)	$41,280	9.8%	26,968

Job 1 shares 237,478 openings with 35 other postsecondary teaching jobs not included in this table.

Typical Sequence of College Courses

English composition, college algebra, basic drawing, oral communication, introduction to economics, art history: Renaissance to modern, general physics, introduction to marketing, introduction to graphic design, visual thinking and problem solving, presentation graphics, industrial design materials and processes, human factors in design (ergonomics), computer modeling, history of industrial design, professional practices for industrial design, senior design project.

Typical Sequence of High School Courses

Algebra, geometry, trigonometry, pre-calculus, English, public speaking, art, computer science, mechanical drawing, photography.

Personality Type

Artistic. These occupations frequently involve working with forms, designs, and patterns. They often require self-expression, and the work can be done without following a clear set of rules.

Other Characteristics

GOE—Related Interest Areas/Career Clusters: 03 Arts and Communication; 05 Education and Training. **Related Work Groups:** 03.05 Design; 05.03 Postsecondary and Adult Teaching and Instructing. **Most Important Skills:** Persuasion, operations analysis, time management, writing, complex problem solving, troubleshooting. **Top Values:** Creativity, ability utilization, achievement. **Work Environment:** Indoors; sitting; repetitive motions; using hands on objects, tools, or controls.

Related Title in the Classification of Instructional Programs (CIP)

50.0404 Industrial Design.

Industrial Engineering

Prepares you to apply scientific and mathematical principles to the design, improvement, and installation of integrated systems of people, material, information, and energy.

Career Snapshot

Industrial engineers plan how an organization can most efficiently use staff, equipment, buildings, raw materials, information, and energy to output a product or service. They facilitate communication between managers and technology experts such as mechanical or chemical engineers. Sometimes they make a career move into management positions. A bachelor's degree is good preparation for this field. The job outlook for industrial engineers is expected to be good, especially in nonmanufacturing industries, as U.S. employers attempt to boost productivity to compete in a global workplace.

Related Specialties in Majors and Careers

Operations research, quality control.

Related Job Titles, Earnings, Projected Growth, and Openings

Job Title	Average Earnings	Projected Growth	Annual Openings
1. Engineering Managers (O*NET-SOC Code 11-9041.00)	$111,020	7.3%	7,404
2. Engineering Teachers, Postsecondary (O*NET-SOC Code 25-1032.00)	$79,510	22.9%	237,478
3. Industrial Engineers (O*NET-SOC Code 17-2112.00)	$71,430	20.3%	11,272

Job 2 shares 237,478 openings with 35 other postsecondary teaching jobs not included in this table.

Typical Sequence of College Courses

English composition, technical writing, calculus, differential equations, general chemistry, introduction to computer science, general physics, statics, dynamics, numerical analysis, thermodynamics, materials engineering, engineering economics, human factors and ergonomics, engineering systems design, operations research, quality control, facilities design, simulation, analysis of industrial activities, senior design project.

Typical Sequence of High School Courses

English, algebra, geometry, trigonometry, pre-calculus, calculus, chemistry, physics, computer science.

Personality Type

Investigative. These occupations frequently involve working with ideas and require an extensive amount of thinking. They can involve searching for facts and figuring out problems mentally.

Other Characteristics

GOE—Related Interest Areas/Career Clusters: 05 Education and Training; 15 Scientific Research, Engineering, and Mathematics. **Related Work Groups:** 05.03 Postsecondary and Adult Teaching and Instructing; 15.01 Managerial Work in Scientific Research, Engineering, and Mathematics; 15.08 Industrial and Safety Engineering. **Most Important Skills:** Technology design, science, installation, mathematics, management of financial resources, operations analysis. **Top Values:** Authority, creativity, autonomy. **Work Environment:** More often indoors than in a vehicle; sitting; protective or safety equipment; hazardous equipment; noisy; extremely bright or inadequate lighting; contaminants.

Related Title in the Classification of Instructional Programs (CIP)

14.3501 Industrial Engineering.

Industrial/Technology Education

Prepares you to teach technology education/industrial arts programs at various educational levels.

Career Snapshot

As American industry progresses into a new century, the traditional "shop teacher" is evolving into a technology educator who teaches young people the high-tech skills they need to succeed in the new economy. In industrial/technology education, as in other teaching fields, a bachelor's degree is usually required for job entry, but a master's is often needed to build a career. In addition, it is helpful to get some genuine work experience in industry or agriculture. The job outlook is better for this field than for many other secondary-school specializations.

Related Specialties in Majors and Careers

A technology (such as welding), agriculture.

Related Job Titles, Earnings, Projected Growth, and Openings

Job Title	Average Earnings	Projected Growth	Annual Openings
1. Education Teachers, Postsecondary (O*NET-SOC Code 25-1081.00)	$54,220	22.9%	237,478
2. Middle School Teachers, Except Special and Vocational Education (O*NET-SOC Code 25-2022.00)	$47,900	11.2%	75,270
3. Secondary School Teachers, Except Special and Vocational Education (O*NET-SOC Code 25-2031.00)	$49,420	5.6%	93,166
4. Vocational Education Teachers, Middle School (O*NET-SOC Code 25-2023.00)	$46,290	–5.1%	1,505
5. Vocational Education Teachers, Postsecondary (O*NET-SOC Code 25-1194.00)	$45,850	22.9%	237,478
6. Vocational Education Teachers, Secondary School (O*NET-SOC Code 25-2032.00)	$50,090	–4.6%	7,639

Jobs 1 and 5 share 237,478 openings with 34 other postsecondary teaching jobs not included in this table.

Typical Sequence of College Courses

Introduction to psychology, English composition, oral communication, history and philosophy of education, human growth and development, history and philosophy of industrial education, methods of teaching industrial education, evaluation in industrial education, instructional materials in industrial education, classroom/laboratory management, special needs in industrial education, safety and liability in the classroom, student teaching.

Typical Sequence of High School Courses

English, algebra, geometry, trigonometry, science, foreign language, industrial arts, mechanical drawing, public speaking.

Personality Type

Social. These occupations frequently involve working with, communicating with, and teaching people and often involve helping or providing service to others.

Other Characteristics

GOE—Related Interest Area/Career Cluster: 05 Education and Training. **Related Work Groups:** 05.02 Preschool, Elementary, and Secondary Teaching and Instructing; 05.03 Postsecondary and Adult Teaching and Instructing. **Most Important Skills:** Learning strategies, instructing, social perceptiveness, monitoring, persuasion, time management. **Top Values:** Social service, authority, creativity. **Work Environment:** Indoors; standing; close to others; walking and running; noisy; disease or infections.

Related Title in the Classification of Instructional Programs (CIP)

13.1309 Technology Teacher Education/Industrial Arts Teacher Education.

Insurance

Prepares you to manage risk in organizational settings and provide insurance and risk-aversion services to businesses, individuals, and other organizations.

Career Snapshot

A bachelor's degree in insurance may lead to employment in an insurance company or agency. Graduates with outstanding mathematical ability may be hired for training as actuaries. Mergers and downsizing among agencies and brokerages may limit the number of job openings.

Related Specialties in Majors and Careers

Commercial risk management, life and health insurance, property and liability insurance.

Related Job Titles, Earnings, Projected Growth, and Openings

Job Title	Average Earnings	Projected Growth	Annual Openings
1. Business Teachers, Postsecondary (O*NET-SOC Code 25-1011.00)	$64,900	22.9%	237,478
2. Insurance Adjusters, Examiners, and Investigators (O*NET-SOC Code 13-1031.02)	$53,560	8.9%	22,024
3. Insurance Appraisers, Auto Damage (O*NET-SOC Code 13-1032.00)	$51,500	12.5%	1,030
4. Insurance Sales Agents (O*NET-SOC Code 41-3021.00)	$44,110	12.9%	64,162
5. Insurance Underwriters (O*NET-SOC Code 13-2053.00)	$54,530	6.3%	6,880
6. Purchasing Agents, Except Wholesale, Retail, and Farm Products (O*NET-SOC Code 13-1023.00)	$52,460	0.1%	22,349
7. Sales Representatives, Wholesale and Manufacturing, Except Technical and Scientific Products (O*NET-SOC Code 41-4012.00)	$50,750	8.4%	156,215
8. Telemarketers (O*NET-SOC Code 41-9041.00)	$21,390	–9.9%	210,810
9. Wholesale and Retail Buyers, Except Farm Products (O*NET-SOC Code 13-1022.00)	$46,960	–0.1%	19,847

Job 1 shares 237,478 openings with 35 other postsecondary teaching jobs not included in this table. Job 2 shares 22,024 openings with another job not included in this table.

Typical Sequence of College Courses

English composition, business writing, introduction to psychology, principles of microeconomics, principles of macroeconomics, calculus for business and social sciences, statistics for business and social sciences, introduction to management information systems, introduction to accounting, legal environment of business, principles of management and organization, operations management, strategic management, business finance, introduction to marketing, property and liability insurance, life and health insurance, commercial risk management, insurance law, employee benefit planning.

Typical Sequence of High School Courses

English, algebra, geometry, trigonometry, science, foreign language, computer science.

Personality Type

Enterprising. These occupations frequently involve starting up and carrying out projects and can involve leading people and making many decisions. They sometimes require risk taking and often deal with business.

Other Characteristics

GOE—Related Interest Areas/Career Clusters: 05 Education and Training; 06 Finance and Insurance; 14 Retail and Wholesale Sales and Service. **Related Work Groups:** 05.03 Postsecondary and Adult Teaching and Instructing; 06.02 Finance/Insurance Investigation and Analysis; 06.05 Finance/Insurance Sales and Support; 14.03 General Sales; 14.04 Personal Soliciting; 14.05 Purchasing. **Most Important Skills:** Persuasion, negotiation, service orientation, management of financial resources, speaking, time management. **Top Values:** Autonomy, advancement, variety. **Work Environment:** More often indoors than in a vehicle; sitting; close to others.

Related Title in the Classification of Instructional Programs (CIP)

52.1701 Insurance.

Interior Design

Prepares you to apply artistic principles and techniques to the professional planning, designing, equipping, and furnishing of residential and commercial interior spaces.

Career Snapshot

Interior designers plan the shaping and decoration of the interiors of all kinds of buildings, including homes and commercial structures. They may design new interiors or renovate existing places. They respond to their clients' needs and budgets by developing designs based on traditional forms, innovative uses of layout and materials, sound principles of engineering, and safety codes. A bachelor's degree in the field is not universally required, but it contributes to your qualifications for licensure (in some states) and membership in a professional association.

Related Specialties in Majors and Careers

Acoustics, bathrooms, computer-aided design, kitchens, public spaces, residential design, restoration.

Related Job Titles, Earnings, Projected Growth, and Openings

Job Title	Average Earnings	Projected Growth	Annual Openings
1. Art, Drama, and Music Teachers, Postsecondary (O*NET-SOC Code 25-1121.00)	$55,190	22.9%	237,478
2. Interior Designers (O*NET-SOC Code 27-1025.00)	$43,970	19.5%	8,434

Job 1 shares 237,478 openings with 35 other postsecondary teaching jobs not included in this table.

Typical Sequence of College Courses

Basic drawing, history of architecture, introduction to interior design, interior materials, history of interiors, presentation graphics, computer-aided design, color and design, lighting design, interior design studio, construction codes and material rating, senior design project.

Typical Sequence of High School Courses

English, algebra, literature, history, geometry, art, physics, trigonometry, pre-calculus, computer science.

Personality Type

Artistic. These occupations frequently involve working with forms, designs, and patterns. They often require self-expression, and the work can be done without following a clear set of rules.

Other Characteristics

GOE—Related Interest Areas/Career Clusters: 03 Arts and Communication; 05 Education and Training. **Related Work Groups:** 03.05 Design; 05.03 Postsecondary and Adult Teaching and Instructing. **Most Important Skills:** Persuasion, speaking, active learning, instructing, writing, critical thinking. **Top Values:** Creativity, ability utilization, social service. **Work Environment:** Indoors; sitting; close to others.

Related Title in the Classification of Instructional Programs (CIP)

50.0408 Interior Design.

International Business

Prepares you to manage international businesses and/or business operations.

Career Snapshot

Now that U.S. businesses are increasingly integrating into the global economy, a major or concentration in international business can be an impressive credential. You may study it at the bachelor's or MBA level. Competence in a foreign language, experience living abroad, and sensitivity to cultural differences can be very helpful.

Related Specialties in Majors and Careers

A particular aspect of business, a particular part of the world.

Related Job Titles, Earnings, Projected Growth, and Openings

Job Title	Average Earnings	Projected Growth	Annual Openings
1. Business Teachers, Postsecondary (O*NET-SOC Code 25-1011.00)	$64,900	22.9%	237,478
2. Chief Executives (O*NET-SOC Code 11-1011.00)	More than $145,600	2.0%	21,209
3. General and Operations Managers (O*NET-SOC Code 11-1021.00)	$88,700	1.5%	112,072

Job 1 shares 237,478 openings with 35 other postsecondary teaching jobs not included in this table.

Typical Sequence of College Courses

English composition, business writing, foreign language, introduction to psychology, principles of microeconomics, principles of macroeconomics, calculus for business and social sciences, statistics for business and social sciences, introduction to management information systems, introduction to accounting, legal environment of business, principles of management and organization, operations management, business finance, introduction to marketing, international business strategy, international economy, international finance, business in emerging markets, study abroad.

Typical Sequence of High School Courses

English, algebra, geometry, trigonometry, science, foreign language, geography, computer science, public speaking.

Personality Type

Enterprising. These occupations frequently involve starting up and carrying out projects and can involve leading people and making many decisions. They sometimes require risk taking and often deal with business.

Other Characteristics

GOE—Related Interest Areas/Career Clusters: 04 Business and Administration; 05 Education and Training. **Related Work Group:** 04.01 Managerial Work in General Business; 05.03 Postsecondary and Adult Teaching and Instructing. **Most Important Skills:** Management of financial resources, management of personnel resources, management of material resources, negotiation, monitoring, persuasion. **Top Values:** Authority, social status, working conditions. **Work Environment:** More often indoors than in a vehicle; sitting.

Related Title in the Classification of Instructional Programs (CIP)

52.1101 International Business/Trade/Commerce.

International Relations

Focuses on the systematic study of international politics and institutions and the conduct of diplomacy and foreign policy.

Career Snapshot

The study of international relations is a multidisciplinary effort that draws on political science, economics, sociology, and history, among other disciplines. It attempts to find meaning in the ways people, private groups, and governments relate to one another politically and economically. The traditional focus on sovereign states is opening up to include attention to other actors on the world stage, including nongovernmental organizations; international organizations; multinational corporations; and groups representing a religion, ethnic group, or ideology. Now that American business is opening to the world more than ever before, this major is gaining in importance. Graduates often go on to law or business school, graduate school in the social sciences, the U.S. Foreign Service, or employment in businesses or organizations with an international focus.

Related Specialties in Majors and Careers

A regional specialization, development, diplomacy, global security, international political economy, U.S. foreign policy.

Related Job Titles, Earnings, Projected Growth, and Openings

Job Title	Average Earnings	Projected Growth	Annual Openings
1. Chief Executives (O*NET-SOC Code 11-1011.00)	More than $145,600	2.0%	21,209
2. Political Science Teachers, Postsecondary (O*NET-SOC Code 25-1065.00)	$63,100	22.9%	237,478
3. Political Scientists (O*NET-SOC Code 19-3094.00)	$91,580	5.3%	318

Job 2 shares 237,478 openings with 35 other postsecondary teaching jobs not included in this table.

Typical Sequence of College Courses

English composition, world history to the early modern era, world history in the modern era, introduction to political science, introduction to international relations, foreign language, introduction to economics, microeconomic theory, macroeconomic theory, comparative governments, world regional geography, history of a non-Western civilization (such as China), international economics, American foreign policy, seminar (reporting on research), study abroad.

Typical Sequence of High School Courses

Algebra, English, foreign language, social science, trigonometry, history.

Personality Type

Social. These occupations frequently involve working with, communicating with, and teaching people and often involve helping or providing service to others.

Other Characteristics

GOE—Related Interest Areas/Career Clusters: 04 Business and Administration; 05 Education and Training; 15 Scientific Research, Engineering, and Mathematics. **Related Work Groups:** 04.01 Managerial Work in General Business; 05.03 Postsecondary and Adult Teaching and Instructing; 15.04 Social Sciences. **Most Important Skills:** Management of financial resources, management of material resources, management of personnel resources, judgment and decision making, negotiation, systems evaluation. **Top Values:** Authority, social status, working conditions. **Work Environment:** More often indoors than in a vehicle; sitting.

Related Title in the Classification of Instructional Programs (CIP)

45.0901 International Relations and Affairs.

Japanese

Focuses on the Japanese language, its literature, and its related dialects, and may include applications in business, science/technology, and other settings.

Career Snapshot

Japan is a major trading partner of the United States, but comparatively few English speakers have mastered the Japanese language. This means that a major in Japanese can be a valuable entry route to careers in international business, travel, and law. A graduate degree in Japanese is good preparation for college teaching or translation.

Related Specialties in Majors and Careers

History and culture, language education, literature, translation.

Related Job Titles, Earnings, Projected Growth, and Openings

Job Title	Average Earnings	Projected Growth	Annual Openings
1. Foreign Language and Literature Teachers, Post-secondary (O*NET-SOC Code 25-1124.00)	$53,610	22.9%	237,478
2. Interpreters and Translators (O*NET-SOC Code 27-3091.00)	$37,490	23.6%	6,630

Job 1 shares 237,478 openings with 35 other postsecondary teaching jobs not included in this table.

Typical Sequence of College Courses

Japanese language, conversation, composition, linguistics, Japanese literature, East Asian literature, East Asian studies, grammar, phonetics, study abroad.

Typical Sequence of High School Courses

English, public speaking, foreign language, history, literature, social science.

Personality Type

Artistic. These occupations frequently involve working with forms, designs, and patterns. They often require self-expression, and the work can be done without following a clear set of rules.

Other Characteristics

GOE—Related Interest Areas/Career Clusters: 03 Arts and Communication; 05 Education and Training. **Related Work Groups:** 03.03 News, Broadcasting, and Public Relations; 05.03 Postsecondary and Adult Teaching and Instructing. **Most Important Skills:** Social perceptiveness, speaking, writing, active listening, reading comprehension, learning strategies. **Top Values:** Social service, ability utilization, achievement. **Work Environment:** Indoors; sitting; close to others.

Related Title in the Classification of Instructional Programs (CIP)

16.0302 Japanese Language and Literature.

Journalism and Mass Communications

Focuses on the theory and practice of gathering, processing, and delivering news and prepares you to be a professional print journalist, news editor, or news manager.

Career Snapshot

Journalism is a good preparation not only for news reporting and writing, but also for advertising and (with specialized coursework) news media production. Competition for entry-level journalism jobs can be keen, especially for prestigious newspapers and media outlets. Expect to start in a smaller operation and move around to increasingly bigger employers as you build your career.

Related Specialties in Majors and Careers

Media management, news editing and editorializing, news reporting, photojournalism, radio and television news.

Related Job Titles, Earnings, Projected Growth, and Openings

Job Title	Average Earnings	Projected Growth	Annual Openings
1. Broadcast News Analysts (O*NET-SOC Code 27-3021.00)	$49,060	6.0%	1,444
2. Communications Teachers, Postsecondary (O*NET-SOC Code 25-1122.00)	$54,720	22.9%	237,478
3. Copy Writers (O*NET-SOC Code 27-3043.04)	$50,660	12.8%	24,023
4. Court Reporters (O*NET-SOC Code 23-2091.00)	$45,330	24.5%	2,620
5. Editors (O*NET-SOC Code 27-3041.00)	$48,320	2.3%	20,193
6. Reporters and Correspondents (O*NET-SOC Code 27-3022.00)	$34,690	1.2%	10,538

Job 2 shares 237,478 openings with 35 other postsecondary teaching jobs not included in this table. Job 3 shares 24,023 openings with another job not included in this table.

Typical Sequence of College Courses

English composition, oral communication, American government, introduction to economics, foreign language, introduction to psychology, introduction to mass communication, writing for mass media, news writing and reporting, copy editing, mass communication law, communication ethics, feature writing, photojournalism, media management, visual design for media.

Typical Sequence of High School Courses

English, algebra, foreign language, art, literature, public speaking, social science.

Personality Type

Artistic. These occupations frequently involve working with forms, designs, and patterns. They often require self-expression, and the work can be done without following a clear set of rules.

Other Characteristics

GOE—Related Interest Areas/Career Clusters: 03 Arts and Communication; 05 Education and Training; 07 Government and Public Administration. **Related Work Groups:** 03.02 Writing and Editing; 03.03 News, Broadcasting, and Public Relations; 05.03 Postsecondary and Adult Teaching and Instructing; 07.04 Public Administration Clerical Support. **Most Important Skills:** Writing, persuasion, active listening, reading comprehension, time management, critical thinking. **Top Values:** Creativity, recognition, ability utilization. **Work Environment:** Indoors; sitting; repetitive motions; using hands on objects, tools, or controls.

Related Title in the Classification of Instructional Programs (CIP)

09.0401 Journalism.

Landscape Architecture

Prepares you for the independent professional practice of landscape architecture and research in various aspects of the field.

Career Snapshot

Landscape architects must have a good flair for design, ability to work with a variety of construction techniques and technologies, knowledge of the characteristics of many plants, and business sense. A bachelor's degree is the usual entry route; some people enter the field with a master's degree after a bachelor's in another field. An internship is a very helpful credential. About 40 percent of landscape architects are self-employed.

Related Specialties in Majors and Careers

Arid lands, ecotourism, historical and cultural landscapes, international studies, small-town and urban revitalization, urban design.

Related Job Titles, Earnings, Projected Growth, and Openings

Job Title	Average Earnings	Projected Growth	Annual Openings
1. Architecture Teachers, Postsecondary (O*NET-SOC Code 25-1031.00)	$68,540	22.9%	237,478
2. Engineering Managers (O*NET-SOC Code 11-9041.00)	$111,020	7.3%	7,404
3. Landscape Architects (O*NET-SOC Code 17-1012.00)	$57,580	16.4%	2,342

Job 1 shares 237,478 openings with 35 other postsecondary teaching jobs not included in this table.

Typical Sequence of College Courses

English composition, calculus, basic drawing, general biology, introduction to soil science, architectural graphics, ecology, history of landscape architecture, landscape architectural design, site analysis, introduction to horticulture, land surveying, landscape structures and materials, architectural computer graphics, land planning, professional practice of landscape architecture, senior design project.

Typical Sequence of High School Courses

English, algebra, geometry, trigonometry, pre-calculus, calculus, physics, computer science, art, biology.

Personality Type

Enterprising. These occupations frequently involve starting up and carrying out projects and can involve leading people and making many decisions. They sometimes require risk taking and often deal with business.

Other Characteristics

GOE—Related Interest Areas/Career Clusters: 02 Architecture and Construction; 05 Education and Training; 15 Scientific Research, Engineering, and Mathematics. **Related Work Groups:** 02.02 Architectural Design; 05.03 Postsecondary and Adult Teaching and Instructing; 15.01 Managerial Work in Scientific Research, Engineering, and Mathematics. **Most Important Skills:** Technology design, operations analysis, science, management of financial resources, installation, mathematics. **Top Values:** Authority, creativity, compensation. **Work Environment:** More often indoors than in a vehicle; sitting; hazardous equipment; protective or safety equipment; extremely bright or inadequate lighting.

Related Title in the Classification of Instructional Programs (CIP)

04.0601 Landscape Architecture (BS, BSLA, BLA, MSLA, MLA, PhD).

Law

Prepares you for the independent professional practice of law, for taking state and national bar examinations, and for advanced research in jurisprudence.

Career Snapshot

Although most lawyers work in private practice, many work for government agencies, businesses, and nonprofits. They enter the field by completing four years of college, three years of law school, and then passing the bar exam. The undergraduate major may be almost anything that contributes to skills in writing and critical thinking. Often it helps open doors to the kinds of careers that will be options after law school—for example, a bachelor's degree in a business field may help prepare for a career in tax law, labor relations law, or antitrust law.

Related Specialties in Majors and Careers

Environmental law, family law, intellectual property, international and comparative law, litigation.

Related Job Titles, Earnings, Projected Growth, and Openings

Job Title	Average Earnings	Projected Growth	Annual Openings
1. Administrative Law Judges, Adjudicators, and Hearing Officers (O*NET-SOC Code 23-1021.00)	$74,170	0.1%	794
2. Arbitrators, Mediators, and Conciliators (O*NET-SOC Code 23-1022.00)	$48,840	10.6%	546
3. Judges, Magistrate Judges, and Magistrates (O*NET-SOC Code 23-1023.00)	$107,230	5.1%	1,567
4. Law Clerks (O*NET-SOC Code 23-2092.00)	$37,550	–1.2%	3,657
5. Law Teachers, Postsecondary (O*NET-SOC Code 25-1112.00)	$87,730	22.9%	237,478
6. Lawyers (O*NET-SOC Code 23-1011.00)	$106,120	11.0%	49,445

Job 5 shares 237,478 openings with 35 other postsecondary teaching jobs not included in this table.

Typical Sequence of College Courses

English composition, oral communication, introduction to political science, introduction to philosophy, American history, foreign language, civil procedure, constitutional law, contracts, criminal law, legal communication, legal research, legal writing, property, torts, criminal procedures, evidence, professional responsibility, trusts and estates.

Typical Sequence of High School Courses

Algebra, English, foreign language, social science, history, geometry, public speaking.

Personality Type

Enterprising. These occupations frequently involve starting up and carrying out projects and can involve leading people and making many decisions. They sometimes require risk taking and often deal with business.

Other Characteristics

GOE—Related Interest Areas/Career Clusters: 05 Education and Training; 12 Law and Public Safety. **Related Work Groups:** 05.03 Postsecondary and Adult Teaching and Instructing; 12.02 Legal Practice and Justice Administration; 12.03 Legal Support. **Most Important Skills:** Persuasion, negotiation, writing, judgment and decision making, critical thinking, reading comprehension. **Top Values:** Autonomy, compensation, ability utilization. **Work Environment:** More often indoors than in a vehicle; sitting.

Related Title in the Classification of Instructional Programs (CIP)

22.0101 Law (LL.B., J.D.).

Library Science

Focuses on the knowledge and skills required to develop, organize, store, retrieve, administer, and facilitate the use of local, remote, and networked collections of information in print, audiovisual, and electronic formats and prepares you for professional service as a librarian or information consultant.

Career Snapshot

This major is sometimes called library and information science because increasingly the information that is needed by businesses, governments, and individuals is not available in books. Library science programs teach not only how to serve library users and manage library collections, but also how to retrieve and compile information from online databases. The master's degree is the entry-level credential in this field; a special librarian often needs an additional graduate or professional degree. The best employment opportunities will probably be in online information retrieval and in nontraditional settings.

Related Specialties in Majors and Careers

Archives, cataloguing, children's libraries, instructional libraries, map libraries, music libraries, online information retrieval, special interest libraries.

Related Job Titles, Earnings, Projected Growth, and Openings

Job Title	Average Earnings	Projected Growth	Annual Openings
1. Librarians (O*NET-SOC Code 25-4021.00)	$50,970	3.6%	18,945
2. Library Science Teachers, Postsecondary (O*NET-SOC Code 25-1082.00)	$56,810	22.9%	237,478

Job 2 shares 237,478 openings with 35 other postsecondary teaching jobs not included in this table.

Typical Sequence of College Courses

English composition, oral communication, introduction to computer science, foreign language, introduction to library and information science, reference services and resources, management of libraries and information services, bibliographic control of library materials, library research and evaluation.

Typical Sequence of High School Courses

English, foreign language, computer science, algebra, public speaking, office computer applications, keyboarding, social science.

Personality Type

Artistic. These occupations frequently involve working with forms, designs, and patterns. They often require self-expression, and the work can be done without following a clear set of rules.

Other Characteristics

GOE—Related Interest Area/Career Cluster: 05 Education and Training. **Related Work Groups:** 05.03 Postsecondary and Adult Teaching and Instructing; 05.04 Library Services. **Most Important Skills:** Management of financial resources, management of material resources, learning strategies, systems evaluation, service orientation, persuasion. **Top Values:** Working conditions, authority, social service. **Work Environment:** Indoors; sitting; close to others; using hands on objects, tools, or controls; kneeling or crouching; repetitive motions.

Related Title in the Classification of Instructional Programs (CIP)

25.0101 Library Science/Librarianship.

Management Information Systems

Prepares you to provide and manage data systems and related facilities for processing and retrieving internal business information; select systems and train personnel; and respond to external data requests.

Career Snapshot

The management information systems major is considered a business major, which means that students get a firm grounding in economics, accounting, business law, finance, and marketing, as well as the technical skills needed to work with the latest business computer applications. Students may specialize in MIS at either the bachelor's or master's level, and may combine it with a degree in a related business field, such as accounting or finance, or in computer science. The job outlook is very good.

Related Specialties in Majors and Careers

Accounting, network programming, security and disaster recovery.

Related Job Titles, Earnings, Projected Growth, and Openings

Job Title	Average Earnings	Projected Growth	Annual Openings
1. Computer and Information Systems Managers (O*NET-SOC Code 11-3021.00)	$108,070	16.4%	30,887
2. Computer Programmers (O*NET-SOC Code 15-1021.00)	$68,080	–4.1%	27,937
3. Database Administrators (O*NET-SOC Code 15-1061.00)	$67,250	28.6%	8,258

Typical Sequence of College Courses

English composition, business writing, introduction to psychology, principles of microeconomics, principles of macroeconomics, calculus for business and social sciences, statistics for business and social sciences, introduction to management information systems, introduction to accounting, legal environment of business, principles of management and organization, operations management, strategic management, business finance, introduction to marketing, database management systems, systems analysis and design, decision support systems for management, networks and telecommunications.

Typical Sequence of High School Courses

English, algebra, geometry, trigonometry, science, foreign language, computer science.

Personality Type

Investigative. These occupations frequently involve working with ideas and require an extensive amount of thinking. They can involve searching for facts and figuring out problems mentally.

Other Characteristics

GOE—Related Interest Area/Career Cluster: 11 Information Technology. **Related Work Groups:** 11.01 Managerial Work in Information Technology; 11.02 Information Technology Specialties. **Most Important Skills:** Programming, operations analysis, systems analysis, technology design, systems evaluation, troubleshooting. **Top Values:** Creativity, authority, advancement. **Work Environment:** Indoors; sitting; repetitive motions.

Related Title in the Classification of Instructional Programs (CIP)

52.1201 Management Information Systems, General.

Marketing

Prepares you to undertake and manage the process of developing consumer audiences and moving products from producers to consumers.

Career Snapshot

Marketing is the study of how buyers and sellers of goods and services find one another, how businesses can tailor their offerings to meet demand, and how businesses can anticipate and influence demand. It uses the findings of economics, psychology, and sociology in a business context. A bachelor's degree is good preparation for a job in marketing research. Usually some experience in this field is required before a person can move into a marketing management position. Job outlook varies, with some industries looking more favorable than others.

Related Specialties in Majors and Careers

Marketing management, marketing research.

Related Job Titles, Earnings, Projected Growth, and Openings

Job Title	Average Earnings	Projected Growth	Annual Openings
1. Advertising and Promotions Managers (O*NET-SOC Code 11-2011.00)	$78,250	6.2%	2,955
2. Business Teachers, Postsecondary (O*NET-SOC Code 25-1011.00)	$64,900	22.9%	237,478
3. Marketing Managers (O*NET-SOC Code 11-2021.00)	$104,400	14.4%	20,189
4. Sales Managers (O*NET-SOC Code 11-2022.00)	$94,910	10.2%	36,392

Job 2 shares 237,478 openings with 35 other postsecondary teaching jobs not included in this table.

Typical Sequence of College Courses

English composition, business writing, introduction to psychology, principles of microeconomics, principles of macroeconomics, calculus for business and social sciences, statistics for business and social sciences, introduction to management information systems, introduction to accounting, legal environment of business, principles of management and organization, operations management, strategic management, business finance, introduction to marketing, marketing research, buyer behavior, decision support systems for management, marketing strategy.

Typical Sequence of High School Courses

English, algebra, geometry, trigonometry, science, foreign language, computer science.

Personality Type

Enterprising. These occupations frequently involve starting up and carrying out projects and can involve leading people and making many decisions. They sometimes require risk taking and often deal with business.

Other Characteristics

GOE—Related Interest Areas/Career Clusters: 05 Education and Training; 14 Retail and Wholesale Sales and Service. **Related Work Group:** 05.03 Postsecondary and Adult Teaching and Instructing; 14.01 Managerial Work in Retail/Wholesale Sales and Service. **Most Important Skills:** Management of personnel resources, negotiation, management of financial resources, persuasion, operations analysis, service orientation. **Top Values:** Authority, creativity, compensation. **Work Environment:** More often indoors than in a vehicle; sitting.

Related Title in the Classification of Instructional Programs (CIP)

52.1401 Marketing/Marketing Management, General.

Materials Science

Focuses on the general application of mathematical and scientific principles to the analysis and evaluation of the characteristics and behavior of solids, including internal structure, chemical properties, transport and energy flow properties, thermodynamics of solids, stress and failure factors, chemical transformation states and processes, compound materials, and research on industrial applications of specific materials.

Career Snapshot

Materials scientists research the physical and chemical properties of ceramics, plastics, and other materials. They devise technologically elegant and economically valuable ways of creating and forming these materials. A bachelor's degree is a common entry route to this field, although those who want to do basic research or teach in college will need to get an advanced degree. The job outlook in this field is only fair, although workers will be needed to replace those who retire.

Related Specialties in Majors and Careers

Building materials, ceramics/glass, polymers, thin films.

Related Job Titles, Earnings, Projected Growth, and Openings

Job Title	Average Earnings	Projected Growth	Annual Openings
1. Engineering Managers (O*NET-SOC Code 11-9041.00)	$111,020	7.3%	7,404
2. Engineering Teachers, Postsecondary (O*NET-SOC Code 25-1032.00)	$79,510	22.9%	237,478
3. Materials Scientists (O*NET-SOC Code 19-2032.00)	$76,160	8.7%	1,039

Job 2 shares 237,478 openings with 35 other postsecondary teaching jobs not included in this table.

Typical Sequence of College Courses

English composition, technical writing, calculus, differential equations, introduction to computer science, general chemistry, physical chemistry, general physics, thermodynamics, numerical analysis, introduction to electrical circuits, statics, dynamics, phase equilibrium, introduction to materials science, mechanics of materials, microstructure and mechanical properties, materials characterization, kinetics of chemical and physical reactions, senior design project.

Typical Sequence of High School Courses

English, algebra, geometry, trigonometry, pre-calculus, calculus, chemistry, physics, computer science.

Personality Type

Investigative. These occupations frequently involve working with ideas and require an extensive amount of thinking. They can involve searching for facts and figuring out problems mentally.

Other Characteristics

GOE—Related Interest Areas/Career Clusters: 05 Education and Training; 15 Scientific Research, Engineering, and Mathematics. **Related Work Groups:** 05.03 Postsecondary and Adult Teaching and Instructing; 15.01 Managerial Work in Scientific Research, Engineering, and Mathematics; 15.02 Physical Sciences. **Most Important Skills:** Science, technology design, operations analysis, installation, management of financial resources, mathematics. **Top Values:** Authority, creativity, autonomy. **Work Environment:** More often indoors than in a vehicle; sitting; protective or safety equipment; hazardous equipment; extremely bright or inadequate lighting; hazardous conditions; high places; noisy.

Related Title in the Classification of Instructional Programs (CIP)

14.3101 Materials Science.

Mathematics

Focuses on the analysis of quantities, magnitudes, and forms and their relationships, using symbolic logic and language.

Career Snapshot

Mathematics is a science in its own right, in which researchers with graduate degrees continue to discover new laws. It is also a tool for understanding and organizing many aspects of our world. Many mathematics majors apply their knowledge by getting additional education or training, either in a master's program or on the job. For example, an insurance company might train them in actuarial science; a computer consulting company might train them in the latest computer language; they might get an economics, engineering, or accounting degree. Employment opportunities are very good for people who apply mathematical knowledge to other fields.

Related Specialties in Majors and Careers

Applied mathematics, mathematical statistics, mathematics education, theoretical mathematics.

Related Job Titles, Earnings, Projected Growth, and Openings

Job Title	Average Earnings	Projected Growth	Annual Openings
1. Mathematical Science Teachers, Postsecondary (O*NET-SOC Code 25-1022.00)	$58,560	22.9%	237,478
2. Mathematicians (O*NET-SOC Code 15-2021.00)	$90,870	10.2%	473
3. Natural Sciences Managers (O*NET-SOC Code 11-9121.00)	$104,040	11.4%	3,661
4. Statisticians (O*NET-SOC Code 15-2041.00)	$69,900	8.5%	3,433

Job 1 shares 237,478 openings with 35 other postsecondary teaching jobs not included in this table.

Typical Sequence of College Courses

Calculus, differential equations, introduction to computer science, programming in a language (e.g., C, Pascal, Visual Basic), statistics, linear algebra, introduction to abstract mathematics.

Typical Sequence of High School Courses
Algebra, geometry, trigonometry, pre-calculus, calculus, computer science, physics.

Personality Type
Investigative. These occupations frequently involve working with ideas and require an extensive amount of thinking. They can involve searching for facts and figuring out problems mentally.

Other Characteristics
GOE—Related Interest Areas/Career Clusters: 05 Education and Training; 15 Scientific Research, Engineering, and Mathematics. **Related Work Groups:** 05.03 Postsecondary and Adult Teaching and Instructing; 15.01 Managerial Work in Scientific Research, Engineering, and Mathematics; 15.06 Mathematics and Data Analysis. **Most Important Skills:** Mathematics, science, active learning, complex problem solving, programming, writing. **Top Values:** Creativity, authority, autonomy. **Work Environment:** Indoors; sitting.

Related Title in the Classification of Instructional Programs (CIP)
27.0101 Mathematics, General.

Mechanical Engineering

Prepares you to apply mathematical and scientific principles to the design, development, and operational evaluation of physical systems used in manufacturing and end-product systems used for specific uses.

Career Snapshot

Mechanical engineers design, test, and supervise the manufacture of various mechanical devices, including tools, motors, machines, and medical equipment. Their goal is to maximize both the technical efficiency and the economic benefits of the devices. Usually they enter their first job with a bachelor's degree. Sometimes they move from engineering to a managerial position. Despite an expected decline in manufacturing, job opportunities are expected to be good.

Related Specialties in Majors and Careers

Automotive design, heating and air conditioning, testing.

Related Job Titles, Earnings, Projected Growth, and Openings

Job Title	Average Earnings	Projected Growth	Annual Openings
1. Cost Estimators (O*NET-SOC Code 13-1051.00)	$54,920	18.5%	38,379
2. Engineering Managers (O*NET-SOC Code 11-9041.00)	$111,020	7.3%	7,404
3. Engineering Teachers, Postsecondary (O*NET-SOC Code 25-1032.00)	$79,510	22.9%	237,478
4. Mechanical Engineers (O*NET-SOC Code 17-2141.00)	$72,300	4.2%	12,394

Job 3 shares 237,478 openings with 35 other postsecondary teaching jobs not included in this table.

Typical Sequence of College Courses

English composition, technical writing, calculus, differential equations, general chemistry, introduction to computer science, general physics, introduction to engineering, statics, dynamics, thermodynamics, numerical analysis, fluid mechanics, materials science, materials engineering, mechanical engineering design, heat transfer, manufacturing processes, senior design project.

Typical Sequence of High School Courses

English, algebra, geometry, trigonometry, pre-calculus, calculus, chemistry, physics, computer science.

Personality Type

Investigative. These occupations frequently involve working with ideas and require an extensive amount of thinking. They can involve searching for facts and figuring out problems mentally.

Other Characteristics

GOE—Related Interest Areas/Career Clusters: 05 Education and Training; 06 Finance and Insurance; 15 Scientific Research, Engineering, and Mathematics. **Related Work Groups:** 05.03 Postsecondary and Adult Teaching and Instructing; 06.02 Finance/Insurance Investigation and Analysis; 15.01 Managerial Work in Scientific Research, Engineering, and Mathematics; 15.07 Research and Design Engineering. **Most Important Skills:** Science, operations analysis, mathematics, installation, management of financial resources, complex problem solving. **Top Values:** Autonomy, working conditions, responsibility. **Work Environment:** More often indoors than in a vehicle; sitting; hazardous equipment; protective or safety equipment; high places; climbing.

Related Title in the Classification of Instructional Programs (CIP)

14.1901 Mechanical Engineering.

Medicine

Prepares you for the independent professional practice of medicine or osteopathic medicine, involving the prevention, diagnosis, and treatment of illnesses, injuries, and other disorders of the human body.

Career Snapshot

Medicine requires long years of education—four years of college, four years of medical school, and three to eight years of internship and residency, depending on the specialty. Entrance to medical school is highly competitive. Although "pre-med" is often referred to as a major, it is possible to meet the entry requirements for medical school while majoring in a nonscientific subject. This may be helpful in demonstrating that you are a well-rounded person and preparing you for another career in case you are not admitted to medical school. Today, physicians are more likely than in the past to work as salaried employees of group practices or HMOs.

Related Specialties in Majors and Careers

Emergency medicine, family medicine, internal medicine, obstetrics/gynecology, pediatrics, psychiatry, radiology, surgery.

Related Job Titles, Earnings, Projected Growth, and Openings

Job Title	Average Earnings	Projected Growth	Annual Openings
1. Anesthesiologists (O*NET-SOC Code 29-1061.00)	More than $145,600	14.2%	38,027
2. Family and General Practitioners (O*NET-SOC Code 29-1062.00)	More than $145,600	14.2%	38,027
3. Internists, General (O*NET-SOC Code 29-1063.00)	More than $145,600	14.2%	38,027
4. Obstetricians and Gynecologists (O*NET-SOC Code 29-1064.00)	More than $145,600	14.2%	38,027
5. Pediatricians, General (O*NET-SOC Code 29-1065.00)	$140,690	14.2%	38,027
6. Psychiatrists (O*NET-SOC Code 29-1066.00)	More than $145,600	14.2%	38,027
7. Surgeons (O*NET-SOC Code 29-1067.00)	More than $145,600	14.2%	38,027

Jobs 1, 2, 3, 4, 5, 6, and 7 share 38,027 openings.

Typical Sequence of College Courses

English composition, introduction to psychology, college algebra, calculus, introduction to sociology, oral communication, general chemistry, general biology, introduction to computer science, organic chemistry, human anatomy and physiology, general microbiology, genetics, introduction to biochemistry, pathology, pharmacology, abnormal psychology, medical interviewing techniques, patient examination and evaluation, clinical laboratory procedures, ethics in health care, clinical experience in internal medicine, clinical experience in emergency medicine, clinical experience in obstetrics/gynecology, clinical experience in family medicine, clinical experience in psychiatry, clinical experience in surgery, clinical experience in pediatrics, clinical experience in geriatrics.

Typical Sequence of High School Courses

English, algebra, geometry, trigonometry, pre-calculus, biology, computer science, public speaking, chemistry, foreign language, physics.

Personality Type

Investigative. These occupations frequently involve working with ideas and require an extensive amount of thinking. They can involve searching for facts and figuring out problems mentally.

Other Characteristics

GOE—Related Interest Area/Career Cluster: 08 Health Science. **Related Work Group:** 08.02 Medicine and Surgery. **Most Important Skills:** Science, social perceptiveness, reading comprehension, complex problem solving, judgment and decision making, persuasion. **Top Values:** Social service, social status, recognition. **Work Environment:** Indoors; more often sitting than standing; disease or infections; close to others; radiation; protective or safety equipment; specialized protective or safety equipment.

Related Titles in the Classification of Instructional Programs (CIP)

51.1201 Medicine (MD); 51.1901 Osteopathic Medicine/Osteopathy (DO).

Metallurgical Engineering

Prepares you to apply mathematical and metallurgical principles to the design, development, and operational evaluation of metal components of structural, load-bearing, power, transmission, and moving systems; and to analysis of engineering problems.

Career Snapshot

Metallurgy is the science of refining and alloying metals, and shaping them to form structures and products. Metallurgical engineers apply principles of physics, chemistry, materials science, and economics to improve extractive and manufacturing processes. A bachelor's degree is often an entry route to this field, which may eventually lead to management. Job growth in this field is expected to be slow, but there will be some need to replace workers who retire.

Related Specialties in Majors and Careers

Chemical metallurgy, materials research, physical metallurgy, process engineering.

Related Job Titles, Earnings, Projected Growth, and Openings

Job Title	Average Earnings	Projected Growth	Annual Openings
1. Engineering Managers (O*NET-SOC Code 11-9041.00)	$111,020	7.3%	7,404
2. Engineering Teachers, Postsecondary (O*NET-SOC Code 25-1032.00)	$79,510	22.9%	237,478
3. Materials Engineers (O*NET-SOC Code 17-2131.00)	$77,170	4.0%	1,390

Job 2 shares 237,478 openings with 35 other postsecondary teaching jobs not included in this table.

Typical Sequence of College Courses

English composition, calculus, differential equations, general chemistry, introduction to computer science, general physics, organic chemistry, introduction to electrical circuits, thermodynamics, numerical analysis, materials engineering, materials thermodynamics, physics of metals, hydroprocessing of materials, metallurgical transport phenomena, metallurgical design, mechanical metallurgy, process modeling, optimization and control, senior design project.

Typical Sequence of High School Courses

English, algebra, geometry, trigonometry, pre-calculus, calculus, chemistry, physics, computer science.

Personality Type

Investigative. These occupations frequently involve working with ideas and require an extensive amount of thinking. They can involve searching for facts and figuring out problems mentally.

Other Characteristics

GOE—Related Interest Areas/Career Clusters: 05 Education and Training; 15 Scientific Research, Engineering, and Mathematics. **Related Work Groups:** 05.03 Postsecondary and Adult Teaching and Instructing; 15.01 Managerial Work in Scientific Research, Engineering, and Mathematics; 15.07 Research and Design Engineering. **Most Important Skills:** Science, technology design, operations analysis, management of financial resources, installation, mathematics. **Top Values:** Authority, creativity, autonomy. **Work Environment:** Indoors; sitting; protective or safety equipment; hazardous equipment; extremely bright or inadequate lighting; noisy; hazardous conditions; high places.

Related Title in the Classification of Instructional Programs (CIP)

14.2001 Metallurgical Engineering.

Meteorology

Focuses on the scientific study of the composition and behavior of the atmospheric envelopes surrounding the earth, the effect of the earth's atmosphere on terrestrial weather, and related problems of environment and climate.

Career Snapshot

A bachelor's degree in meteorology is the minimum educational requirement to work as an atmospheric scientist. A master's degree is necessary for some positions, and a Ph.D. degree is required for most basic research positions. About 37 percent of meteorologists are employed by the federal government, mostly in the National Weather Service. Job prospects are generally favorable, but opportunities as weather broadcasters are rare and highly competitive.

Related Specialties in Majors and Careers

Air quality, atmospheric science, business applications, climatology, environmental science, forecasting.

Related Job Titles, Earnings, Projected Growth, and Openings

Job Title	Average Earnings	Projected Growth	Annual Openings
1. Atmospheric, Earth, Marine, and Space Sciences Teachers, Postsecondary (O*NET-SOC Code 25-1051.00)	$73,280	22.9%	237,478
2. Atmospheric and Space Scientists (O*NET-SOC Code 19-2021.00)	$78,390	10.6%	735
3. Natural Sciences Managers (O*NET-SOC Code 11-9121.00)	$104,040	11.4%	3,661

Job 1 shares 237,478 openings with 35 other postsecondary teaching jobs not included in this table.

Typical Sequence of College Courses

English composition, introduction to computer science, scientific programming, calculus, differential equations, general chemistry, mechanics, thermal physics, introduction to meteorology, remote sensing, thermodynamics of the atmosphere, synoptic meteorology, weather forecasting.

Typical Sequence of High School Courses

English, algebra, geometry, trigonometry, chemistry, physics, pre-calculus, computer science, calculus.

Personality Type

Investigative. These occupations frequently involve working with ideas and require an extensive amount of thinking. They can involve searching for facts and figuring out problems mentally.

Other Characteristics

GOE—Related Interest Areas/Career Clusters: 05 Education and Training; 15 Scientific Research, Engineering, and Mathematics. **Related Work Groups:** 05.03 Postsecondary and Adult Teaching and Instructing; 15.01 Managerial Work in Scientific Research, Engineering, and Mathematics; 15.02 Physical Sciences. **Most Important Skills:** Science, mathematics, management of personnel resources, active learning, complex problem solving, reading comprehension. **Top Values:** Authority, creativity, responsibility. **Work Environment:** More often indoors than in a vehicle; sitting; hazardous conditions; noisy; climbing.

Related Title in the Classification of Instructional Programs (CIP)

40.0401 Atmospheric Sciences and Meteorology, General.

Microbiology/Bacteriology

Focuses on the scientific study of bacteria and other microorganisms, including those that are significant factors in causing or facilitating human disease.

Career Snapshot

A bachelor's degree in microbiology or bacteriology may be an entry route to clinical laboratory work or to nonresearch work in industry or government. It also is good preparation for medical school. For a position in research or college teaching, a graduate degree is expected.

Related Specialties in Majors and Careers

Algae, bacteria, fungi (mycology), immunology, virology.

Related Job Titles, Earnings, Projected Growth, and Openings

Job Title	Average Earnings	Projected Growth	Annual Openings
1. Medical Scientists, Except Epidemiologists (O*NET-SOC Code 19-1042.00)	$64,200	20.2%	10,596
2. Natural Sciences Managers (O*NET-SOC Code 11-9121.00)	$104,040	11.4%	3,661

Typical Sequence of College Courses

English composition, calculus, introduction to computer science, general chemistry, general biology, organic chemistry, general physics, general microbiology, genetics, introduction to biochemistry, immunology, bacterial physiology, bacterial genetics.

Typical Sequence of High School Courses

English, biology, algebra, geometry, trigonometry, pre-calculus, chemistry, physics, computer science, calculus.

Personality Type

Investigative. These occupations frequently involve working with ideas and require an extensive amount of thinking. They can involve searching for facts and figuring out problems mentally.

Other Characteristics

GOE—Related Interest Area/Career Cluster: 15 Scientific Research, Engineering, and Mathematics. **Related Work Groups:** 15.01 Managerial Work in Scientific Research, Engineering, and Mathematics; 15.03 Life Sciences. **Most Important Skills:** Science, reading comprehension, writing, management of financial resources, complex problem solving, judgment and decision making. **Top Values:** Social status, creativity, responsibility. **Work Environment:** Indoors; sitting; disease or infections; radiation; specialized protective or safety equipment; hazardous conditions.

Related Title in the Classification of Instructional Programs (CIP)

26.0503 Medical Microbiology and Bacteriology.

Modern Foreign Language

Focuses on a specific modern language, its literature, and its related dialects, and may include applications in business, science/technology, and other settings.

Career Snapshot

The most popular foreign language majors—Chinese, French, German, Japanese, Russian, and Spanish—are described elsewhere in this book. But many colleges offer majors in other modern languages such as Arabic, Hebrew, Hindi, Portuguese, Swahili, Swedish, or Turkish, to name just a few. As global trade continues to increase, a degree in a foreign language can lead to many job opportunities in international business, travel, and law. Many employers look for graduates with an understanding of a second language and culture. Translation or college teaching are options for those with a graduate degree in a foreign language.

Related Specialties in Majors and Careers

History and culture, language education, literature, regional studies, translation.

Related Job Titles, Earnings, Projected Growth, and Openings

Job Title	Average Earnings	Projected Growth	Annual Openings
1. Foreign Language and Literature Teachers, Post-secondary (O*NET-SOC Code 25-1124.00)	$53,610	22.9%	237,478
2. Interpreters and Translators (O*NET-SOC Code 27-3091.00)	$37,490	23.6%	6,630

Job 1 shares 237,478 openings with 35 other postsecondary teaching jobs not included in this table.

Typical Sequence of College Courses

Foreign language, conversation, composition, linguistics, foreign literature and culture, grammar, phonetics, history of a world region, study abroad.

Typical Sequence of High School Courses

English, public speaking, foreign language, history, social science.

Personality Type

Artistic. These occupations frequently involve working with forms, designs, and patterns. They often require self-expression, and the work can be done without following a clear set of rules.

Other Characteristics

GOE—Related Interest Areas/Career Clusters: 03 Arts and Communication; 05 Education and Training. **Related Work Groups:** 03.03 News, Broadcasting, and Public Relations; 05.03 Postsecondary and Adult Teaching and Instructing. **Most Important Skills:** Social perceptiveness, speaking, writing, active listening, reading comprehension, learning strategies. **Top Values:** Social service, ability utilization, achievement. **Work Environment:** Indoors; sitting; close to others.

Related Titles in the Classification of Instructional Programs (CIP)

16.1101 Arabic Language and Literature; 16.0301 Chinese Language and Literature; 16.0399 East Asian Languages, Literatures, and Linguistics, Other; 16.0101 Foreign Languages and Literatures, General; 16.9999 Foreign Languages, Literatures, and Linguistics, Other; 16.0901 French Language and Literature; 16.0501 German Language and Literature; 16.0599 Germanic Languages, Literatures, and Linguistics, Other; 16.1102 Hebrew Language and Literature; 16.0902 Italian Language and Literature; 16.0302 Japanese Language and Literature; 16.0103 Language Interpretation and Translation; 16.0102 Linguistics; 16.1199 Middle/Near Eastern and Semitic Languages, Literatures, and Linguistics, Other; 16.0904 Portuguese Language and Literature; 16.0999 Romance Languages, Literatures, and Linguistics, Other; 16.0402 Russian Language and Literature; 16.0502 Scandinavian Languages, Literatures, and Linguistics; 16.0400 Slavic Languages, Literatures, and Linguistics, General; 16.0499 Slavic, Baltic, and Albanian Languages, Literatures, and Linguistics, Other; 16.0905 Spanish Language and Literature.

Music

Prepares you to master a musical instrument and play it as a solo and/or ensemble performer.

Career Snapshot

Music majors study theory, composition, and performance. They learn how the success of a work of music depends on certain principles of what appeals to the ear, on the skill of the arranger, and on the interpretation of the performers. Relatively few graduates are able to support themselves as composers, arrangers, or performers, but many teach in schools or universities or give private instruction.

Related Specialties in Majors and Careers

Composition, music education, music theory, performance.

Related Job Titles, Earnings, Projected Growth, and Openings

Job Title	Average Earnings	Projected Growth	Annual Openings
1. Art, Drama, and Music Teachers, Postsecondary (O*NET-SOC Code 25-1121.00)	$55,190	22.9%	237,478
2. Music Composers and Arrangers (O*NET-SOC Code 27-2041.04)	$40,150	12.9%	8,597
3. Music Directors (O*NET-SOC Code 27-2041.01)	$40,150	12.9%	8,597
4. Musicians, Instrumental (O*NET-SOC Code 27-2042.02)	No data available	10.1%	23,985
5. Singers (O*NET-SOC Code 27-2042.01)	No data available	10.1%	23,985

Job 1 shares 237,478 openings with 35 other postsecondary teaching jobs not included in this table. Jobs 2 and 3 share 8,597 openings. Jobs 4 and 5 share 23,985 openings.

Typical Sequence of College Courses

English composition, foreign language, piano proficiency, introduction to music theory, harmony and counterpoint, conducting, music history and literature, recital attendance, performance technique with instrument/voice, recital performance.

Typical Sequence of High School Courses

Music, foreign language, history, English.

Personality Type

Artistic. These occupations frequently involve working with forms, designs, and patterns. They often require self-expression, and the work can be done without following a clear set of rules.

Other Characteristics

GOE—Related Interest Areas/Career Clusters: 03 Arts and Communication; 05 Education and Training. **Related Work Groups:** 03.07 Music; 05.03 Postsecondary and Adult Teaching and Instructing. **Most Important Skills:** Coordination, active listening, social perceptiveness, monitoring, active learning, time management. **Top Values:** Ability utilization, creativity, achievement. **Work Environment:** Indoors; sitting; close to others; repetitive motions.

Related Title in the Classification of Instructional Programs (CIP)

50.0903 Music Performance, General.

Nursing (RN Training)

Prepares you in the knowledge, techniques, and procedures needed for promoting health and providing care for sick, disabled, infirm, or other individuals or groups.

Career Snapshot

The study of nursing includes a combination of classroom and clinical work. Students learn what science tells us about the origins and treatment of disease, how to care effectively for the physical and emotional needs of sick and injured people, and how to teach people to maintain health. Nurses work in a variety of health-care settings, including patients' homes, schools and companies, and desk jobs for HMOs. The employment outlook is good.

Related Specialties in Majors and Careers

Community health nursing, mental health nursing, nursing administration, pediatric nursing.

Related Job Titles, Earnings, Projected Growth, and Openings

Job Title	Average Earnings	Projected Growth	Annual Openings
1. Nursing Instructors and Teachers, Postsecondary (O*NET-SOC Code 25-1072.00)	$57,500	22.9%	237,478
2. Registered Nurses (O*NET-SOC Code 29-1111.00)	$60,010	23.5%	233,499

Job 1 shares 237,478 openings with 35 other postsecondary teaching jobs not included in this table.

Typical Sequence of College Courses

English composition, introduction to psychology, college algebra, introduction to sociology, oral communication, general chemistry, general biology, human anatomy and physiology, general microbiology, ethics in health care, patient examination and evaluation, pharmacology, reproductive health nursing, pediatric nursing, adult health nursing, mental health nursing, nursing leadership and management, community health nursing, clinical nursing experience.

Typical Sequence of High School Courses

English, algebra, geometry, trigonometry, biology, computer science, public speaking, chemistry, foreign language.

Personality Type

Social. These occupations frequently involve working with, communicating with, and teaching people, and often involve helping or providing service to others.

Other Characteristics

GOE—Related Interest Areas/Career Clusters: 05 Education and Training; 08 Health Science. **Related Work Groups:** 05.03 Postsecondary and Adult Teaching and Instructing; 08.02 Medicine and Surgery. **Most Important Skills:** Social perceptiveness, service orientation, science, time management, monitoring, reading comprehension. **Top Values:** Social service, coworkers, ability utilization. **Work Environment:** Indoors; disease or infections; protective or safety equipment; radiation; close to others; cramped work space, awkward positions; walking and running; contaminants.

Related Title in the Classification of Instructional Programs (CIP)

51.1601 Nursing/Registered Nurse (RN, ASN, BSN, MSN).

Occupational Health and Industrial Hygiene

Prepares you to monitor and evaluate health and related safety standards in industrial, commercial, and government workplaces and facilities.

Career Snapshot

Graduates with a bachelor's degree in occupational health and industrial hygiene are trained to protect workers from a variety of threats to their health and safety: chemical and biological contaminants, fire, noise, cramped bodily positions, dangerous machinery, and radiation. The major covers the nature of the risks from these and other hazards, the laws that exist to ban such hazards, how to recognize the presence and assess the risks of workplace hazards, and how to take steps to eliminate them.

Related Specialties in Majors and Careers

Hazardous materials, occupational health, safety.

Related Job Titles, Earnings, Projected Growth, and Openings

Job Title	Average Earnings	Projected Growth	Annual Openings
1. Health Specialties Teachers, Postsecondary (O*NET-SOC Code 25-1071.00)	$80,700	22.9%	237,478
2. Occupational Health and Safety Specialists (O*NET-SOC Code 29-9011.00)	$60,140	8.1%	3,440
3. Occupational Health and Safety Technicians (O*NET-SOC Code 29-9012.00)	$44,020	14.6%	886

Job 1 shares 237,478 openings with 35 other postsecondary teaching jobs not included in this table.

Typical Sequence of College Courses

English composition, oral communication, calculus, technical writing, general chemistry, introduction to computer science, general physics, general biology, introduction to environmental health, introduction to occupational health and safety, biostatistics, organic chemistry, pollution science and treatment, statistics, microbial hazards, chemistry of hazardous materials, safety organization and management, industrial fire prevention, occupational safety and health law, environmental regulations.

Typical Sequence of High School Courses

English, algebra, geometry, trigonometry, pre-calculus, chemistry, physics, computer science, public speaking.

Personality Type

Investigative. These occupations frequently involve working with ideas and require an extensive amount of thinking. They can involve searching for facts and figuring out problems mentally.

Other Characteristics

GOE—Related Interest Areas/Career Clusters: 05 Education and Training; 07 Government and Public Administration. **Related Work Groups:** 05.03 Postsecondary and Adult Teaching and Instructing; 07.03 Regulations Enforcement. **Most Important Skills:** Science, writing, reading comprehension, instructing, complex problem solving, speaking. **Top Values:** Authority, social service, creativity. **Work Environment:** Indoors; sitting; disease or infections; radiation.

Related Title in the Classification of Instructional Programs (CIP)

51.2206 Occupational Health and Industrial Hygiene.

Occupational Therapy

Prepares you to assist patients limited by physical, cognitive, psychosocial, mental, developmental, and learning disabilities, as well as adverse environmental conditions, to maximize their independence and maintain optimum health through a planned mix of acquired skills, performance motivation, environmental adaptations, assistive technologies, and physical agents.

Career Snapshot

Occupational therapists help people cope with disabilities and lead more productive and enjoyable lives. Some therapists enter the field with a bachelor's degree in occupational therapy; others get a master's after a bachelor's in another field. They learn about the nature of various kinds of disabilities—developmental, emotional, and so on—and how to help people overcome them or compensate for them in their daily lives. The long-range outlook for jobs is considered good, although it may be affected by cutbacks in Medicare coverage of therapies.

Related Specialties in Majors and Careers

Geriatric OT, pediatric OT, prosthetics.

Related Job Titles, Earnings, Projected Growth, and Openings

Job Title	Average Earnings	Projected Growth	Annual Openings
1. Health Specialties Teachers, Postsecondary (O*NET-SOC Code 25-1071.00)	$80,700	22.9%	237,478
2. Occupational Therapists (O*NET-SOC Code 29-1122.00)	$63,790	23.1%	8,338

Job 1 shares 237,478 openings with 35 other postsecondary teaching jobs not included in this table.

Typical Sequence of College Courses

English composition, statistics for business and social sciences, general chemistry, general biology, human anatomy and physiology, introduction to psychology, human growth and development, introduction to computer science, abnormal psychology, fundamentals of medical science, neuroscience for therapy, occupational therapy for developmental problems, occupational therapy for physiological diagnoses, occupational therapy for psychosocial diagnoses, administration of occupational therapy services, research methods in occupational therapy, methods of facilitating therapeutic adaptation, occupational therapy fieldwork experience, seminar (reporting on research).

Typical Sequence of High School Courses

English, algebra, geometry, trigonometry, chemistry, physics, biology, foreign language, computer science.

Personality Type

Investigative. These occupations frequently involve working with ideas and require an extensive amount of thinking. They can involve searching for facts and figuring out problems mentally.

Other Characteristics

GOE—Related Interest Areas/Career Clusters: 05 Education and Training; 08 Health Science. **Related Work Groups:** 05.03 Postsecondary and Adult Teaching and Instructing; 08.07 Medical Therapy. **Most Important Skills:** Science, writing, reading comprehension, instructing, learning strategies, social perceptiveness. **Top Values:** Social service, authority, achievement. **Work Environment:** Indoors; sitting; disease or infections; close to others.

Related Title in the Classification of Instructional Programs (CIP)

51.2306 Occupational Therapy/Therapist.

Oceanography

Focuses on the scientific study of the chemical components, mechanisms, structure, and movement of ocean waters and their interaction with terrestrial and atmospheric phenomena.

Career Snapshot

Oceans cover more of the earth than dry land, yet many of the physical and biological characteristics of the oceans are poorly understood. Oceanographers use techniques of physical sciences to study the properties of ocean waters and how these affect coastal areas, climate, and weather. Those who specialize in ocean life work to improve the fishing industry, to protect the environment, and to understand the relationship between oceanic and terrestrial life forms. It is possible to get started in this field with a bachelor's degree; for advancement and many research jobs, however, a master's degree or Ph.D. is helpful or required.

Related Specialties in Majors and Careers

Ocean biology, ocean chemistry, ocean geology, ocean meteorology.

Related Job Titles, Earnings, Projected Growth, and Openings

Job Title	Average Earnings	Projected Growth	Annual Openings
1. Atmospheric, Earth, Marine, and Space Sciences Teachers, Postsecondary (O*NET-SOC Code 25-1051.00)	$73,280	22.9%	237,478
2. Geoscientists, Except Hydrologists and Geographers (O*NET-SOC Code 19-2042.00)	$75,800	21.9%	2,471
3. Hydrologists (O*NET-SOC Code 19-2043.00)	$68,140	24.3%	687
4. Natural Sciences Managers (O*NET-SOC Code 11-9121.00)	$104,040	11.4%	3,661

Job 1 shares 237,478 openings with 35 other postsecondary teaching jobs not included in this table.

Typical Sequence of College Courses

English composition, introduction to computer science, calculus, differential equations, general chemistry, general physics, agricultural power and machines, physical oceanography, chemical oceanography, geological oceanography, biological oceanography, seminar (reporting on research).

Typical Sequence of High School Courses

English, algebra, geometry, trigonometry, chemistry, pre-calculus, physics, computer science, biology, calculus.

Personality Type

Investigative. These occupations frequently involve working with ideas and require an extensive amount of thinking. They can involve searching for facts and figuring out problems mentally.

Other Characteristics

GOE—Related Interest Areas/Career Clusters: 05 Education and Training; 15 Scientific Research, Engineering, and Mathematics. **Related Work Groups:** 05.03 Postsecondary and Adult Teaching and Instructing; 15.01 Managerial Work in Scientific Research, Engineering, and Mathematics; 15.02 Physical Sciences. **Most Important Skills:** Science, mathematics, management of financial resources, management of personnel resources, active learning, writing. **Top Values:** Creativity, responsibility, autonomy. **Work Environment:** More often indoors than in a vehicle; sitting; hazardous conditions; hazardous equipment; radiation; extremely bright or inadequate lighting; specialized protective or safety equipment.

Related Title in the Classification of Instructional Programs (CIP)

40.0607 Oceanography, Chemical and Physical.

Operations Management

Prepares you to manage and direct the physical and/or technical functions of a firm or organization, particularly those relating to development, production, and manufacturing.

Career Snapshot

Whereas other managers focus on segments of the production and distribution process (such as marketing or finance), operations managers look at the entire process and devise ways to streamline it. They use quantitative methods and computer technology to study the inputs of materials, energy, and labor into production, the processes that create products, and the paths that products take to reach customers. Their skills are greatly valued in today's competitive global business environment.

Related Specialties in Majors and Careers

Logistics, materials management, process analysis, production supervision, quality assurance.

Related Job Titles, Earnings, Projected Growth, and Openings

Job Title	Average Earnings	Projected Growth	Annual Openings
1. Business Teachers, Postsecondary (O*NET-SOC Code 25-1011.00)	$64,900	22.9%	237,478
2. Computer and Information Systems Managers (O*NET-SOC Code 11-3021.00)	$108,070	16.4%	30,887
3. Construction Managers (O*NET-SOC Code 11-9021.00)	$76,230	15.7%	44,158
4. First-Line Supervisors/Managers of Mechanics, Installers, and Repairers (O*NET-SOC Code 49-1011.00)	$55,380	7.3%	24,361
5. First-Line Supervisors/Managers of Production and Operating Workers (O*NET-SOC Code 51-1011.00)	$48,670	–4.8%	46,144
6. Industrial Production Managers (O*NET-SOC Code 11-3051.00)	$80,560	–5.9%	14,889
7. Logisticians (O*NET-SOC Code 13-1081.00)	$64,250	17.3%	9,671

Job 1 shares 237,478 openings with 35 other postsecondary teaching jobs not included in this table.

Typical Sequence of College Courses

English composition, business writing, introduction to psychology, principles of microeconomics, principles of macroeconomics, calculus for business and social sciences, statistics for business and social sciences, introduction to management information systems, introduction to accounting, legal environment of business, principles of management and organization, operations management, business finance, introduction to marketing, introduction to logistics, organizational behavior, human resource management, inventory management, supply chain management.

Typical Sequence of High School Courses

English, algebra, geometry, trigonometry, science, pre-calculus, computer science.

Personality Type

Enterprising. These occupations frequently involve starting up and carrying out projects and can involve leading people and making many decisions. They sometimes require risk taking and often deal with business.

Other Characteristics

GOE—Related Interest Areas/Career Clusters: 02 Architecture and Construction; 04 Business and Administration; 05 Education and Training; 11 Information Technology; 13 Manufacturing. **Related Work Groups:** 02.01 Managerial Work in Architecture and Construction; 04.05 Accounting, Auditing, and Analytical Support; 05.03 Postsecondary and Adult Teaching and Instructing; 11.01 Managerial Work in Information Technology; 13.01 Managerial Work in Manufacturing. **Most Important Skills:** Management of personnel resources, management of material resources, systems analysis, installation, operations analysis, management of financial resources. **Top Values:** Authority, responsibility, autonomy. **Work Environment:** More often indoors than in a vehicle; protective or safety equipment; hazardous equipment; noisy; contaminants; high places; walking and running.

Related Title in the Classification of Instructional Programs (CIP)

52.0205 Operations Management and Supervision.

Operations Research

Prepares you to develop and apply complex mathematical or simulation models to solve problems involving operational systems, where the system concerned is subject to human intervention.

Career Snapshot

Operations research (OR) teaches you a mix of skills—modeling, statistics, programming, and general analytical skills—that you can use in a business or other organization to improve its efficiency. You may work in management or as a professional who advises managers. You may study OR at the undergraduate level, perhaps as a specialization within an industrial engineering or statistics major, or you may enter a graduate program if you have a good background in math.

Related Specialties in Majors and Careers

Data analysis, simulation, statistical modeling.

Related Job Titles, Earnings, Projected Growth, and Openings

Job Title	Average Earnings	Projected Growth	Annual Openings
1. Natural Sciences Managers (O*NET-SOC Code 11-9121.00)	$104,040	11.4%	3,661
2. Operations Research Analysts (O*NET-SOC Code 15-2031.00)	$66,950	10.6%	5,727

Typical Sequence of College Courses

Technical writing, calculus, differential equations, general chemistry, introduction to computer science, general physics, probability theory and applications, methods of optimization, linear programming, stochastic processes, simulation, design project.

Typical Sequence of High School Courses

English, algebra, geometry, trigonometry, pre-calculus, calculus, chemistry, physics, computer science.

Personality Type

Investigative. These occupations frequently involve working with ideas and require an extensive amount of thinking. They can involve searching for facts and figuring out problems mentally.

Other Characteristics

GOE—Related Interest Areas/Career Clusters: 04 Business and Administration; 15 Scientific Research, Engineering, and Mathematics. **Related Work Groups:** 04.05 Accounting, Auditing, and Analytical Support; 15.01 Managerial Work in Scientific Research, Engineering, and Mathematics. **Most Important Skills:** Science, programming, mathematics, systems analysis, operations analysis, systems evaluation. **Top Values:** Creativity, autonomy, responsibility. **Work Environment:** Indoors; sitting.

Related Title in the Classification of Instructional Programs (CIP)

14.3701 Operations Research.

Optometry

Prepares you for the independent professional practice of optometry and focuses on the principles and techniques for examining, diagnosing, and treating conditions of the visual system.

Career Snapshot

Optometrists measure patients' visual ability and prescribe visual aids such as glasses and contact lenses. They may evaluate patients' suitability for laser surgery and/or provide post-operative care, but they do not perform surgery. The usual educational preparation is at least three years of college, followed by a four-year program of optometry school. The job outlook is good because the aging population will need increased attention to vision. The best opportunities probably will be at retail vision centers and outpatient clinics.

Related Specialties in Majors and Careers

Contact lenses, low vision.

Related Job Title, Earnings, Projected Growth, and Openings

Job Title	Average Earnings	Projected Growth	Annual Openings
1. Optometrists (O*NET-SOC Code 29-1041.00)	$93,800	11.3%	1,789

Typical Sequence of College Courses

English composition, introduction to psychology, calculus, introduction to sociology, oral communication, general chemistry, general biology, organic chemistry, general microbiology, introduction to biochemistry, microbiology for optometry, geometric, physical and visual optics, ocular health assessment, neuroanatomy, ocular anatomy and physiology, pathology, theory and methods of refraction, general and ocular pharmacology, optical and motor aspects of vision, ophthalmic optics, environmental and occupational vision, assessment of oculomotor system, strabismus and vision therapy, visual information processing and perception, ocular disease, contact lenses, pediatric and developmental vision, ethics in health care, professional practice management, low vision and geriatric vision, clinical experience in optometry.

Typical Sequence of High School Courses

English, algebra, geometry, trigonometry, pre-calculus, biology, computer science, public speaking, chemistry, calculus, physics, foreign language.

Personality Type

Investigative. These occupations frequently involve working with ideas and require an extensive amount of thinking. They can involve searching for facts and figuring out problems mentally.

Other Characteristics

GOE—Related Interest Area/Career Cluster: 08 Health Science. **Related Work Group:** 08.04 Health Specialties. **Most Important Skills:** Science, judgment and decision making, management of personnel resources, active listening, reading comprehension, management of material resources. **Top Values:** Social service, responsibility, social status. **Work Environment:** Indoors; sitting; disease or infections; close to others; using hands on objects, tools, or controls; repetitive motions.

Related Title in the Classification of Instructional Programs (CIP)

51.1701 Optometry (OD).

Orthotics/Prosthetics

Prepares you to work in consultation with physicians and other therapists to design and fit orthoses for patients with disabling conditions of the limbs and/or spine, and prostheses for patients who have partial or total absence of a limb or significant superficial deformity.

Career Snapshot

Orthotics is the design and fitting of supportive or corrective braces for patients with musculoskeletal deformity or injury. Prosthetics is the fabrication and fitting of artificial limbs. People enter this field by getting a bachelor's degree in one or both specializations, or enrolling in a certification program after a bachelor's in another field (perhaps occupational therapy). The job outlook is expected to be good.

Related Specialties in Majors and Careers

Fabrication, fitting, orthotics, prosthetics.

Related Job Titles, Earnings, Projected Growth, and Openings

Job Title	Average Earnings	Projected Growth	Annual Openings
1. Health Specialties Teachers, Postsecondary (O*NET-SOC Code 25-1071.00)	$80,700	22.9%	237,478
2. Medical Appliance Technicians (O*NET-SOC Code 51-9082.00)	$32,640	9.4%	895
3. Orthotists and Prosthetists (O*NET-SOC Code 29-2091.00)	$60,520	11.8%	295

Job 1 shares 237,478 openings with 35 other postsecondary teaching jobs not included in this table.

Typical Sequence of College Courses

English composition, general chemistry, introduction to psychology, general biology, general physics, statistics for business and social sciences, human anatomy and physiology, human growth and development, introduction to computer science, abnormal psychology, kinesiology, fundamentals of medical science, function of the locomotor system, neuroanatomy, lower extremity orthotics, upper extremity orthotics, lower extremity prosthetics, upper extremity prosthetics, psychological aspects of rehabilitation, immediate post-operative and early fitting, spinal orthotics.

Typical Sequence of High School Courses

English, algebra, geometry, trigonometry, chemistry, physics, biology, foreign language, computer science.

Personality Type

Investigative. These occupations frequently involve working with ideas and require an extensive amount of thinking. They can involve searching for facts and figuring out problems mentally.

Other Characteristics

GOE—Related Interest Areas/Career Clusters: 05 Education and Training; 08 Health Science; 13 Manufacturing. **Related Work Groups:** 05.03 Postsecondary and Adult Teaching and Instructing; 08.06 Medical Technology; 13.06 Production Precision Work. **Most Important Skills:** Science, instructing, writing, reading comprehension, learning strategies, complex problem solving. **Top Values:** Authority, social service, creativity. **Work Environment:** Indoors; sitting; disease or infections.

Related Title in the Classification of Instructional Programs (CIP)

51.2307 Orthotist/Prosthetist.

Petroleum Engineering

Prepares you to apply mathematical and scientific principles to the design, development and operational evaluation of systems for locating, extracting, processing, and refining crude petroleum and natural gas.

Career Snapshot

Petroleum engineers devise technically effective and economically justifiable ways of locating, extracting, transporting, refining, and storing petroleum and natural gas. They apply basic principles of science to problems related to oil wells deep in the ground or high-towering refineries. Usually they begin with a bachelor's degree. Management is sometimes an option later in their careers. The job outlook in the United States depends on the price of oil. The overall trend seems to be upward because of rapidly rising global demand for petroleum.

Related Specialties in Majors and Careers

Distribution, drilling/extraction, exploration, refining.

Related Job Titles, Earnings, Projected Growth, and Openings

Job Title	Average Earnings	Projected Growth	Annual Openings
1. Engineering Managers (O*NET-SOC Code 11-9041.00)	$111,020	7.3%	7,404
2. Engineering Teachers, Postsecondary (O*NET-SOC Code 25-1032.00)	$79,510	22.9%	237,478
3. Petroleum Engineers (O*NET-SOC Code 17-2171.00)	$103,960	5.2%	1,016

Job 2 shares 237,478 openings with 35 other postsecondary teaching jobs not included in this table.

Typical Sequence of College Courses

English composition, introduction to computer science, technical writing, calculus, differential equations, general chemistry, general physics, physical geology, introduction to engineering, statics, dynamics, fluid mechanics, thermodynamics, numerical analysis, materials engineering, engineering economics, heat transfer, sedimentary rocks and processes, petroleum geology, petroleum development, petroleum production methods, petroleum property management, formation evaluation, natural gas engineering, reservoir fluids, reservoir engineering, well testing and analysis, drilling engineering, reservoir stimulation, senior design project.

Typical Sequence of High School Courses

English, algebra, geometry, trigonometry, pre-calculus, calculus, chemistry, physics, computer science.

Personality Type

Investigative. These occupations frequently involve working with ideas and require an extensive amount of thinking. They can involve searching for facts and figuring out problems mentally.

Other Characteristics

GOE—Related Interest Areas/Career Clusters: 01 Agriculture and Natural Resources; 05 Education and Training; 15 Scientific Research, Engineering, and Mathematics. **Related Work Groups:** 01.02 Resource Science/Engineering for Plants, Animals, and the Environment; 05.03 Postsecondary and Adult Teaching and Instructing; 15.01 Managerial Work in Scientific Research, Engineering, and Mathematics. **Most Important Skills:** Science, technology design, operations analysis, management of financial resources, mathematics, installation. **Top Values:** Authority, creativity, autonomy. **Work Environment:** More often indoors than in a vehicle; sitting; protective or safety equipment; hazardous equipment; extremely bright or inadequate lighting; high places; hazardous conditions.

Related Title in the Classification of Instructional Programs (CIP)

14.2501 Petroleum Engineering.

Pharmacy

Prepares you for the independent or employed practice of preparing and dispensing drugs and medications in consultation with prescribing physicians and other health-care professionals, and for managing pharmacy practices and counseling patients.

Career Snapshot

Pharmacists dispense medications as prescribed by physicians and other health practitioners and give advice to patients about how to use medications. Pharmacists must be knowledgeable about the chemical and physical properties of drugs, how they behave in the body, and how they may interact with other drugs and substances. Schools of pharmacy take about four years to complete and usually require at least one or two years of prior college work. Some pharmacists go on to additional graduate training to prepare for research, administration, or college teaching.

Related Specialties in Majors and Careers

Pharmaceutical chemistry, pharmacology, pharmacy administration.

Related Job Titles, Earnings, Projected Growth, and Openings

Job Title	Average Earnings	Projected Growth	Annual Openings
1. Health Specialties Teachers, Postsecondary (O*NET-SOC Code 25-1071.00)	$80,700	22.9%	237,478
2. Pharmacists (O*NET-SOC Code 29-1051.00)	$100,480	21.7%	16,358

Job 1 shares 237,478 openings with 35 other postsecondary teaching jobs not included in this table.

Typical Sequence of College Courses

English composition, introduction to psychology, calculus, introduction to sociology, oral communication, general chemistry, general biology, organic chemistry, introduction to biochemistry, human anatomy and physiology, pharmaceutical calculations, pharmacology, pharmaceutics, microbiology and immunology, patient assessment and education, medicinal chemistry, therapeutics, pharmacy law and ethics, pharmacokinetics, electrical inspection.

Typical Sequence of High School Courses

English, algebra, geometry, trigonometry, biology, computer science, public speaking, chemistry, calculus, physics, foreign language.

Personality Type

Investigative. These occupations frequently involve working with ideas and require an extensive amount of thinking. They can involve searching for facts and figuring out problems mentally.

Other Characteristics

GOE—Related Interest Areas/Career Clusters: 05 Education and Training; 08 Health Science. **Related Work Groups:** 05.03 Postsecondary and Adult Teaching and Instructing; 08.02 Medicine and Surgery. **Most Important Skills:** Science, reading comprehension, instructing, critical thinking, speaking, active listening. **Top Values:** Authority, social service, social status. **Work Environment:** Indoors; standing; disease or infections; close to others; repetitive motions.

Related Title in the Classification of Instructional Programs (CIP)

51.2001 Pharmacy (PharmD [USA], PharmD or BS/BPharm [Canada]).

Philosophy

Focuses on ideas and their logical structures, including arguments and investigations about abstract and real phenomena.

Career Snapshot

Philosophy is concerned with the most basic questions about the human experience, such as what reality is, what the ultimate values are, and how we know what we know. Philosophy majors are trained to think independently and critically, and to write clearly and persuasively. They may go to work in a number of business careers where these skills are appreciated and help philosophy graduates advance to positions of leadership. Some find that a philosophy major combines well with further training in law, computer science, or religious studies. Those with a graduate degree in philosophy may teach at the college level.

Related Specialties in Majors and Careers

Esthetics, ethics, history of philosophy, logic.

Related Job Titles, Earnings, Projected Growth, and Openings

Job Title	Average Earnings	Projected Growth	Annual Openings
1. Clergy (O*NET-SOC Code 21-2011.00)	$40,460	18.9%	35,092
2. Directors, Religious Activities and Education (O*NET-SOC Code 21-2021.00)	$35,370	19.7%	11,463
3. Philosophy and Religion Teachers, Postsecondary (O*NET-SOC Code 25-1126.00)	$56,380	22.9%	237,478
4. Religious Workers, All Other (O*NET-SOC Code 21-2099.99)	$26,660	19.7%	7,924

Job 3 shares 237,478 openings with 35 other postsecondary teaching jobs not included in this table.

Typical Sequence of College Courses

English composition, foreign language, introduction to logic, major thinkers and issues in philosophy, ethical/moral theory, classical philosophy, modern philosophy, contemporary philosophy, esthetics.

Typical Sequence of High School Courses
Algebra, English, foreign language, social science, history, geometry.

Personality Type
Social. These occupations frequently involve working with, communicating with, and teaching people and often involve helping or providing service to others.

Other Characteristics
GOE—Related Interest Areas/Career Clusters: 05 Education and Training; 10 Human Service. **Related Work Groups:** 05.03 Postsecondary and Adult Teaching and Instructing; 10.02 Religious Work. **Most Important Skills:** Management of personnel resources, management of financial resources, negotiation, service orientation, social perceptiveness, persuasion. **Top Values:** Social service, social status, autonomy. **Work Environment:** Indoors; sitting.

Related Title in the Classification of Instructional Programs (CIP)
38.0101 Philosophy.

Photography

Focuses on the principles and techniques of communicating information, ideas, moods, and feelings through the creation of images or videos and may prepare you to be a professional photographic or video artist.

Career Snapshot

Photography is a highly competitive field, and a major in this field makes the most sense at a college that is known for it; elsewhere you would be better advised to pursue a bachelor of fine arts (BFA) degree with a concentration in photography. The spread of digital photography is expected to slow down job growth somewhat, partly because it will increase the productivity of photographers and partly because many users of photographs will be able to find appropriate existing images in collections rather than hire photographers to create new images.

Related Specialties in Majors and Careers

Digital photography, photojournalism, scientific photography.

Related Job Titles, Earnings, Projected Growth, and Openings

Job Title	Average Earnings	Projected Growth	Annual Openings
1. Art, Drama, and Music Teachers, Postsecondary (O*NET-SOC Code 25-1121.00)	$55,190	22.9%	237,478
2. Photographers (O*NET-SOC Code 27-4021.00)	$27,720	10.3%	16,100

Job 1 shares 237,478 openings with 35 other postsecondary teaching jobs not included in this table.

Typical Sequence of College Courses

English composition, foreign language, art and culture, basic drawing, color and design, two-dimensional design, three-dimensional design, art history and criticism, history of photography, fundamentals of photography, photojournalism, creative photography, senior project.

Typical Sequence of High School Courses

English, algebra, geometry, trigonometry, physics, foreign language, literature, history, art, photography.

Personality Type

Artistic. These occupations frequently involve working with forms, designs, and patterns. They often require self-expression, and the work can be done without following a clear set of rules.

Other Characteristics

GOE—Related Interest Areas/Career Clusters: 03 Arts and Communication; 05 Education and Training. **Related Work Groups:** 03.09 Media Technology; 05.03 Postsecondary and Adult Teaching and Instructing. **Most Important Skills:** Persuasion, monitoring, active learning, service orientation, speaking, management of financial resources. **Top Values:** Creativity, ability utilization, achievement. **Work Environment:** More often indoors than outdoors; extremely bright or inadequate lighting.

Related Title in the Classification of Instructional Programs (CIP)

50.0605 Photography.

Physical Education

Prepares you to teach physical education programs and/or to coach sports at various educational levels.

Career Snapshot

This major covers not only educational techniques, but also the workings of the human body. Thanks to a national concern for fitness and health, physical education graduates are finding employment not only as teachers, but also as instructors and athletic directors in health and sports clubs. Most jobs are still to be found in elementary and secondary schools, where a bachelor's degree is often sufficient for entry, but a master's may be required for advancement to a more secure and better-paid position. Some graduates may go on to get a master's in athletic training and work for a college or professional sports team.

Related Specialties in Majors and Careers

Coaching, health education, recreation, sports activities.

Related Job Titles, Earnings, Projected Growth, and Openings

Job Title	Average Earnings	Projected Growth	Annual Openings
1. Coaches and Scouts (O*NET-SOC Code 27-2022.00)	$27,840	14.6%	51,100
2. Education Teachers, Postsecondary (O*NET-SOC Code 25-1081.00)	$54,220	22.9%	237,478
3. Fitness Trainers and Aerobics Instructors (O*NET-SOC Code 39-9031.00)	$27,680	26.8%	51,235
4. Middle School Teachers, Except Special and Vocational Education (O*NET-SOC Code 25-2022.00)	$47,900	11.2%	75,270
5. Secondary School Teachers, Except Special and Vocational Education (O*NET-SOC Code 25-2031.00)	$49,420	5.6%	93,166

Job 2 shares 237,478 openings with 35 other postsecondary teaching jobs not included in this table.

Typical Sequence of College Courses

Introduction to psychology, English composition, oral communication, history and philosophy of education, human growth and development, introduction to special education, history and philosophy of physical education, first aid and CPR, methods of teaching physical education, human anatomy and physiology, kinesiology, special needs in physical education, psychomotor development, organization and administration of physical education, evaluation in physical education, methods of teaching dance, methods of teaching sports activities, methods of teaching aerobics and weight training, swimming and water safety, student teaching.

Typical Sequence of High School Courses

English, algebra, geometry, trigonometry, science, foreign language, public speaking, dance.

Personality Type

Social. These occupations frequently involve working with, communicating with, and teaching people and often involve helping or providing service to others.

Other Characteristics

GOE—Related Interest Areas/Career Clusters: 05 Education and Training; 09 Hospitality, Tourism, and Recreation. **Related Work Groups:** 05.02 Preschool, Elementary, and Secondary Teaching and Instructing; 05.06 Counseling, Health, and Fitness Education; 09.06 Sports. **Most Important Skills:** Learning strategies, instructing, social perceptiveness, monitoring, persuasion, time management. **Top Values:** Authority, social service, creativity. **Work Environment:** More often indoors than outdoors; standing; disease or infections; close to others; walking and running.

Related Title in the Classification of Instructional Programs (CIP)

13.1314 Physical Education Teaching and Coaching.

Physical Therapy

Prepares you to alleviate physical and functional impairments and limitations caused by injury or disease through the design and implementation of therapeutic interventions to promote fitness and health.

Career Snapshot

Physical therapists help people overcome pain and limited movement caused by disease or injury, and help them avoid further disabilities. They review patients' medical records and the prescriptions of physicians, evaluate patients' mobility, and then guide patients through appropriate exercise routines and apply therapeutic agents such as heat and electrical stimulation. They need to be knowledgeable about many disabling conditions and therapeutic techniques. The master's program is becoming the standard requirement for entry into this field. Entry to master's programs is extremely competitive. The short-term job outlook has been hurt by cutbacks in Medicare coverage of therapy; however, the long-term outlook is expected to be good.

Related Specialties in Majors and Careers

Geriatric physical therapy, neurological physical therapy, orthopedics, physical therapy education, sports medicine.

Related Job Titles, Earnings, Projected Growth, and Openings

Job Title	Average Earnings	Projected Growth	Annual Openings
1. Health Specialties Teachers, Postsecondary (O*NET-SOC Code 25-1071.00)	$80,700	22.9%	237,478
2. Physical Therapists (O*NET-SOC Code 29-1123.00)	$69,760	27.1%	12,072

Job 1 shares 237,478 openings with 35 other postsecondary teaching jobs not included in this table.

Typical Sequence of College Courses

English composition, statistics for business and social sciences, general chemistry, general biology, human anatomy and physiology, introduction to psychology, human growth and development, introduction to computer science, abnormal psychology, fundamentals of medical science, neuroanatomy, neuroscience for

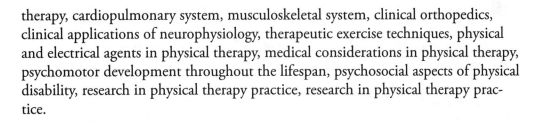

therapy, cardiopulmonary system, musculoskeletal system, clinical orthopedics, clinical applications of neurophysiology, therapeutic exercise techniques, physical and electrical agents in physical therapy, medical considerations in physical therapy, psychomotor development throughout the lifespan, psychosocial aspects of physical disability, research in physical therapy practice, research in physical therapy practice.

Typical Sequence of High School Courses

English, algebra, geometry, trigonometry, chemistry, physics, biology, foreign language, computer science.

Personality Type

Investigative. These occupations frequently involve working with ideas and require an extensive amount of thinking. They can involve searching for facts and figuring out problems mentally.

Other Characteristics

GOE—Related Interest Areas/Career Clusters: 05 Education and Training; 08 Health Science. **Related Work Groups:** 05.03 Postsecondary and Adult Teaching and Instructing; 08.07 Medical Therapy. **Most Important Skills:** Science, reading comprehension, instructing, writing, learning strategies, complex problem solving. **Top Values:** Social service, authority, achievement. **Work Environment:** Indoors; disease or infections; close to others; keeping or regaining balance; specialized protective or safety equipment; standing; cramped work space, awkward positions.

Related Title in the Classification of Instructional Programs (CIP)

51.2308 Physical Therapy/Therapist.

Physician Assisting

Prepares you to practice medicine, including diagnoses and treatment therapies, under the supervision of a physician.

Career Snapshot

Physician assistants work under the supervision of physicians, but in some cases they provide care in settings where a physician may be present only a couple of days per week. They perform many of the diagnostic, therapeutic, and preventative functions that we are used to associating with physicians. The typical educational program results in a bachelor's degree. It often takes only two years to complete, but entrants usually must have at least two years of prior college and often must have work experience in the field of health care. Employment opportunities are expected to be good.

Related Specialties in Majors and Careers

Emergency medicine, family medicine, internal medicine, pediatrics.

Related Job Titles, Earnings, Projected Growth, and Openings

Job Title	Average Earnings	Projected Growth	Annual Openings
1. Health Specialties Teachers, Postsecondary (O*NET-SOC Code 25-1071.00)	$80,700	22.9%	237,478
2. Physician Assistants (O*NET-SOC Code 29-1071.00)	$78,450	27.0%	7,147

Job 1 shares 237,478 openings with 35 other postsecondary teaching jobs not included in this table.

Typical Sequence of College Courses

English composition, college algebra, general chemistry, general biology, introduction to psychology, human growth and development, general microbiology, human physiology, human anatomy, pharmacology, medical interviewing techniques, patient examination and evaluation, clinical laboratory procedures, ethics in health care, clinical experience in internal medicine, clinical experience in emergency medicine, clinical experience in obstetrics/gynecology, clinical experience in family medicine, clinical experience in psychiatry, clinical experience in surgery, clinical experience in pediatrics, clinical experience in geriatrics.

Typical Sequence of High School Courses

English, algebra, geometry, trigonometry, pre-calculus, biology, computer science, public speaking, chemistry, foreign language.

Personality Type

Investigative. These occupations frequently involve working with ideas and require an extensive amount of thinking. They can involve searching for facts and figuring out problems mentally.

Other Characteristics

GOE—Related Interest Areas/Career Clusters: 05 Education and Training; 08 Health Science. **Related Work Groups:** 05.03 Postsecondary and Adult Teaching and Instructing; 08.02 Medicine and Surgery. **Most Important Skills:** Science, instructing, writing, reading comprehension, critical thinking, complex problem solving. **Top Values:** Social service, authority, achievement. **Work Environment:** Indoors; sitting; disease or infections; radiation.

Related Title in the Classification of Instructional Programs (CIP)

51.0912 Physician Assistant.

Physics

Focuses on the scientific study of matter and energy and the formulation and testing of the laws governing the behavior of matter and energy.

Career Snapshot

Physics is the study of the basic laws of the physical world, including those that govern what matter and energy are and how they are created, move, and interact. This knowledge is the basis for our understanding of many fields, such as chemistry, biology, and engineering. Physics has direct applications in the technologies that we use every day for transportation, communication, and entertainment. Because most jobs are in basic research and development, a Ph.D. is most commonly required. Unfortunately, research is not expected to grow fast, if at all, so there will be keen competition for jobs.

Related Specialties in Majors and Careers

Acoustics, astronomy, elementary particles, nuclear physics, optics, plasma physics, solid-state physics, theoretical physics.

Related Job Titles, Earnings, Projected Growth, and Openings

Job Title	Average Earnings	Projected Growth	Annual Openings
1. Natural Sciences Managers (O*NET-SOC Code 11-9121.00)	$104,040	11.4%	3,661
2. Physicists (O*NET-SOC Code 19-2012.00)	$96,850	6.8%	1,302
3. Physics Teachers, Postsecondary (O*NET-SOC Code 25-1054.00)	$70,090	22.9%	237,478

Job 3 shares 237,478 openings with 35 other postsecondary teaching jobs not included in this table.

Typical Sequence of College Courses

English composition, introduction to computer science, calculus, differential equations, general chemistry, mechanics, optics, thermal physics, electricity and magnetism, modern physics, modern experimental physics, quantum and atomic physics.

Typical Sequence of High School Courses

English, algebra, geometry, trigonometry, chemistry, physics, pre-calculus, computer science, calculus.

Personality Type

Investigative. These occupations frequently involve working with ideas and require an extensive amount of thinking. They can involve searching for facts and figuring out problems mentally.

Other Characteristics

GOE—Related Interest Areas/Career Clusters: 05 Education and Training; 15 Scientific Research, Engineering, and Mathematics. **Related Work Groups:** 05.03 Postsecondary and Adult Teaching and Instructing; 15.01 Managerial Work in Scientific Research, Engineering, and Mathematics; 15.02 Physical Sciences. **Most Important Skills:** Science, mathematics, programming, complex problem solving, reading comprehension, writing. **Top Values:** Creativity, authority, autonomy. **Work Environment:** Indoors; sitting; hazardous conditions; in an enclosed vehicle or equipment; radiation.

Related Title in the Classification of Instructional Programs (CIP)

40.0801 Physics, General.

Podiatry

Prepares you for the independent professional practice of podiatric medicine, involving the prevention, diagnosis, and treatment of diseases, disorders, and injuries to the foot and lower extremities.

Career Snapshot

Podiatrists are health-care practitioners who specialize in the feet and lower extremities. The educational process is much like that for medical doctors—for almost all students, first a bachelor's degree, then four years of study and clinical practice in a school of podiatric medicine, followed by one to three years of a hospital residency program. The bachelor's degree can be in any subject as long as it includes certain coursework in science and math.

Related Specialties in Majors and Careers

Orthopedics, sports medicine, surgery.

Related Job Title, Earnings, Projected Growth, and Openings

Job Title	Average Earnings	Projected Growth	Annual Openings
1. Podiatrists (O*NET-SOC Code 29-1081.00)	$110,510	9.5%	648

Typical Sequence of College Courses

English composition, introduction to psychology, college algebra, calculus, introduction to sociology, oral communication, general chemistry, general biology, introduction to computer science, organic chemistry, human anatomy and physiology, general microbiology, genetics, introduction to biochemistry, gross anatomy, histology, patient examination and evaluation, lower extremity anatomy, neuroanatomy, human physiology, microbiology and immunology, pathology, biomechanics, radiology, podiatric surgery, dermatology, general medicine, traumatology, professional practice management, clinical experience in podiatric medicine.

Typical Sequence of High School Courses

English, algebra, geometry, trigonometry, biology, computer science, public speaking, chemistry, foreign language, physics, pre-calculus.

Personality Type

Social. These occupations frequently involve working with, communicating with, and teaching people and often involve helping or providing service to others.

Other Characteristics

GOE—Related Interest Area/Career Cluster: 08 Health Science. **Related Work Group:** 08.04 Health Specialties. **Most Important Skills:** Science, complex problem solving, active listening, management of financial resources, reading comprehension, equipment selection. **Top Values:** Social service, responsibility, recognition. **Work Environment:** Indoors; disease or infections; radiation; close to others; protective or safety equipment; specialized protective or safety equipment; using hands on objects, tools, or controls.

Related Title in the Classification of Instructional Programs (CIP)

51.2101 Podiatric Medicine/Podiatry (DPM).

Political Science

Focuses on the systematic study of political institutions and behavior.

Career Snapshot

Political science is the study of how political systems and public policy are created and evolve. It is concerned with many levels of political activity, from the campaigns of candidates for representation of a city precinct to the maneuvers of nations trying to resolve regional conflicts. Most political scientists work as researchers and teachers in universities, which means they generally have graduate degrees. Many graduates of political science programs use the bachelor's degree as an entry route to law school or public administration.

Related Specialties in Majors and Careers

Comparative politics, international relations, political theory, public administration, public opinion, public policy.

Related Job Titles, Earnings, Projected Growth, and Openings

Job Title	Average Earnings	Projected Growth	Annual Openings
1. Political Science Teachers, Postsecondary (O*NET-SOC Code 25-1065.00)	$63,100	22.9%	237,478
2. Political Scientists (O*NET-SOC Code 19-3094.00)	$91,580	5.3%	318

Job 1 shares 237,478 openings with 35 other postsecondary teaching jobs not included in this table.

Typical Sequence of College Courses

English composition, introduction to psychology, introduction to sociology, American government, foreign language, statistics, introduction to economics, statistics for business and social sciences, state and local government, comparative governments, introduction to international relations, political theory, political science research methods, public policy analysis, seminar (reporting on research).

Typical Sequence of High School Courses

Algebra, English, foreign language, social science, trigonometry, history.

Personality Type

Social. These occupations frequently involve working with, communicating with, and teaching people and often involve helping or providing service to others.

Other Characteristics

GOE—Related Interest Areas/Career Clusters: 05 Education and Training; 15 Scientific Research, Engineering, and Mathematics. **Related Work Groups:** 05.03 Postsecondary and Adult Teaching and Instructing; 15.04 Social Sciences. **Most Important Skills:** Writing, reading comprehension, instructing, critical thinking, persuasion, speaking. **Top Values:** Creativity, authority, autonomy. **Work Environment:** Indoors; sitting.

Related Title in the Classification of Instructional Programs (CIP)

45.1001 Political Science and Government, General.

Psychology

Focuses on the scientific study of individual and collective behavior, the physical and environmental bases of behaviors, and the analysis and treatment of behavioral problems and disorders.

Career Snapshot

Psychology is the study of human behavior. It may take place in a clinical, educational, industrial, or experimental setting. Those with a bachelor's degree usually must find employment in another field, such as marketing research. A bachelor's degree can also be a good first step toward graduate education in education, law, social work, or another field. To be licensed as a clinical or counseling psychologist, you usually need a Ph.D. About half of psychologists are self-employed. Because psychology is about behavior, many people don't realize that it uses scientific methods and that students are expected to become competent in statistics.

Related Specialties in Majors and Careers

Clinical/counseling psychology, educational psychology, industrial psychology, research clinical psychology.

Related Job Titles, Earnings, Projected Growth, and Openings

Job Title	Average Earnings	Projected Growth	Annual Openings
1. Clinical Psychologists (O*NET-SOC Code 19-3031.02)	$62,210	15.8%	8,309
2. Counseling Psychologists (O*NET-SOC Code 19-3031.03)	$62,210	15.8%	8,309
3. Industrial-Organizational Psychologists (O*NET-SOC Code 19-3032.00)	$80,820	21.3%	118
4. Psychology Teachers, Postsecondary (O*NET-SOC Code 25-1066.00)	$60,610	22.9%	237,478
5. School Psychologists (O*NET-SOC Code 19-3031.01)	$62,210	15.8%	8,309

Jobs 1, 2, and 5 share 8,309 openings. Job 4 shares 237,478 openings with 35 other postsecondary teaching jobs not included in this table.

Typical Sequence of College Courses

Introduction to psychology, English composition, statistics, research methods in speech pathology and audiology, experimental psychology, psychology of learning, abnormal psychology, social psychology, developmental psychology, sensation and perception, cognitive psychology, biopsychology, psychology of personality, quantitative analysis in psychology, psychological testing and measurements.

Typical Sequence of High School Courses

Algebra, biology, English, foreign language, social science, trigonometry.

Personality Type

Social. These occupations frequently involve working with, communicating with, and teaching people and often involve helping or providing service to others.

Other Characteristics

GOE—Related Interest Areas/Career Clusters: 05 Education and Training; 10 Human Service; 15 Scientific Research, Engineering, and Mathematics. **Related Work Groups:** 05.03 Postsecondary and Adult Teaching and Instructing; 10.01 Counseling and Social Work; 15.04 Social Sciences. **Most Important Skills:** Social perceptiveness, learning strategies, active listening, negotiation, service orientation, persuasion. **Top Values:** Social service, creativity, autonomy. **Work Environment:** Indoors; sitting; disease or infections; close to others.

Related Title in the Classification of Instructional Programs (CIP)

42.0101 Psychology, General.

Public Administration

Prepares you to serve as a manager in the executive arm of local, state, and federal government; and focuses on the systematic study of executive organization and management.

Career Snapshot

The public sector includes many kinds of agencies, working in the fields of health, law enforcement, environmental protection, transportation, and taxation, to name just a few. Because of this variety of fields, public administrators can benefit from a background that combines training in administrative skills (perhaps at the master's level) with specific training in another field, such as health, science, engineering, or accounting. Public administration programs usually include internships that give students actual experience working in a public agency.

Related Specialties in Majors and Careers

Economic development, finance and budgeting, personnel and labor relations, policy analysis, program management.

Related Job Titles, Earnings, Projected Growth, and Openings

Job Title	Average Earnings	Projected Growth	Annual Openings
1. Administrative Services Managers (O*NET-SOC Code 11-3011.00)	$70,990	11.7%	19,513
2. Chief Executives (O*NET-SOC Code 11-1011.00)	More than $145,600	2.0%	21,209
3. Emergency Management Specialists (O*NET-SOC Code 13-1061.00)	$48,380	12.3%	1,538
4. General and Operations Managers (O*NET-SOC Code 11-1021.00)	$88,700	1.5%	112,072
5. Legislators (O*NET-SOC Code 11-1031.00)	$16,220	1.0%	3,387
6. Postmasters and Mail Superintendents (O*NET-SOC Code 11-9131.00)	$57,900	–0.8%	1,627
7. Social and Community Service Managers (O*NET-SOC Code 11-9151.00)	$54,530	24.7%	23,788
8. Storage and Distribution Managers (O*NET-SOC Code 11-3071.02)	$76,310	8.3%	6,994

Job Title	Average Earnings	Projected Growth	Annual Openings
9. Transportation Managers (O*NET-SOC Code 11-3071.01)	$76,310	8.3%	6,994

Jobs 8 and 9 share 6,994 openings.

Typical Sequence of College Courses

English composition, oral communication, accounting, introduction to business management, American government, state and local government, college algebra, introduction to economics, organizational behavior, statistics for business and social sciences, organizational theory, introduction to psychology, urban politics, public policy–making process, public finance and budgeting, political science research methods, planning and change in public organizations, seminar (reporting on research).

Typical Sequence of High School Courses

Algebra, English, foreign language, social science, trigonometry, history, public speaking, computer science.

Personality Type

Enterprising. These occupations frequently involve starting up and carrying out projects and can involve leading people and making many decisions. They sometimes require risk taking and often deal with business.

Other Characteristics

GOE—Related Interest Areas/Career Clusters: 04 Business and Administration; 07 Government and Public Administration; 12 Law and Public Safety; 16 Transportation, Distribution, and Logistics. **Related Work Groups:** 04.01 Managerial Work in General Business; 04.02 Managerial Work in Business Detail; 07.01 Managerial Work in Government and Public Administration; 12.01 Managerial Work in Law and Public Safety; 16.01 Managerial Work in Transportation. **Most Important Skills:** Management of financial resources, management of personnel resources, management of material resources, monitoring, negotiation, coordination. **Top Values:** Authority, autonomy, creativity. **Work Environment:** More often indoors than in a vehicle; sitting.

Related Title in the Classification of Instructional Programs (CIP)

44.0401 Public Administration.

Public Relations

Focuses on the theories and methods for managing the media image of a business, organization, or individual and the communication process with stakeholders, constituencies, audiences, and the general public; and prepares you to function as a public relations assistant, technician, or manager.

Career Snapshot

Public relations specialists work for business, government, and nonprofit organizations and encourage public support for the employer's policies and practices. Often several "publics" with differing interests and needs have to be targeted with different messages. The work requires understanding of psychology, the business and social environments, effective writing, and techniques used in various media for persuasive communications. A bachelor's degree is good preparation for an entry-level job in this competitive field. With experience, you may be able to manage public relations campaigns.

Related Specialties in Majors and Careers

Creative process, management, new media.

Related Job Titles, Earnings, Projected Growth, and Openings

Job Title	Average Earnings	Projected Growth	Annual Openings
1. Advertising and Promotions Managers (O*NET-SOC Code 11-2011.00)	$78,250	6.2%	2,955
2. Communications Teachers, Postsecondary (O*NET-SOC Code 25-1122.00)	$54,720	22.9%	237,478
3. Public Relations Managers (O*NET-SOC Code 11-2031.00)	$86,470	16.9%	5,781
4. Public Relations Specialists (O*NET-SOC Code 27-3031.00)	$49,800	17.6%	51,216

Job 2 shares 237,478 openings with 35 other postsecondary teaching jobs not included in this table.

Typical Sequence of College Courses

English composition, oral communication, introduction to marketing, introduction to economics, principles of public relations, communications theory, public relations message strategy, communication ethics, public relations media, public relations writing, public relations techniques and campaigns, organizational communications, mass communication law, introduction to communication research, visual design for media.

Typical Sequence of High School Courses

English, algebra, foreign language, art, literature, public speaking, social science.

Personality Type

Enterprising. These occupations frequently involve starting up and carrying out projects and can involve leading people and making many decisions. They sometimes require risk taking and often deal with business.

Other Characteristics

GOE—Related Interest Areas/Career Clusters: 03 Arts and Communication; 05 Education and Training; 14 Retail and Wholesale Sales and Service. **Related Work Groups:** 03.01 Managerial Work in Arts and Communication; 03.03 News, Broadcasting, and Public Relations; 14.01 Managerial Work in Retail/Wholesale Sales and Service. **Most Important Skills:** Management of financial resources, service orientation, persuasion, negotiation, writing, monitoring. **Top Values:** Creativity, recognition, ability utilization. **Work Environment:** Indoors; sitting.

Related Title in the Classification of Instructional Programs (CIP)

09.0902 Public Relations/Image Management.

Recreation and Parks Management

Prepares you to develop and manage park facilities and other indoor and outdoor recreation and leisure facilities.

Career Snapshot

Recreation is a growth industry, especially as the baby boomers enter retirement. Those who major in parks and recreation management may want to emphasize either the managerial or the leadership and therapeutic aspects. With bachelor's degrees, they may find employment with government, commercial recreational and tourism organizations, camps, or theme parks. Other jobs will be in social assistance organizations and in nursing and residential care facilities. Although the field offers many opportunities for part-time and seasonal work, competition is expected to remain keen for full-time career positions. People with graduate degrees are expected to have the best opportunities for supervisory positions.

Related Specialties in Majors and Careers

Exercise, interpretation, outdoor leadership, resource management, therapeutic recreation, tourism.

Related Job Title, Earnings, Projected Growth, and Openings

Job Title	Average Earnings	Projected Growth	Annual Openings
1. Recreation Workers (O*NET-SOC Code 39-9032.00)	$21,220	12.7%	61,454

Typical Sequence of College Courses

English composition, introduction to computer science, American government, oral communication, conservation of natural resources, introduction to economics, introduction to psychology, statistics for business and social sciences, introduction to sociology, introduction to business management, natural resource economics, ecology, foundations of parks and recreation, tourism management and planning, methods of environmental interpretation, evaluation and research in parks and recreation, parks, recreation and diverse populations, recreation and tourism programs, park planning and design, seminar (reporting on research).

Typical Sequence of High School Courses
English, biology, social science, chemistry, geometry, public speaking.

Personality Type
Social. These occupations frequently involve working with, communicating with, and teaching people and often involve helping or providing service to others.

Other Characteristics
GOE—Related Interest Area/Career Cluster: 09 Hospitality, Tourism, and Recreation. **Related Work Group:** 09.02 Recreational Services. **Most Important Skills:** Management of personnel resources, management of financial resources, management of material resources, service orientation, social perceptiveness, systems evaluation. **Top Values:** Social service, creativity, autonomy. **Work Environment:** More often indoors than outdoors or in a vehicle; walking and running; noisy; bending or twisting the body; close to others.

Related Title in the Classification of Instructional Programs (CIP)
31.0301 Parks, Recreation and Leisure Facilities Management.

Religion/Religious Studies

Focuses on the nature of religious belief and specific religious and quasi-religious systems.

Career Snapshot

Interest in religion continues to grow in America, and many colleges were founded by churches, so the religious studies major continues to attract students, some of whom have no intention of becoming professional clergy. A graduate of a religious studies major has skills in language, literature, critical thinking, and writing that are valuable in many careers in the secular world. The amount of education required to be ordained in the clergy depends on the person's religious denomination. For some, there may be no formal requirement; most require several years of seminary training, often following four years of college. Clergy find work in places of worship and religious schools; as chaplains for hospitals, prisons, and the military; and as missionaries.

Related Specialties in Majors and Careers

Ecumenical studies, missionary work, pastoral counseling, pastoral studies, scriptural texts/language.

Related Job Titles, Earnings, Projected Growth, and Openings

Job Title	Average Earnings	Projected Growth	Annual Openings
1. Clergy (O*NET-SOC Code 21-2011.00)	$40,460	18.9%	35,092
2. Philosophy and Religion Teachers, Postsecondary (O*NET-SOC Code 25-1126.00)	$56,380	22.9%	237,478

Job 2 shares 237,478 openings with 35 other postsecondary teaching jobs not included in this table.

Typical Sequence of College Courses

English composition, foreign language, introduction to religious studies, introduction to philosophy, ethical/moral theory, Hebrew Bible, New Testament, non-Western religions, philosophy of religion, history of religion in the West, contemporary theologies, religious ethics.

Typical Sequence of High School Courses

Algebra, English, foreign language, social science, history, geometry, public speaking.

Personality Type

Social. These occupations frequently involve working with, communicating with, and teaching people and often involve helping or providing service to others.

Other Characteristics

GOE—Related Interest Areas/Career Clusters: 05 Education and Training; 10 Human Service. **Related Work Groups:** 05.03 Postsecondary and Adult Teaching and Instructing; 10.02 Religious Work. **Most Important Skills:** Management of personnel resources, management of financial resources, service orientation, negotiation, judgment and decision making, persuasion. **Top Values:** Social status, social service, autonomy. **Work Environment:** Indoors; sitting.

Related Title in the Classification of Instructional Programs (CIP)

38.0201 Religion/Religious Studies.

Russian

Focuses on the Russian language, its literature, and its related dialects, and may include applications in business, science/technology, and other settings.

Career Snapshot

Despite the breakup of the Soviet Union, Russian is still an important world language that not many Americans know. As business and governmental ties with Russia continue to increase as it opens to free trade, a degree in Russian can lead to careers in international business, travel, and law. College teaching and translation are options for those with a graduate degree in Russian.

Related Specialties in Majors and Careers

History and culture, language education, literature, translation.

Related Job Titles, Earnings, Projected Growth, and Openings

Job Title	Average Earnings	Projected Growth	Annual Openings
1. Foreign Language and Literature Teachers, Post-secondary (O*NET-SOC Code 25-1124.00)	$53,610	22.9%	237,478
2. Interpreters and Translators (O*NET-SOC Code 27-3091.00)	$37,490	23.6%	6,630

Job 1 shares 237,478 openings with 35 other postsecondary teaching jobs not included in this table.

Typical Sequence of College Courses

Russian language, conversation, composition, linguistics, Russian literature, Russian history and civilization, European history and civilization, grammar, phonetics, study abroad.

Typical Sequence of High School Courses

English, public speaking, foreign language, history, literature, social science.

Personality Type

Artistic. These occupations frequently involve working with forms, designs, and patterns. They often require self-expression, and the work can be done without following a clear set of rules.

Other Characteristics

GOE—Related Interest Areas/Career Clusters: 03 Arts and Communication; 05 Education and Training. **Related Work Groups:** 03.03 News, Broadcasting, and Public Relations; 05.03 Postsecondary and Adult Teaching and Instructing. **Most Important Skills:** Social perceptiveness, speaking, writing, active listening, reading comprehension, learning strategies. **Top Values:** Social service, ability utilization, achievement. **Work Environment:** Indoors; sitting; close to others.

Related Title in the Classification of Instructional Programs (CIP)

16.0402 Russian Language and Literature.

Secondary Education

Prepares you to teach students in the secondary grades, which may include grades seven through twelve, depending on the school system or state regulations; may prepare you to teach a comprehensive curriculum or a specific subject matter.

Career Snapshot

A bachelor's is the minimum for starting a secondary teaching career, and a master's may be required or encouraged for job security and a pay raise. A teacher-education program covers not only the subjects you will teach, but also basic principles of how young people learn and how to run a classroom. Demand for secondary school teachers is expected to be better than that for lower grades, but it will vary according to subject field and geographic area.

Related Specialties in Majors and Careers

Art education, bilingual education, language education, mathematics education, music education, remedial and developmental reading, science education, social studies education.

Related Job Title, Earnings, Projected Growth, and Openings

Job Title	Average Earnings	Projected Growth	Annual Openings
1. Secondary School Teachers, Except Special and Vocational Education (O*NET-SOC Code 25-2031.00)	$49,420	5.6%	93,166

Typical Sequence of College Courses

Introduction to psychology, English composition, oral communication, history and philosophy of education, human growth and development, teaching methods, educational alternatives for exceptional students, educational psychology, courses in subject to be taught, student teaching.

Typical Sequence of High School Courses

English, algebra, geometry, trigonometry, science, foreign language, public speaking.

Personality Type

Social. These occupations frequently involve working with, communicating with, and teaching people and often involve helping or providing service to others.

Other Characteristics

GOE—Related Interest Area/Career Cluster: 05 Education and Training. **Related Work Group:** 05.02 Preschool, Elementary, and Secondary Teaching and Instructing. **Most Important Skills:** Learning strategies, social perceptiveness, persuasion, monitoring, instructing, time management. **Top Values:** Social service, authority, creativity. **Work Environment:** Indoors; standing; close to others; noisy.

Related Title in the Classification of Instructional Programs (CIP)

13.1205 Secondary Education and Teaching.

Social Work

Prepares you for the professional practice of social welfare administration and counseling and focuses on the study of organized means of providing basic support services for vulnerable individuals and groups.

Career Snapshot

Social workers improve people's lives by helping them cope with problems of bad health, substance abuse, disability, old age, family conflicts, mental illness, or poverty. A large number of them work for public agencies and health care institutions. A master's degree is becoming standard preparation for this field. Job opportunities are expected to be good, especially in rural areas.

Related Specialties in Majors and Careers

Advocacy, child welfare, domestic violence, health care, mental health, mental retardation, school, substance abuse.

Related Job Titles, Earnings, Projected Growth, and Openings

Job Title	Average Earnings	Projected Growth	Annual Openings
1. Child, Family, and School Social Workers (O*NET-SOC Code 21-1021.00)	$38,620	19.1%	35,402
2. Marriage and Family Therapists (O*NET-SOC Code 21-1013.00)	$43,600	29.8%	5,953
3. Probation Officers and Correctional Treatment Specialists (O*NET-SOC Code 21-1092.00)	$44,510	10.9%	18,335
4. Social Work Teachers, Postsecondary (O*NET-SOC Code 25-1113.00)	$56,240	22.9%	237,478

Job 4 shares 237,478 openings with 35 other postsecondary teaching jobs not included in this table.

Typical Sequence of College Courses

English composition, human growth and development, American government, introduction to psychology, introduction to sociology, introduction to philosophy, statistics for business and social sciences, cultural diversity, human anatomy and physiology, development of social welfare, human behavior and the social environment, social work methods, social welfare policy and issues, field experience/internship, social work research methods, foreign language, seminar (reporting on research).

Typical Sequence of High School Courses

Algebra, biology, English, foreign language, social science, trigonometry.

Personality Type

Social. These occupations frequently involve working with, communicating with, and teaching people and often involve helping or providing service to others.

Other Characteristics

GOE—Related Interest Areas/Career Clusters: 05 Education and Training; 10 Human Service. **Related Work Groups:** 05.03 Postsecondary and Adult Teaching and Instructing; 10.01 Counseling and Social Work. **Most Important Skills:** Social perceptiveness, service orientation, negotiation, monitoring, speaking, persuasion. **Top Values:** Social service, autonomy, activity. **Work Environment:** More often indoors than in a vehicle or outdoors; sitting; disease or infections.

Related Title in the Classification of Instructional Programs (CIP)

44.0701 Social Work.

Sociology

Focuses on the systematic study of human social institutions and social relationships.

Career Snapshot

Sociology studies how people behave within groups such as families, religious denominations, social organizations, businesses, and political groups. Many graduates of bachelor's sociology programs go on to graduate schools with the goal of research or teaching. Others branch out to related fields, perhaps with additional education in social work, the law, or marketing research.

Related Specialties in Majors and Careers

Anthropology, criminology, culture and social change, family and marriage, gerontology, human relations, social institutions/organizations, social problems.

Related Job Titles, Earnings, Projected Growth, and Openings

Job Title	Average Earnings	Projected Growth	Annual Openings
1. Sociologists (O*NET-SOC Code 19-3041.00)	$61,140	10.0%	403
2. Sociology Teachers, Postsecondary (O*NET-SOC Code 25-1067.00)	$58,160	22.9%	237,478

Job 2 shares 237,478 openings with 35 other postsecondary teaching jobs not included in this table.

Typical Sequence of College Courses

English composition, introduction to psychology, introduction to sociology, American government, introduction to economics, statistics, foreign language, social inequality, introduction to social research, history of social thought, contemporary social problems, seminar (reporting on research).

Typical Sequence of High School Courses

Algebra, English, foreign language, social science, trigonometry.

Personality Type

Social. These occupations frequently involve working with, communicating with, and teaching people and often involve helping or providing service to others.

Other Characteristics

GOE—Related Interest Areas/Career Clusters: 05 Education and Training; 15 Scientific Research, Engineering, and Mathematics. **Related Work Groups:** 05.03 Postsecondary and Adult Teaching and Instructing; 15.04 Social Sciences. **Most Important Skills:** Science, writing, instructing, learning strategies, social perceptiveness, critical thinking. **Top Values:** Authority, creativity, social service. **Work Environment:** Indoors; sitting.

Related Title in the Classification of Instructional Programs (CIP)

45.1101 Sociology.

Soil Science

Focuses on the scientific classification of soils, soil properties, and their relationship to agricultural crops.

Career Snapshot

Soil is a lot more than just dirt. It is a complex ecosystem with chemical, physical, mineralogical, and biological properties that affect agricultural productivity and the larger environment. Soil scientists survey and map soils, advise farmers and landowners on how to use land in productive and ecologically sound methods, and consult with civil engineers about construction projects that involve soil. Many work for governments. Those with advanced degrees may go into college teaching or basic research.

Related Specialties in Majors and Careers

Land-use management, soil conservation, soil surveying, sustainable agriculture, waste/bioresource management.

Related Job Titles, Earnings, Projected Growth, and Openings

Job Title	Average Earnings	Projected Growth	Annual Openings
1. Agricultural Sciences Teachers, Postsecondary (O*NET-SOC Code 25-1041.00)	$78,460	22.9%	237,478
2. Soil and Plant Scientists (O*NET-SOC Code 19-1013.00)	$58,000	8.4%	850

Job 1 shares 237,478 openings with 35 other postsecondary teaching jobs not included in this table.

Typical Sequence of College Courses

English composition, calculus, general biology, general chemistry, organic chemistry, general physics, introduction to geology, introduction to soil science, statistics, computer applications in agriculture, soil mechanics, soil chemistry, soil conservation engineering, soil morphology, soil analysis, soil fertility, ecology, introduction to ground water/hydrology, natural resource management and water quality, ecology and renewable resource management.

Typical Sequence of High School Courses

Biology, chemistry, algebra, geometry, trigonometry, computer science, English, public speaking.

Personality Type

Investigative. These occupations frequently involve working with ideas and require an extensive amount of thinking. They can involve searching for facts and figuring out problems mentally.

Other Characteristics

GOE—Related Interest Areas/Career Clusters: 01 Agriculture and Natural Resources; 05 Education and Training. **Related Work Groups:** 01.02 Resource Science/Engineering for Plants, Animals, and the Environment; 05.03 Postsecondary and Adult Teaching and Instructing. **Most Important Skills:** Science, management of financial resources, writing, management of personnel resources, reading comprehension, management of material resources. **Top Values:** Creativity, autonomy, responsibility. **Work Environment:** More often indoors than in a vehicle or outdoors; sitting; very hot or cold; specialized protective or safety equipment; hazardous conditions.

Related Title in the Classification of Instructional Programs (CIP)

01.1201 Soil Science and Agronomy, General.

Spanish

Focuses on the Spanish language, its literature, and its related dialects, and may include applications in business, science/technology, and other settings.

Career Snapshot

Spanish has become the second-most-used language in the United States, as well as maintaining its importance as a world language, especially in the Western Hemisphere. A degree in Spanish can be useful preparation (perhaps with an additional degree) for many careers in business, travel, and public service, and not just with an international orientation.

Related Specialties in Majors and Careers

History and culture, language education, literature, translation.

Related Job Titles, Earnings, Projected Growth, and Openings

Job Title	Average Earnings	Projected Growth	Annual Openings
1. Foreign Language and Literature Teachers, Post-secondary (O*NET-SOC Code 25-1124.00)	$53,610	22.9%	237,478
2. Interpreters and Translators (O*NET-SOC Code 27-3091.00)	$37,490	23.6%	6,630

Job 1 shares 237,478 openings with 35 other postsecondary teaching jobs not included in this table.

Typical Sequence of College Courses

Spanish language, conversation, composition, linguistics, Spanish literature, Spanish American literature, Spanish history and civilization, European history and civilization, grammar, phonetics, study abroad.

Typical Sequence of High School Courses

English, public speaking, Spanish, history, literature, social science.

Personality Type

Artistic. These occupations frequently involve working with forms, designs, and patterns. They often require self-expression, and the work can be done without following a clear set of rules.

Other Characteristics

GOE—Related Interest Areas/Career Clusters: 03 Arts and Communication; 05 Education and Training. **Related Work Groups:** 03.03 News, Broadcasting, and Public Relations; 05.03 Postsecondary and Adult Teaching and Instructing. **Most Important Skills:** Social perceptiveness, speaking, writing, active listening, reading comprehension, learning strategies. **Top Values:** Social service, ability utilization, achievement. **Work Environment:** Indoors; sitting; close to others; disease or infections; radiation.

Related Title in the Classification of Instructional Programs (CIP)

16.0905 Spanish Language and Literature.

Special Education

Focuses on the design and provision of teaching and other educational services to children or adults with special learning needs or disabilities and may prepare you to function as a special education teacher.

Career Snapshot

Special education covers a wide variety of learning and developmental disabilities and other conditions that require nonstandard educational techniques. Many states require a master's degree for licensure, but some states offer alternative entry routes. Job opportunity in this field is excellent, especially in rural areas and inner cities.

Related Specialties in Majors and Careers

Autism, multiple disabilities, specific learning disabilities, speech-language impairments, traumatic brain injury, visual impairments.

Related Job Titles, Earnings, Projected Growth, and Openings

Job Title	Average Earnings	Projected Growth	Annual Openings
1. Special Education Teachers, Middle School (O*NET-SOC Code 25-2042.00)	$48,940	15.8%	8,846
2. Special Education Teachers, Preschool, Kindergarten, and Elementary School (O*NET-SOC Code 25-2041.00)	$48,350	19.6%	20,049
3. Special Education Teachers, Secondary School (O*NET-SOC Code 25-2043.00)	$49,640	8.5%	10,601

Typical Sequence of College Courses

Introduction to psychology, English composition, oral communication, history and philosophy of education, human growth and development, introduction to special education, curriculum and methods for special education, educational psychology, psychology of the exceptional child, assessment in special education, classroom/laboratory management, behavior modification techniques in education, education for moderate and severe disabilities, reading assessment and teaching, mathematics education, student teaching.

Typical Sequence of High School Courses

English, algebra, geometry, trigonometry, science, foreign language, public speaking.

Personality Type

Social. These occupations frequently involve working with, communicating with, and teaching people and often involve helping or providing service to others.

Other Characteristics

GOE—Related Interest Area/Career Cluster: 05 Education and Training. **Related Work Group:** 05.02 Preschool, Elementary, and Secondary Teaching and Instructing. **Most Important Skills:** Learning strategies, social perceptiveness, instructing, negotiation, monitoring, time management. **Top Values:** Social service, authority, creativity. **Work Environment:** Indoors; standing; close to others.

Related Title in the Classification of Instructional Programs (CIP)

13.1001 Special Education and Teaching, General.

Speech Pathology and Audiology

Prepares you to work as an audiologist or speech-language pathologist, involving the diagnosis, treatment, and management of conditions that affect speech, language, or hearing.

Career Snapshot

Speech pathologists and audiologists help people with a variety of communication disorders. About half work in schools, and most of the rest work for health-care facilities. A master's degree is the standard entry route into this field, and it is possible to complete the requirements for entering the graduate program within a variety of undergraduate majors. Because of the aging of the population, demand for qualified practitioners is expected to increase.

Related Specialties in Majors and Careers

Audiology, speech-language pathology.

Related Job Titles, Earnings, Projected Growth, and Openings

Job Title	Average Earnings	Projected Growth	Annual Openings
1. Audiologists (O*NET-SOC Code 29-1121.00)	$59,440	9.8%	980
2. Health Specialties Teachers, Postsecondary (O*NET-SOC Code 25-1071.00)	$80,700	22.9%	237,478
3. Speech-Language Pathologists (O*NET-SOC Code 29-1127.00)	$60,690	10.6%	11,160

Job 2 shares 237,478 openings with 35 other postsecondary teaching jobs not included in this table.

Typical Sequence of College Courses

General biology, English composition, general physics, introduction to psychology, human growth and development, statistics, introduction to sociology, introduction to speech, language and hearing, phonetics, anatomy of the speech and hearing mechanism, linguistics, psychoacoustics, neuroscience, auditory anatomy and physiology, stuttering and other fluency disorders, voice disorders, hearing problems, psycholinguistics and speech perception, diagnostic procedures in audiology, aural rehabilitation, research methods in speech pathology and audiology, student teaching.

Typical Sequence of High School Courses

English, algebra, geometry, trigonometry, biology, chemistry, physics, computer science, public speaking, social science, pre-calculus.

Personality Type

Investigative. These occupations frequently involve working with ideas and require an extensive amount of thinking. They can involve searching for facts and figuring out problems mentally.

Other Characteristics

GOE—Related Interest Areas/Career Clusters: 05 Education and Training; 08 Health Science. **Related Work Groups:** 05.03 Postsecondary and Adult Teaching and Instructing; 08.07 Medical Therapy. **Most Important Skills:** Science, instructing, learning strategies, writing, reading comprehension, speaking. **Top Values:** Social service, authority, creativity. **Work Environment:** Indoors; sitting.

Related Title in the Classification of Instructional Programs (CIP)

51.0204 Audiology/Audiologist and Speech-Language Pathology/Pathologist.

Sports Management

Prepares you to apply business, coaching, and physical education principles to the organization, administration, and management of athletic programs and teams, fitness/rehabilitation facilities and health clubs, sport recreation services, and related services.

Career Snapshot

A degree in sports management can lead to a position as an assistant general manager, a director of marketing and promotions, a sales representative for sporting goods, or a director of sports programs at a college. You may study this subject for a bachelor's degree or as a specialization in an MBA program. The field is highly competitive, so you should study enough business subjects to also be employable in another management field.

Related Specialties in Majors and Careers

Facilities management, marketing and promotions, player development, school athletic programs.

Related Job Titles, Earnings, Projected Growth, and Openings

Job Title	Average Earnings	Projected Growth	Annual Openings
1. Coaches and Scouts (O*NET-SOC Code 27-2022.00)	$27,840	14.6%	51,100
2. Fitness Trainers and Aerobics Instructors (O*NET-SOC Code 39-9031.00)	$27,680	26.8%	51,235
3. Recreation and Fitness Studies Teachers, Postsecondary (O*NET-SOC Code 25-1193.00)	$52,170	22.9%	237,478
4. Recreation Workers (O*NET-SOC Code 39-9032.00)	$21,220	12.7%	61,454

Job 3 shares 237,478 openings with 35 other postsecondary teaching jobs not included in this table.

Typical Sequence of College Courses

Business writing, introduction to psychology, principles of microeconomics, principles of macroeconomics, statistics for business and social sciences, personnel management, introduction to accounting, introduction to sports management, sports accounting and finance, sociology of sports, sports law and ethics, sports marketing.

Typical Sequence of High School Courses

English, algebra, geometry, trigonometry, science, foreign language, computer science, public speaking.

Personality Type

Social. These occupations frequently involve working with, communicating with, and teaching people and often involve helping or providing service to others.

Other Characteristics

GOE—Related Interest Areas/Career Clusters: 05 Education and Training; 09 Hospitality, Tourism, and Recreation. **Related Work Groups:** 05.03 Postsecondary and Adult Teaching and Instructing; 05.06 Counseling, Health, and Fitness Education; 09.02 Recreational Services; 09.06 Sports. **Most Important Skills:** Management of financial resources, social perceptiveness, instructing, service orientation, management of personnel resources, monitoring. **Top Values:** Social service, creativity, authority. **Work Environment:** More often indoors than outdoors; standing; walking and running; close to others; keeping or regaining balance; bending or twisting the body.

Related Title in the Classification of Instructional Programs (CIP)

31.0504 Sport and Fitness Administration/Management.

Statistics

Focuses on the relationships between groups of measurements, and similarities and differences, using probability theory and techniques derived from it.

Career Snapshot

Statistical analysis is a valuable tool that is used by every discipline that deals in quantitative information—social sciences, laboratory sciences, and business studies. Statisticians find meaningful patterns in data sets that are harvested from experiments, surveys, and other procedures such as bookkeeping. Graduates of statistics programs are in demand in many parts of the economy, from basic research to business management, from government to academia. Some get advanced degrees to specialize in research or college teaching, or get a degree in a second field such as psychology, computer science, or business.

Related Specialties in Majors and Careers

Computer applications, experimental design, mathematical statistics, probability, psychometrics.

Related Job Titles, Earnings, Projected Growth, and Openings

Job Title	Average Earnings	Projected Growth	Annual Openings
1. Mathematical Science Teachers, Postsecondary (O*NET-SOC Code 25-1022.00)	$58,560	22.9%	237,478
2. Natural Sciences Managers (O*NET-SOC Code 11-9121.00)	$104,040	11.4%	3,661
3. Statisticians (O*NET-SOC Code 15-2041.00)	$69,900	8.5%	3,433

Job 1 shares 237,478 openings with 35 other postsecondary teaching jobs not included in this table.

Typical Sequence of College Courses

Calculus, introduction to computer science, programming in a language (e.g., C++, Pascal, Visual Basic), statistics, linear algebra, experimental design and analysis, mathematical statistics, seminar (reporting on research).

Typical Sequence of High School Courses

Algebra, geometry, trigonometry, pre-calculus, calculus, computer science, physics.

Personality Type

Investigative. These occupations frequently involve working with ideas and require an extensive amount of thinking. They can involve searching for facts and figuring out problems mentally.

Other Characteristics

GOE—Related Interest Areas/Career Clusters: 05 Education and Training; 15 Scientific Research, Engineering, and Mathematics. **Related Work Groups:** 05.03 Postsecondary and Adult Teaching and Instructing; 15.01 Managerial Work in Scientific Research, Engineering, and Mathematics; 15.06 Mathematics and Data Analysis. **Most Important Skills:** Mathematics, science, active learning, complex problem solving, writing, critical thinking. **Top Values:** Authority, creativity, autonomy. **Work Environment:** Indoors; sitting.

Related Title in the Classification of Instructional Programs (CIP)

27.0501 Statistics, General.

Teaching English as a Second Language

Focuses on the principles and practice of teaching English to students who are not proficient in English or who do not speak, read, or write English; and prepares you to function as a teacher or administrator in programs for such students.

Career Snapshot

About 1 in 5 Americans speak a language other than English at home, and a growing percentage of them have limited ability to speak, read, and write English. Teachers of English as a second language (ESL) may earn their credentials as part of an undergraduate major in English, linguistics, or teacher education or as part of a master's degree or certification program. You may teach students at any age level and possibly in a foreign country. The outlook is generally good, although it may vary depending on trends in immigration.

Related Specialties in Majors and Careers

Age level of students, bilingual education, students' first language.

Related Job Title, Earnings, Projected Growth, and Openings

Job Title	Average Earnings	Projected Growth	Annual Openings
1. Adult Literacy, Remedial Education, and GED Teachers and Instructors (O*NET-SOC Code 25-3011.00)	$44,710	14.2%	17,340

Typical Sequence of College Courses

Introduction to psychology, English composition, oral communication, history and philosophy of education, language acquisition and development, ESL teaching methods, traditional and modern English grammar, educational psychology, English phonology, language and culture, assessment in ESL, student teaching.

Typical Sequence of High School Courses

English, algebra, geometry, trigonometry, science, foreign language, public speaking.

Personality Type

Social. These occupations frequently involve working with, communicating with, and teaching people and often involve helping or providing service to others.

Other Characteristics

GOE—Related Interest Area/Career Cluster: 05 Education and Training. **Related Work Group:** 05.03 Postsecondary and Adult Teaching and Instructing. **Most Important Skills:** Instructing, social perceptiveness, learning strategies, service orientation, speaking, monitoring. **Top Values:** Authority, social service, creativity. **Work Environment:** Indoors; more often standing than sitting; close to others.

Related Title in the Classification of Instructional Programs (CIP)

13.1401 Teaching English as a Second or Foreign Language/ESL Language Instructor.

Transportation and Logistics Management

Prepares you to manage and coordinate all logistical functions in an enterprise, ranging from acquisitions to receiving and handling, through internal allocation of resources to operations units, to the handling and delivery of output.

Career Snapshot

Transportation and logistics managers find the fastest and most cost-effective ways to keep materials flowing through our economy. Any business that produces goods or uses supplies—and that means practically every business—faces problems that these specialists are trained to solve. Some enter the field with a bachelor's in transportation and logistics management. Those interested in a technical specialization such as inventory control, packaging, or forecasting may major in (or get a master's degree in) management information systems, operations research, or industrial engineering.

Related Specialties in Majors and Careers

Inventory control, location analysis, management information systems, materials handling, order fulfillment, planning and forecasting, traffic and transportation management, warehouse operations.

Related Job Titles, Earnings, Projected Growth, and Openings

Job Title	Average Earnings	Projected Growth	Annual Openings
1. Storage and Distribution Managers (O*NET-SOC Code 11-3071.02)	$76,310	8.3%	6,994
2. Business Teachers, Postsecondary (O*NET-SOC Code 25-1011.00)	$64,900	22.9%	237,478
3. Logisticians (O*NET-SOC Code 13-1081.00)	$64,250	17.3%	9,671
4. Transportation Managers (O*NET-SOC Code 11-3071.01)	$76,310	8.3%	6,994

Jobs 1 and 4 share 6,994 openings. Job 2 shares 237,478 openings with 35 other postsecondary teaching jobs not included in this table.

Typical Sequence of College Courses

English composition, business writing, introduction to psychology, principles of microeconomics, principles of macroeconomics, calculus for business and social sciences, statistics for business and social sciences, introduction to management information systems, introduction to accounting, legal environment of business, business finance, introduction to marketing, human resource management, introduction to logistics, transportation management, inventory management, analysis and design of logistics systems.

Typical Sequence of High School Courses
English, algebra, geometry, trigonometry, foreign language, computer science, public speaking, pre-calculus.

Personality Type
Enterprising. These occupations frequently involve starting up and carrying out projects and can involve leading people and making many decisions. They sometimes require risk taking and often deal with business.

Other Characteristics
GOE—Related Interest Areas/Career Clusters: 04 Business and Administration; 05 Education and Training; 16 Transportation, Distribution, and Logistics. **Related Work Group:** 04.05 Accounting, Auditing, and Analytical Support; 05.03 Postsecondary and Adult Teaching and Instructing; 16.01 Managerial Work in Transportation. **Most Important Skills:** Management of personnel resources, monitoring, management of financial resources, systems analysis, management of material resources, operations analysis. **Top Values:** Authority, autonomy, creativity. **Work Environment:** Indoors; sitting; very hot or cold; high places; hazardous equipment; specialized protective or safety equipment; noisy.

Related Title in the Classification of Instructional Programs (CIP)
52.0203 Logistics and Materials Management.

Urban Studies

Focuses on the application of social science principles to the study of urban institutions and the forces influencing urban social and political life.

Career Snapshot

Many different kinds of activities are concentrated in cities and towns—economic, social, political, architectural, and cultural—so urban studies is an interdisciplinary major. Degree holders go on to a variety of different careers, most often after getting a graduate or professional degree. Some work in urban planning or redevelopment, law, public administration, environmental planning, social work, or journalism.

Related Specialties in Majors and Careers

Community economic development, environmental design, ethnic studies, urban economics, urban planning, urban politics.

Related Job Titles, Earnings, Projected Growth, and Openings

Job Title	Average Earnings	Projected Growth	Annual Openings
1. Architecture Teachers, Postsecondary (O*NET-SOC Code 25-1031.00)	$68,540	22.9%	237,478
2. Engineering Managers (O*NET-SOC Code 11-9041.00)	$111,020	7.3%	7,404
3. Sociologists (O*NET-SOC Code 19-3041.00)	$61,140	10.0%	403
4. Urban and Regional Planners (O*NET-SOC Code 19-3051.00)	$57,970	14.5%	1,967

Job 1 shares 237,478 openings with 35 other postsecondary teaching jobs not included in this table.

Typical Sequence of College Courses

English composition, introduction to economics, introduction to sociology, statistics for business and social sciences, urban politics, history of cities, urban economics, introduction to urban planning, public policy analysis, seminar (reporting on research).

Typical Sequence of High School Courses

Algebra, English, foreign language, social science, trigonometry, history.

Personality Type

Enterprising. These occupations frequently involve starting up and carrying out projects and can involve leading people and making many decisions. They sometimes require risk taking and often deal with business.

Other Characteristics

GOE—Related Interest Areas/Career Clusters: 05 Education and Training; 07 Government and Public Administration; 15 Scientific Research, Engineering, and Mathematics. **Related Work Groups:** 05.03 Postsecondary and Adult Teaching and Instructing; 07.02 Public Planning; 15.01 Managerial Work in Scientific Research, Engineering, and Mathematics; 15.04 Social Sciences. **Most Important Skills:** Science, technology design, operations analysis, management of financial resources, mathematics, installation. **Top Values:** Authority, autonomy, creativity. **Work Environment:** Indoors; sitting.

Related Titles in the Classification of Instructional Programs (CIP)

04.0301 City/Urban, Community and Regional Planning; 45.1201 Urban Studies/ Affairs.

Veterinary Medicine

Prepares you for the independent professional practice of veterinary medicine, involving the diagnosis, treatment, and health care management of animals and animal populations and the prevention and management of animal-borne disease.

Career Snapshot

Veterinarians care for the health of animals—from dogs and cats to horses and cattle to exotic zoo animals—protect humans from diseases carried by animals, and conduct basic research on animal health. Most of them work in private practices. Some inspect animals or animal products for government agencies. Most students who enter the four-year veterinary school program have already completed a bachelor's degree that includes math and science coursework. Competition for entry to veterinary school is keen, but the job outlook is expected to be good.

Related Specialties in Majors and Careers

Companion animals, large animals (horses, cattle), public health, research.

Related Job Titles, Earnings, Projected Growth, and Openings

Job Title	Average Earnings	Projected Growth	Annual Openings
1. Health Specialties Teachers, Postsecondary (O*NET-SOC Code 25-1071.00)	$80,700	22.9%	237,478
2. Veterinarians (O*NET-SOC Code 29-1131.00)	$75,230	35.0%	5,301

Job 1 shares 237,478 openings with 35 other postsecondary teaching jobs not included in this table.

Typical Sequence of College Courses

English composition, introduction to psychology, college algebra, calculus, introduction to sociology, oral communication, general chemistry, general biology, introduction to computer science, organic chemistry, human anatomy and physiology, general microbiology, genetics, introduction to biochemistry, veterinary gross anatomy, neuroanatomy, veterinary histology and cell biology, veterinary radiology, animal nutrition and nutritional diseases, neuroanatomy, pathology, veterinary microbiology, pharmacology, veterinary ophthalmology, public health, veterinary surgery, reproduction, veterinary toxicology, clinical veterinary experience.

Typical Sequence of High School Courses

English, algebra, geometry, trigonometry, biology, computer science, public speaking, chemistry, foreign language, physics, pre-calculus.

Personality Type

Investigative. These occupations frequently involve working with ideas and require an extensive amount of thinking. They can involve searching for facts and figuring out problems mentally.

Other Characteristics

GOE—Related Interest Areas/Career Clusters: 05 Education and Training; 08 Health Science. **Related Work Groups:** 05.03 Postsecondary and Adult Teaching and Instructing; 08.05 Animal Care. **Most Important Skills:** Science, instructing, reading comprehension, complex problem solving, writing, critical thinking. **Top Values:** Authority, creativity, achievement. **Work Environment:** Indoors; sitting; disease or infections; radiation; specialized protective or safety equipment; hazardous conditions.

Related Title in the Classification of Instructional Programs (CIP)

51.2401 Veterinary Medicine (DVM).

Wildlife Management

Prepares you to conserve and manage wilderness areas and the flora and fauna therein and manage wildlife reservations and zoological facilities for recreational, commercial, and ecological purposes.

Career Snapshot

The study of wildlife management combines a number of disciplines, including biology and public policy. Wildlife managers have to understand how wild creatures interact with their natural environment and how they react to the pressures put on them by human hunting and habitat destruction. Most wildlife managers work for governmental agencies.

Related Specialties in Majors and Careers

Fisheries management, public policy, terrestrial wildlife management.

Related Job Titles, Earnings, Projected Growth, and Openings

Job Title	Average Earnings	Projected Growth	Annual Openings
1. Fish and Game Wardens (O*NET-SOC Code 33-3031.00)	$47,830	–0.2%	576
2. Park Naturalists (O*NET-SOC Code 19-1031.03)	$56,150	5.3%	1,161
3. Range Managers (O*NET-SOC Code 19-1031.02)	$56,150	5.3%	1,161
4. Soil and Water Conservationists (O*NET-SOC Code 19-1031.01)	$56,150	5.3%	1,161
5. Zoologists and Wildlife Biologists (O*NET-SOC Code 19-1023.00)	$55,100	8.7%	1,444

Jobs 2, 3, and 4 share 1,161 openings.

Typical Sequence of College Courses

English composition, calculus, general biology, general chemistry, organic chemistry, oral communication, statistics, introduction to computer science, introduction to soil science, ecology, general zoology, introduction to wildlife conservation, invertebrate zoology, introduction to forestry, mammalogy, ornithology, natural resource biometrics, wildlife habitat management, animal population dynamics and management, animal physiology, ichthyology/herpetology, regional wildlife management and policy.

Typical Sequence of High School Courses

Biology, chemistry, algebra, geometry, trigonometry, computer science, English, public speaking, geography.

Personality Type

Investigative. These occupations frequently involve working with ideas and require an extensive amount of thinking. They can involve searching for facts and figuring out problems mentally.

Other Characteristics

GOE—Related Interest Areas/Career Clusters: 01 Agriculture and Natural Resources; 07 Government and Public Administration. **Related Work Groups:** 01.01 Managerial Work in Agriculture and Natural Resources; 01.02 Resource Science/Engineering for Plants, Animals, and the Environment; 07.03 Regulations Enforcement. **Most Important Skills:** Science, persuasion, management of financial resources, writing, management of personnel resources, negotiation. **Top Values:** Autonomy, creativity, responsibility. **Work Environment:** More often in a vehicle or outdoors than indoors; very hot or cold; minor burns, cuts, bites, or stings; extremely bright or inadequate lighting; specialized protective or safety equipment; sitting; whole body vibration.

Related Title in the Classification of Instructional Programs (CIP)

03.0601 Wildlife and Wildlands Science and Management.

Women's Studies

Focuses on the history, sociology, politics, culture, and economics of women and the development of modern feminism in relation to the roles played by women in different periods and locations in North America and the world.

Career Snapshot

Women's studies is an interdisciplinary major that looks at the experience of women from the perspectives of history, literature, psychology, and sociology, among others. Graduates of this major may go into business fields where understanding of women's issues can be helpful—for example, advertising or human resources management. With further education, they may also find careers in fields where they can affect the lives of women, such as social work, law, public health, or public administration.

Related Specialties in Majors and Careers

Feminist theory, history of feminism, women's issues in art and culture, women's political issues.

Related Job Title, Earnings, Projected Growth, and Openings

Job Title	Average Earnings	Projected Growth	Annual Openings
1. Area, Ethnic, and Cultural Studies Teachers, Postsecondary (O*NET-SOC Code 25-1062.00)	$59,150	22.9%	237,478

This job shares 237,478 openings with 35 other postsecondary teaching jobs not included in this table.

Typical Sequence of College Courses

English composition, foreign language, American history, introduction to women's studies, women of color, theories of feminism, historical and philosophical origins of feminism, feminism from a global perspective, seminar (reporting on research).

Typical Sequence of High School Courses

English, algebra, foreign language, history, literature, public speaking, social science.

Personality Type

Social. These occupations frequently involve working with, communicating with, and teaching people and often involve helping or providing service to others.

Other Characteristics

GOE—Related Interest Area/Career Cluster: 05 Education and Training. **Related Work Group:** 05.03 Postsecondary and Adult Teaching and Instructing. **Most Important Skills:** Writing, critical thinking, instructing, persuasion, active learning, learning strategies. **Top Values:** Authority, social service, creativity. **Work Environment:** Indoors; sitting.

Related Title in the Classification of Instructional Programs (CIP)

05.0207 Women's Studies.

Zoology

Focuses on the scientific study of the biology of animal species and phyla, with reference to their molecular and cellular systems, anatomy, physiology, and behavior.

Career Snapshot

Zoologists study any form of animal life and therefore need a good background in biology and chemistry. A bachelor's degree in zoology can be a good first step toward a professional degree in medicine, veterinary science, or dentistry, or it may lead to entry-level work in some government and business fields. A graduate degree in zoology is good preparation for a career in research, college teaching, or agricultural extension service.

Related Specialties in Majors and Careers

Entomology, herpetology, ichthyology, mammalogy, ornithology.

Related Job Titles, Earnings, Projected Growth, and Openings

Job Title	Average Earnings	Projected Growth	Annual Openings
1. Biological Science Teachers, Postsecondary (O*NET-SOC Code 25-1042.00)	$71,780	22.9%	237,478
2. Natural Sciences Managers (O*NET-SOC Code 11-9121.00)	$104,040	11.4%	3,661
3. Zoologists and Wildlife Biologists (O*NET-SOC Code 19-1023.00)	$55,100	8.7%	1,444

Job 1 shares 237,478 openings with 35 other postsecondary teaching jobs not included in this table.

Typical Sequence of College Courses

English composition, calculus, introduction to computer science, general chemistry, general biology, organic chemistry, genetics, general physics, cell biology, statistics, animal anatomy and physiology, evolution, ecology.

Typical Sequence of High School Courses

English, biology, algebra, geometry, trigonometry, chemistry, pre-calculus, physics, computer science, calculus.

Personality Type

Investigative. These occupations frequently involve working with ideas and require an extensive amount of thinking. They can involve searching for facts and figuring out problems mentally.

Other Characteristics

GOE—Related Interest Areas/Career Clusters: 01 Agriculture and Natural Resources; 05 Education and Training; 15 Scientific Research, Engineering, and Mathematics. **Related Work Groups:** 01.02 Resource Science/Engineering for Plants, Animals, and the Environment; 05.03 Postsecondary and Adult Teaching and Instructing; 15.01 Managerial Work in Scientific Research, Engineering, and Mathematics. **Most Important Skills:** Science, writing, reading comprehension, active learning, mathematics, critical thinking. **Top Values:** Creativity, authority, autonomy. **Work Environment:** More often indoors than in a vehicle; sitting; hazardous conditions; disease or infections.

Related Title in the Classification of Instructional Programs (CIP)

26.0701 Zoology/Animal Biology.

Majors Listed by Personality Type

If you have taken an assessment or done some other career-related activity to clarify your personality type in terms of the six Holland types—Realistic, Investigative, Artistic, Social, Enterprising, or Conventional—this appendix will help you identify majors that may suit you.

If you're not sure what personality type describes you best, you may want to try the *O*NET Career Interests Inventory* or the *Picture Interest Career Survey*, both published by JIST. Or you may want to use a checklist at www.roguecc.edu/ Counseling/HollandCodes/about.asp or http://careerservices.rutgers.edu/ PCCPinterests.html.

The Six Personality Types Defined

The following definitions refer to the kinds of jobs that satisfy the six types:

Artistic. These occupations frequently involve working with forms, designs, and patterns. They often require self-expression, and the work can be done without following a clear set of rules.

Conventional. These occupations frequently involve following set procedures and routines and can include working with data and details more than with ideas. Usually there is a clear line of authority to follow.

Enterprising. These occupations frequently involve starting up and carrying out projects and can involve leading people and making many decisions. They sometimes require risk taking and often deal with business.

Investigative. These occupations frequently involve working with ideas and require an extensive amount of thinking. They can involve searching for facts and figuring out problems mentally.

Realistic. These occupations frequently involve work activities that include practical, hands-on problems and solutions. They often deal with plants; animals; and real-world materials such as wood, tools, and machinery. Many of the occupations require working outside and do not involve a lot of paperwork or working closely with others.

Social. These occupations frequently involve working with, communicating with, and teaching people and often involve helping or providing service to others.

The following listing identifies the majors in this book that correspond to each of the six personality types. Part II of this book identifies the *primary* personality type for each major, but majors can also be described by *secondary* personality types. The list that follows is based on both the primary *and* the highest-rated secondary personality type to which the major is linked.

Realistic

Aeronautical/Aerospace Engineering

Agricultural Business and Economics

Agricultural Engineering

Agronomy and Crop Science

Animal Science

Architecture

Bioengineering

Business Education

Chemical Engineering

Civil Engineering

Computer Engineering

Earth Sciences

Electrical Engineering

Environmental Science

Forestry

Geography

Geology

Horticulture

Industrial Engineering

Landscape Architecture

Materials Science

Mechanical Engineering

Metallurgical Engineering

Microbiology/Bacteriology

Oceanography

Operations Management

Optometry

Petroleum Engineering

Recreation and Parks Management

Sports Management

Wildlife Management

Investigative

Actuarial Science

Aeronautical/Aerospace Engineering

Agricultural Business and Economics

Agricultural Engineering

Agronomy and Crop Science

American Studies

Animal Science

Anthropology

Archeology

Area Studies

Asian Studies

Astronomy

Biochemistry

Bioengineering

Biology

Botany

Chemical Engineering

Chemistry

Chiropractic

Civil Engineering

Clinical Laboratory Technology

Computer Engineering

Computer Science

Dentistry

Dietetics

Earth Sciences

Economics

Electrical Engineering

Elementary Education

Environmental Science

Food Science

Forestry

Geography

Geology

Hispanic American Studies

History

Humanities

Industrial Engineering

Industrial/Technology Education

International Relations

Management Information Systems

Materials Science

Mathematics

Mechanical Engineering

Medicine

Metallurgical Engineering

Meteorology

Microbiology/Bacteriology

Nursing (RN Training)

Occupational Health and Industrial Hygiene

Occupational Therapy

Oceanography

Operations Research

Optometry

Orthotics/Prosthetics

Petroleum Engineering

Pharmacy

Physical Therapy

Physician Assisting

Physics

Podiatry

Political Science

Psychology

Sociology

Soil Science

Speech Pathology and Audiology

Statistics

Urban Studies

Veterinary Medicine

Wildlife Management

Women's Studies

Zoology

Artistic

Advertising

Art

Art History

Chinese

Classics

Dance

Drama/Theater Arts

Early Childhood Education

English

Film/Cinema Studies

French

German

Graphic Design, Commercial Art, and Illustration

Industrial Design

Interior Design

Japanese

Journalism and Mass Communications

Library Science

Modern Foreign Language

Music

Photography

Physical Education

Public Relations

Religion/Religious Studies

Russian

Secondary Education

Spanish

Special Education

Teaching English as a Second Language

Social

African American Studies

American Studies

Anthropology

Archeology

Area Studies

Art

Art History

Asian Studies

Biochemistry

Biology

Botany

Business Education

Chemistry

Chinese

Chiropractic

Classics

Clinical Laboratory Technology

Criminal Justice/Law Enforcement

Dance

Dentistry

Dietetics

Drama/Theater Arts

Early Childhood Education

Economics

Elementary Education

English

Family and Consumer Sciences

Film/Cinema Studies

Food Science

French

German

Graphic Design/Commercial Art/Illustration

Hispanic American Studies

History

Hospital/Health Facilities Administration

Hotel/Motel and Restaurant Management

Human Resources Management

Humanities

Industrial and Labor Relations

Industrial Design

Industrial/Technology Education

Interior Design

International Relations

Japanese

Medicine

Modern Foreign Language

Music

Nursing (RN Training)

Occupational Health and Industrial Hygiene

Occupational Therapy

Orthotics/Prosthetics

Pharmacy

Philosophy

Photography

Physical Education

Physical Therapy

Physician Assisting

Physics

Podiatry

Political Science

Psychology

Recreation and Parks Management

Religion/Religious Studies

Secondary Education

Social Work

Sociology

Soil Science

Spanish

Special Education

Speech Pathology and Audiology

Sports Management

Teaching English as a Second Language

Veterinary Medicine

Women's Studies

Zoology

Enterprising

Accounting

Advertising

Architecture

Astronomy

Business Management

Family and Consumer Sciences

Finance

Health Information Systems Administration

Horticulture

Hospital/Health Facilities Administration

Hotel/Motel and Restaurant Management

Human Resources Management

Industrial and Labor Relations

Insurance

International Business

Journalism and Mass Communications

Landscape Architecture

Law

Marketing

Meteorology

Operations Management

Operations Research

Public Administration

Public Relations

Social Work

Transportation and Logistics Management

Urban Studies

Conventional

Accounting

Actuarial Science

Business Management

Computer Science

Finance

Health Information Systems Administration

Insurance

International Business

Law

Library Science

Management Information Systems

Marketing

Mathematics

Public Administration

Statistics

Transportation and Logistics Management

Majors Listed by CIP Code

The Classification of Instructional Programs (CIP) is used by the U.S. Department of Education and many colleges to identify college majors. The following list, ordered numerically, shows all the CIP codes used in this book and the majors linked to them.

01.0101 Agricultural Business and Management, General	Agricultural Business and Economics
01.0102 Agribusiness/Agricultural Business Operations	Agricultural Business and Economics
01.0103 Agricultural Economics	Agricultural Business and Economics
01.0601 Applied Horticulture/Horticulture Operations, General	Horticulture
01.0603 Ornamental Horticulture	Horticulture
01.0604 Greenhouse Operations and Management	Horticulture
01.0605 Landscaping and Groundskeeping	Horticulture
01.0606 Plant Nursery Operations and Management	Horticulture
01.0607 Turf and Turfgrass Management	Horticulture
01.0608 Floriculture/Floristry Operations and Management	Horticulture
01.0901 Animal Sciences, General	Animal Science
01.1001 Food Science	Food Science
01.1102 Agronomy and Crop Science	Agronomy and Crop Science
01.1201 Soil Science and Agronomy, General	Soil Science
03.0103 Environmental Studies	Environmental Science
03.0104 Environmental Science	Environmental Science
03.0501 Forestry, General	Forestry

03.0601 Wildlife and Wildlands Science and Management	Wildlife Management
04.0201 Architecture (BArch, BA/BS, MArch, MA/MS, PhD)	Architecture
04.0301 City/Urban, Community and Regional Planning	Urban Studies
04.0601 Landscape Architecture (BS, BSLA, BLA, MSLA, MLA, PhD)	Landscape Architecture
05.0102 American/United States Studies/ Civilization	Area Studies
05.0102 American/United States Studies/ Civilization	American Studies
05.0103 Asian Studies/Civilization	Asian Studies
05.0104 East Asian Studies	Area Studies
05.0105 Central/Middle and Eastern European Studies	Area Studies
05.0106 European Studies/Civilization	Area Studies
05.0107 Latin American Studies	Area Studies
05.0108 Near and Middle Eastern Studies	Area Studies
05.0109 Pacific Area/Pacific Rim Studies	Area Studies
05.0110 Russian Studies	Area Studies
05.0111 Scandinavian Studies	Area Studies
05.0115 Canadian Studies	Area Studies
05.0201 African-American/Black Studies	African American Studies
05.0203 Hispanic-American, Puerto Rican, and Mexican-American/Chicano Studies	Hispanic American Studies
05.0207 Women's Studies	Women's Studies
09.0401 Journalism	Journalism and Mass Communications
09.0902 Public Relations/Image Management	Public Relations
09.0903 Advertising	Advertising

11.0701 Computer Science	Computer Science
13.1001 Special Education and Teaching, General	Special Education
13.1202 Elementary Education and Teaching	Elementary Education
13.1205 Secondary Education and Teaching	Secondary Education
13.1210 Early Childhood Education and Teaching	Early Childhood Education
13.1303 Business Teacher Education	Business Education
13.1308 Family and Consumer Sciences/Home Economics Teacher Education	Family and Consumer Sciences
13.1309 Technology Teacher Education/Industrial Arts Teacher Education	Industrial/Technology Education
13.1314 Physical Education Teaching and Coaching	Physical Education
13.1401 Teaching English as a Second or Foreign Language/ESL Language Instructor	Teaching English as a Second Language
14.0201 Aerospace, Aeronautical and Astronautical Engineering	Aeronautical/Aerospace Engineering
14.0301 Agricultural/Biological Engineering and Bioengineering	Agricultural Engineering
14.0501 Biomedical/Medical Engineering	Bioengineering
14.0701 Chemical Engineering	Chemical Engineering
14.0801 Civil Engineering, General	Civil Engineering
14.0901 Computer Engineering, General	Computer Engineering
14.1001 Electrical, Electronics and Communications Engineering	Electrical Engineering
14.1901 Mechanical Engineering	Mechanical Engineering
14.2001 Metallurgical Engineering	Metallurgical Engineering
14.2501 Petroleum Engineering	Petroleum Engineering
14.3101 Materials Science	Materials Science

14.3501 Industrial Engineering	Industrial Engineering
14.3701 Operations Research	Operations Research
16.0101 Foreign Languages and Literatures, General	Modern Foreign Language
16.0102 Linguistics	Modern Foreign Language
16.0103 Language Interpretation and Translation	Modern Foreign Language
16.0301 Chinese Language and Literature	Modern Foreign Language
16.0301 Chinese Language and Literature	Chinese
16.0302 Japanese Language and Literature	Japanese
16.0302 Japanese Language and Literature	Modern Foreign Language
16.0399 East Asian Languages, Literatures, and Linguistics, Other	Modern Foreign Language
16.0400 Slavic Languages, Literatures, and Linguistics, General	Modern Foreign Language
16.0402 Russian Language and Literature	Russian
16.0402 Russian Language and Literature	Modern Foreign Language
16.0499 Slavic, Baltic, and Albanian Languages, Literatures, and Linguistics, Other	Modern Foreign Language
16.0501 German Language and Literature	German
16.0501 German Language and Literature	Modern Foreign Language
16.0502 Scandinavian Languages, Literatures, and Linguistics	Modern Foreign Language
16.0599 Germanic Languages, Literatures, and Linguistics, Other	Modern Foreign Language
16.0901 French Language and Literature	French
16.0901 French Language and Literature	Modern Foreign Language
16.0902 Italian Language and Literature	Modern Foreign Language
16.0904 Portuguese Language and Literature	Modern Foreign Language
16.0905 Spanish Language and Literature	Spanish

16.0905 Spanish Language and Literature	Modern Foreign Language
16.0999 Romance Languages, Literatures, and Linguistics, Other	Modern Foreign Language
16.1101 Arabic Language and Literature	Modern Foreign Language
16.1102 Hebrew Language and Literature	Modern Foreign Language
16.1199 Middle/Near Eastern and Semitic Languages, Literatures, and Linguistics, Other	Modern Foreign Language
16.1200 Classics and Classical Languages, Literatures, and Linguistics, General	Classics
16.9999 Foreign Languages, Literatures, and Linguistics	Modern Foreign Language
19.0101 Family and Consumer Sciences/Human Sciences, General	Family and Consumer Sciences
19.0203 Consumer Merchandising/Retailing Management	Family and Consumer Sciences
19.0701 Human Development and Family Studies, General	Family and Consumer Sciences
19.0702 Adult Development and Aging	Family and Consumer Sciences
19.0706 Child Development	Family and Consumer Sciences
19.0707 Family and Community Services	Family and Consumer Sciences
19.0901 Apparel and Textiles, General	Family and Consumer Sciences
19.0905 Apparel and Textile Marketing Management	Family and Consumer Sciences
19.0906 Fashion and Fabric Consultant	Family and Consumer Sciences
19.9999 Family and Consumer Sciences/Human Sciences, Other	Family and Consumer Sciences
22.0101 Law (LL.B., J.D.)	Law
23.0101 English Language and Literature, General	English
24.0103 Humanities/Humanistic Studies	Humanities

25.0101 Library Science/Librarianship	Library Science
26.0101 Biology/Biological Sciences, General	Biology
26.0202 Biochemistry	Biochemistry
26.0301 Botany/Plant Biology	Botany
26.0503 Medical Microbiology and Bacteriology	Microbiology/Bacteriology
26.0701 Zoology/Animal Biology	Zoology
27.0101 Mathematics, General	Mathematics
27.0501 Statistics, General	Statistics
31.0301 Parks, Recreation, and Leisure Facilities Management	Recreation and Parks Management
31.0504 Sport and Fitness Administration/ Management	Sports Management
38.0101 Philosophy	Philosophy
38.0201 Religion/Religious Studies	Religion/Religious Studies
40.0201 Astronomy	Astronomy
40.0401 Atmospheric Sciences and Meteorology, General	Meteorology
40.0501 Chemistry, General	Chemistry
40.0601 Geology/Earth Science, General	Earth Sciences
40.0601 Geology/Earth Science, General	Geology
40.0607 Oceanography, Chemical and Physical	Oceanography
40.0801 Physics, General	Physics
42.0101 Psychology, General	Psychology
43.0107 Criminal Justice/Police Science	Criminal Justice/Law Enforcement
44.0401 Public Administration	Public Administration
44.0701 Social Work	Social Work
45.0201 Anthropology	Anthropology
45.0301 Archeology	Archeology

45.0601 Economics, General	Economics
45.0701 Geography	Geography
45.0901 International Relations and Affairs	International Relations
45.1001 Political Science and Government, General	Political Science
45.1101 Sociology	Sociology
45.1201 Urban Studies/Affairs	Urban Studies
50.0301 Dance, General	Dance
50.0402 Commercial and Advertising Art	Graphic Design, Commercial Art, and Illustration
50.0404 Industrial Design	Industrial Design
50.0408 Interior Design	Interior Design
50.0409 Graphic Design	Graphic Design, Commercial Art, and Illustration
50.0410 Illustration	Graphic Design, Commercial Art, and Illustration
50.0501 Drama and Dramatics/Theatre Arts, General	Drama/Theater Arts
50.0601 Film/Cinema Studies	Film/Cinema Studies
50.0602 Cinematography and Film/Video Production	Film/Cinema Studies
50.0605 Photography	Photography
50.0702 Fine/Studio Arts, General	Art
50.0703 Art History, Criticism and Conservation	Art History
50.0903 Music Performance, General	Music
51.0101 Chiropractic (DC)	Chiropractic
51.0204 Audiology/Audiologist and Speech-Language Pathology/Pathologist	Speech Pathology and Audiology
51.0401 Dentistry (DDS, DMD)	Dentistry

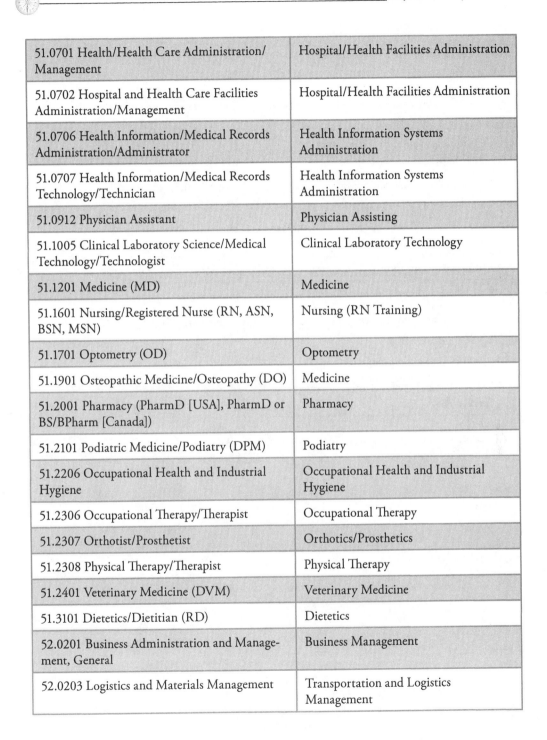

51.0701 Health/Health Care Administration/Management	Hospital/Health Facilities Administration
51.0702 Hospital and Health Care Facilities Administration/Management	Hospital/Health Facilities Administration
51.0706 Health Information/Medical Records Administration/Administrator	Health Information Systems Administration
51.0707 Health Information/Medical Records Technology/Technician	Health Information Systems Administration
51.0912 Physician Assistant	Physician Assisting
51.1005 Clinical Laboratory Science/Medical Technology/Technologist	Clinical Laboratory Technology
51.1201 Medicine (MD)	Medicine
51.1601 Nursing/Registered Nurse (RN, ASN, BSN, MSN)	Nursing (RN Training)
51.1701 Optometry (OD)	Optometry
51.1901 Osteopathic Medicine/Osteopathy (DO)	Medicine
51.2001 Pharmacy (PharmD [USA], PharmD or BS/BPharm [Canada])	Pharmacy
51.2101 Podiatric Medicine/Podiatry (DPM)	Podiatry
51.2206 Occupational Health and Industrial Hygiene	Occupational Health and Industrial Hygiene
51.2306 Occupational Therapy/Therapist	Occupational Therapy
51.2307 Orthotist/Prosthetist	Orthotics/Prosthetics
51.2308 Physical Therapy/Therapist	Physical Therapy
51.2401 Veterinary Medicine (DVM)	Veterinary Medicine
51.3101 Dietetics/Dietitian (RD)	Dietetics
52.0201 Business Administration and Management, General	Business Management
52.0203 Logistics and Materials Management	Transportation and Logistics Management

52.0205 Operations Management and Supervision	Operations Management
52.0301 Accounting	Accounting
52.0801 Finance, General	Finance
52.0904 Hotel/Motel Administration/ Management	Hotel/Motel and Restaurant Management
52.0905 Restaurant/Food Services Management	Hotel/Motel and Restaurant Management
52.1001 Human Resources Management/Personnel Administration, General	Human Resources Management
52.1002 Labor and Industrial Relations	Industrial and Labor Relations
52.1101 International Business/Trade/Commerce	International Business
52.1201 Management Information Systems, General	Management Information Systems
52.1304 Actuarial Science	Actuarial Science
52.1401 Marketing/Marketing Management, General	Marketing
52.1701 Insurance	Insurance
54.0101 History, General	History

Indexes

Careers Index

High School Courses Index

Interest Areas/Clusters Index

Work Groups Index